Dr. Dave's
Stallside
Manner

Hope you enjoy

D. Dave

Dr. Dave's
Stallside
Manner

More Adventures
of a Country Vet

Dr. David Perrin

Illustrations by Wendy Liddle

DAVE'S PRESS INC.

Published by Dave's Press Inc.
Box 616, Lister
British Columbia
Canada V0B 1Y0

Cover and book design by Warren Clark
Illustrations by Wendy Liddle
Edited by Betsy Brierley
Proofread by Elizabeth McLean

Printed and bound in Canada

Canadian Cataloguing in Publication Data

ISBN 0-9687943-1-9

Perrin, David, 1948-
    Dr. dave's stallside manner

    1. Perrin, David, 1948- 2. Veterinarians—British Columbia—
Biography. 3. Animals--Anecdotes. I. Liddle, Wendy. II. Title.
SF613.P47A3 2001   636.089'92   C2001-911580-6

To the clients and patients

who provided the rich material

for this book

Acknowledgements

As the time comes to launch *Stallside Manner*, it is appropriate to recognize the people who have helped bring it into existence. As with *Don't Turn Your Back in the Barn*, the input from my production team has been outstanding.

Betsy Brierley, my editor, has expended the tireless energy that I have come to expect from her. How fortunate I was to find a person to work with who understands my vision and my writing style. Wendy Liddle has again added her own delightful flavour to my book through her illustrations. She has been a cheerleader from the sidelines since the first chapters were in their infancy. Warren Clark has wielded his considerable skills to create an appealing book design for *Stallside Manner*.

My "in-house readers" have provided an invaluable service by previewing the manuscript to help me expand and clarify the stories for my audience. Thank you Nancy Wise, Pat Badger, Al Theede, Bob and Marian Moats, and Jack Ingram.

I want to express my sincere appreciation to those who read *Don't Turn Your Back in the Barn* and sent me letters and e-mail messages of encouragement. Many times in the past months, your words buoyed my spirits and motivated me to go on.

I extend a special thank you to all those people who have come forward with photographs and reminders of our past association. Many of your stories are in this book; others will come to life in future collections. Please continue to send me your reminiscences. They will help to keep the stories flowing.

Throughout the writing of this manuscript, my family has encouraged me and steadfastly accepted the inevitable disruptions. Thank you Ruth, Joan, Marshall, Gordon, and Alicia.

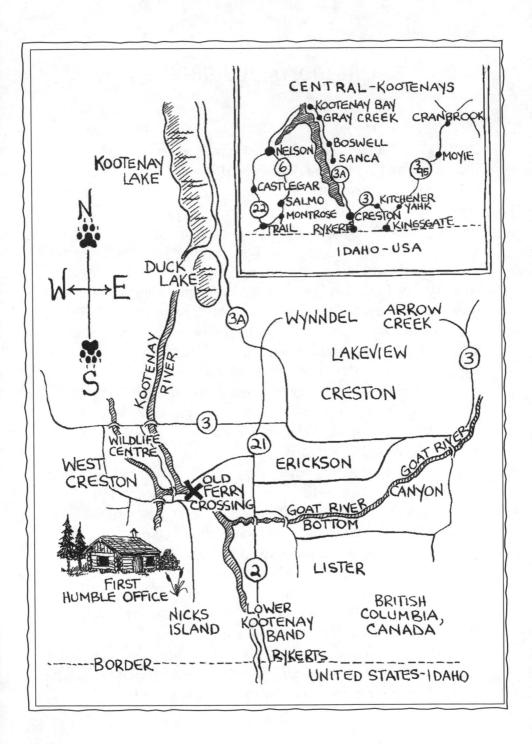

Contents

Trouble at Tilly's

I pulled over to the side of the road and glared at the scratches on my notepad. Damn! Why hadn't I looked at the odometer when I left Wynndel? I had been to Tilly Hubner's farm several times during the previous summer, and I should have recognized her exit but, along this twisted highway, they all looked similar. The directions said four miles past the store—I was sure I should have come to the turnoff by now. I stared over my shoulder with the certainty that I had driven past it.

Gravel-laden mounds of snow lined the ditches at the sides of the road. Although most of Highway 3A was skirted by a green hedge of fir and pine, here birch and cottonwood persisted, their limbs still bare and lifeless. It would be a few months before tourists crowded this scenic route to the Kootenay Lake ferry. A car rounded the corner behind me, slowed, then proceeded past.

I put the Volkswagen in low gear and eased back onto the highway. Lug whined and twirled around on the seat. Certain that something exciting was in the making, he rooted at my hand as it rested on the gearshift.

"Settle down, you big boob...We're lost again."

I accelerated. If I didn't find the place in the next few minutes, I'd turn back and figure out where I'd messed up. I had rounded several sharp curves in succession and was looking for a place to turn around when I recognized the access up a steep hill to the right.

"Well, look at that, boy. There it is."

Although I couldn't see Tilly's house, I could picture the tall, stark building at the top of the drive, its bunker-like garage plunked in front, as if dropped by a giant bird, its massive concrete walls and roof so out of touch with the rest of the building and the surrounding landscape.

Tilly existed in that barren little house as if the Depression had never ended, and even having a cup of tea with her made me feel guilty. Her cupboards were always bare, her ancient refrigerator empty except for a lonely can of evaporated milk. There was hardly a stick of furniture or a picture on the wall; one would wonder if she had occupied the building only yesterday. It was as if her possessions were in storage somewhere, waiting for the day she would move in and start living there.

I rounded the corner to her pasture access. There she stood, a bucket of water on either side of her, her long, lean body straight, tall, immobile, looking like some classical figure carved from stone. She held up her hand and shook her head as I pulled to the left and parked in front of her.

"You better stop right here, Dave. You'll never get out of the driveway this time of year. It's slick as can be, and there's no place to turn around."

Lug planted his front feet on my lap and strained to get a better look. Whining excitedly, he skidded his nose across the side window, leaving a streak of slime glistening on its surface.

"You'll have to carry your stuff from here," said Tilly.

I shut off the engine and opened the door. Lug tried to muscle his way out, but I caught him as he stepped down. "Stay!"

"God, you have no idea how I hated to call you out here for this cow. She's such a pain with strangers."

"She's not the big blond one that put me out of the corral when we were vaccinating them last fall, the one that knocked Joe Pogany's horse out from under him during community pasture roundup?"

"Afraid so…and she'll be even worse now that she's this close to calving. Maternal instincts bring out the worst in my girls. Every other year, I've been lucky and she's delivered on her own. I just threw out feed and stayed as far away from her as I possibly could. She doesn't have much use for me either! I suspected she was going to calve soon and was lucky enough to lure her into the corral last night."

I rummaged in the back of the car, unloading the calving jack and stuffing chains and handles into my pockets. I grabbed my bucket, threw in the container of soap, and draped the lariat over my shoulder. I felt a sudden urge to drag my feet, but Tilly was not about to let me dawdle. With a bucket in either hand, she headed down the trail. I slammed the end door shut and took off after her. She was already several strides ahead of me, her long legs motoring deftly down the steep incline towards Duck Lake below us.

"With your being all alone like this, Tilly, the place for a cow like her is in the deep freeze. If she knocked you down and hurt you when you were all by yourself, who'd ever know you were even out here?"

"I can look after myself. I worked a long time to be able to sell an animal as a purebred. When we're done with her, I'll show you her last year's calf. He's one fine-looking bull."

"Sure hope he doesn't have his mother's temperament."

Tilly stopped and looked at me as if I had stabbed her in the side. Even the slightest criticism of her cattle, or of the Charolais breed in general, was known to summon a tirade in their defence. She hesitated for a moment, ready to give me a piece of her mind, then sighed and strode off. This was a time like no other in the North American beef industry. Prices for cattle in 1974 were good, and the introduction of exotic breeds like Charolais and Simmental was sending people clamouring to import purebred stock.

Small producers like Tilly found it the perfect opportunity to increase the income they could generate from their farmsteads.

For her, the sale of a few good bulls and a purebred heifer could easily match the income she would get from selling a goodly number of grade weaner calves. The difficulty that she faced, like everyone in the industry, was getting quality stock to begin with. The cows she started with had originated in the southern United States with the artificial insemination of Brahman stock and their progressive upbreeding. In North America, most producers associated that breed with rodeo stock; for me, that association was reaffirmed every time I stepped onto Tilly's holding.

There was a sudden flurry of movement in front of us, as hundreds of plump little grey birds erupted from the bushes along the side of the trail. Perching like round Christmas ornaments in the trees overhead, they inspected us as we passed beneath them. Their dark heads and tails bobbing, they hopped from one branch to the next, filling the air with their chatter.

"What are those birds, Tilly?"

"I'm not sure, but Dad always called them juncos."

The dense bush beside us opened up, and railway tracks stretched in either direction. I could see fenced pasture below us and, in the distance, the marshy shore of the lake. A few winter fishermen still huddled over their holes in the ice. I followed Tilly over the tracks and up to the pasture fence. She stopped in front of a metal gate and set down her buckets of water.

"You stay here," she whispered, bringing a long, bony finger to her lips. Her grey eyes sparkling with excitement, she ran her hand across her forehead, slicked back her short-cropped hair, and slipped through the gate. Tiptoeing stealthily along the brush hedgerow that screened the corral on the far side, she stopped, knelt at the edge of the bushes, and stared.

A smile spread across my face as I watched her creep further along the row of brush, now crouching, now kneeling, now stretched out on the cold, hard ground. I thought of all the poor dentists who, at this very moment, were peering into the black, smelly cavern of someone's aching mouth, of doctors flitting like bees from one examination to another, their waiting rooms stuffed with patients. What other profession could allow me this moment in the sun watching a woman in her sixties play hide and seek with a creature that wanted only to be left alone? I marvelled at Tilly's agility, as she sprang to her feet and scurried in a crouch in my direction.

"She's lying there pushing. We may be able to just sneak up on her while she's distracted."

"What can you see? Is she making any progress on her own?"

"I can see two legs. They're enormous; I'm sure it's coming backwards."

I handed the buckets of water over the fence to Tilly, then gathered the calving jack and my own empty bucket to climb clumsily over the gate. The bucket and cradle crashed against it with a harsh, metallic clang.

"Shhhhh," Tilly whispered forcefully. "Keep banging around like that, and you'll have the whole herd on the prod."

I followed her as quietly as possible, taking great care to separate the cradle of the jack from the bar itself. As we crept around the end of the brush, I could see the cow lying full on her side, head pointed in the other direction.

"We might be lucky," I whispered. "Let me see if I can sneak in there and get the chains on. She's so hard into labour, she'll probably just keep on pushing and forget about me."

The rounded poles of the corral were close together, and I had to find a spot in the corner where I could get enough purchase to scale the wall. The huge cow was pushing for all she was worth and paid not the slightest heed as I slipped over the rails. Bawling loudly, she sustained a prolonged push. The legs of the calf protruded to the level of his thighs; I could spot the very tip of his tail.

"This is a huge calf, Tilly."

"I know, that's why you're here," she replied anxiously.

I slipped a calving chain from my back pocket and worked it over the massive foot that stuck out in front of me. Putting on a second half hitch, I grabbed the other chain and readied it. As the cow strained, I attached the handles and applied pressure.

"Man, what's she bred to? I can't budge this critter."

The cow took a deep breath and emitted a long, mournful wail that ended with a rattle deep in her throat. She panted for a moment, lifted her head, and glared at me grumpily.

"She's at the stage of do or die, Tilly. Hand me the hardware, and I'll get the jack set up. There's no way I want to risk pulling this calf by hand."

Tilly poked the breech through the corral rails, and I slipped the metal yoke around the calf's feet and under the cow's vagina. I lengthened the strap that went over the mother's tailhead as much as I could, then reached for the bar as Tilly extended it to me.

"Looks like a toy on a cow her size." I looked in chagrin as the wings of the cradle hung up on her thighs. I slid the bar into the breech and connected the chains. The cow continued to push, apparently intent on getting this ordeal over with. I jacked rapidly several times to tighten the chains. Waiting for her to push, I pulled down on the end of the bar. The calf's thighs protruded; I could see the base of its tail.

Tilly's eyes were fiery. She hung over the rails of the corral fence, anticipating the event like a grandmother. A new herdsire was in the offing, and she couldn't wait for the end result.

I jacked a few more times and, as I applied pressure downward, could see the calf's rectum. His tail flicking rapidly back and forth, he tried in vain to flex his hind legs. He didn't think much of this treatment. I was about to take up more slack with the jack when the cow suddenly shifted. Throwing her head up, she struggled to get her front legs beneath her.

"Look out!" yelled Tilly. "You better get out of there."

The monstrous cow was already on her feet, twirling in my direction. I grabbed the corral rail and attempted my escape. As I struggled to get purchase in the tiny spaces between the logs, the end of the calving jack caught me on the side. I found myself flat on my face on the cold ground.

"Get up! Get up!"

Tilly was hanging over the top rail, swinging madly with a pole in an attempt to divert the cow's attention. The end of the jack, which was gyrating wildly back and forth, whacked forcefully against the post in front of her. Tilly catapulted backwards, dropping her pole in the process. The jingle and rattle of the chains against the metal of the breech seemed to further incense the cow. She caught me beneath the gut with her nose as I struggled to get up. Effortlessly, she flipped me through the air.

I landed in a heap in front of a clump of birch trees and scrambled for their cover. The huge cow snorted angrily and whirled after me. Seeking an exit, I was anxious to keep the trees between us. I had made a complete circuit with her in hot pursuit when the calving jack jammed against the edge of the corral. The cow circled, trying to shed the unwieldy contraption. Bucking like her ancestral relatives, she took off away from me. The bar separated and fell to the ground; the breech lasted for one more lunge before it, too, flew through the air.

I searched the corral wall for somewhere to escape, but couldn't see a spot where the rails were far enough apart for my big feet to fit. I was possessed by the sudden urge to climb the birch tree in front of me. I had passed the first whorl of branches by the time the cow forgot about the calving jack. She circled quickly around and around. Only a bit of the hind legs of the calf was now showing. Still incensed by the chains that dangled behind her, she twirled and bucked. Mud flew in all directions.

"Look out!" screeched Tilly.

My feet had reached the second ring of branches, and I was looking upward when the cow reached the base of the tree. With a crazed bellow, she flipped her head at me, catching my lower foot and almost knocking me from my precarious refuge. Grabbing a branch at the tip of my fingers, I pulled for all I was worth to shinny up a bare portion of the trunk.

The cow was bawling in rage; she whirled around the trees

again and again. She extended her neck, her eyes bloodshot and full of tears. Froth hung from the margins of her mouth. Lunging upward with her front feet against the tree, she snorted, spraying me with foam. Hanging there for a moment, she stuck out her tongue and tried deliberately to munch the heel of my boot. Cows don't bite—I couldn't believe this critter.

"Stay there!" Tilly hollered.

"Don't worry. I don't plan on going anywhere soon."

For the next twenty minutes, the acrimonious beast circled around and around the clump of trees, infuriated that she couldn't reach me. Anxious as I was to get out of the predicament, I clung firmly to the trunk, thankful for my place of refuge. Tilly fussed around the outside of the corral, totally beside herself.

Suddenly, as though on a mission, she began pounding away at the ancient head gate in the corner of the log structure. Five minutes of banging and crashing accomplished something, because eventually she was able to swing the gate open and closed at will. Scurrying around at the far end of the corral, she finally pushed open a gate to the entrance of the chute.

As Tilly entered the enclosure, the cow stopped pacing to stare at this new annoyance. Straining again, she staggered from the base of my tree to the front of the chute. With an aggressive shake of her head, she stopped, looked towards the lake and the other cattle, and sent several long blats in their direction.

"There now, girl," chirped Tilly. "Settle down now."

The cow lumbered back beneath my tree and peered up at me with disdain. She strained again heartily and took a step towards Tilly.

"I'm going to try and get her to follow me down the alleyway, Dave. As soon as she comes in, get a pole behind her so we have her confined."

The cow raised and lowered her head as the crusty woman took a baby step in her direction. Snorting through both nostrils, the beast tossed her head and took after my would-be rescuer as she retreated into the confined V at the head of the chute.

"Be careful, Tilly!"

The moment the cow had cleared the entranceway, I jumped down, slammed the gate closed, and slid the bolt home. The irate creature was partway down the chute before she realized her folly. Tilly slammed the front gate closed, and I rammed a pole behind her.

"Are you all right?"

"Just fine." Tilly's reply came between puffs; she was leaning over with her hands on her knees.

The cow backed up until she ran into the pole, then crashed like a bovine bulldozer into the metal head gate. As the structure creaked and groaned against her weight, I moved the pole ahead to further confine her.

"Hand me that lariat, Tilly. We better get her under control before she does something crazy."

I leaned over the top rails and slid the noose of the lariat over the cow's neck. Dodging repeated butts from her head, I finally slipped the rope through the noose and over her nose. When I tightened it, she was secured in such a manner that she couldn't choke herself.

"Okay, Tilly, let's back her out."

"Why can't you do her right there where she can't get away from us?"

"With a big calf like that, if she goes down on us halfway through, we may end up losing them both. I've got the holding gate closed, so we'll just back her up to the end of the chute and tie her to the last post. That way if she lies down, I've got room to work."

The cow literally flew backwards down the chute and crashed forcefully into the rails at the far end. Worrying that she might have injured the poor calf's legs, I dropped the rope to the ground and took a few quick wraps around the base of the post. She charged ahead and I cinched up the lariat. Secured at last!

While the cow snorted and reefed at her confinement, I gathered the pieces of my equipment. By the time I had them cleaned up enough to use again, she was straining against the rope. I positioned the jack once more and began to apply downward pressure to the chains. I maintained the tension as she pushed, and her pelvic inlet was soon filled with the huge buttocks of her calf. Letting out a mournful moan, she slowly crumpled. I stepped back as she flopped heavily onto her left side.

The cow's enormous belly bulged as she strained. Taking a few more quick pumps on the jack, I pulled down between her hind legs. She bellowed as the calf's massive thighs and hips slid through the vaginal lips.

"Get the cold water ready, Tilly!" My voice was terse, almost shrill.

I straightened the bar and pumped madly on the jack. The long, slender abdomen of the calf slipped easily from his mother's womb and, for a while, there was almost no tension at all. With the impingement of the umbilicus, we were at the point of no return. The first of the ribs came into view and the going got tougher.

"My God, Tilly! We may be in trouble."

I pulled downward on the jack, following the contour of the calf's body. It continued to come, but it was ever so tight. I straightened the jack and applied tension to the chains again.

"Oh man…"

I was met with a long period of resistance when nothing budged. I felt the calf's muscles tense; his body twitched convulsively. The mother bellowed loudly, panted, and strained for all she was worth. There was sudden movement when the shoulders finally released; I fell backwards, pulling desperately on the chains. The calf slid onto the ground in front of me. I clamoured for my footing as I tore at the membranes that covered his face. His heart was pounding, but he had yet to attempt a breath.

"The cold water, Tilly!" I dug madly at the calf's mouth and raked gobs of mucous from the back of his throat. Tilly thrust a bucket in front of me, and I flung icy water onto the outstretched body. He drew in a breath; his eyes blinked. I grabbed a twig and stuck it up the calf's nostril, then listened to the rattle of fluid as he took another breath.

On my feet again, I grasped the monstrous baby under his abdomen and struggled to lift him to the fence. With Tilly's help, I managed to heave him up and hook his hind legs over the top rail.

"Hold the legs steady!" I let go and opened the calf's mouth. Long strings of mucous dangled down as he struggled to breathe. I slapped him aggressively on first one side, then the other, and cleared away the slime. Air was moving nicely with each breath now, and I wrapped my arms around his huge, slippery body to half lower, half drop him to the ground.

"My God, Tilly, this calf's humongous. I helped deliver one by Caesarian in Saint Paul, Alberta, that weighed a hundred and eighty pounds. I swear this one's bigger."

The calf shook his head and opened his big brown eyes. His breaths were coming in rapid succession, and his nose and tongue had begun to pink up. The cow still lay stretched out, panting from exhaustion.

"Isn't he a beauty?" Tilly's face beamed with a smile that literally radiated enthusiasm. "He's certainly all bull."

I smiled, sharing her zeal for the fact that the calf was going to live. I looked at his barrel chest, his heavily muscled hips. If a huge cow like this had so much trouble allowing him passage into the world, how would some poor Hereford have fared?

I scrubbed my arms down with surgical soap and knelt behind the cow. She stirred when I directed my hand forward over her pelvic canal. I breathed a sigh of relief as I explored her birth canal—no bleeding, no tears.

Tilly rushed around gathering her supplies from the barn while I watched the pair gain strength. The cow rolled up on her brisket and struggled to get her head back far enough to see her calf. I gave her more slack and finally noticed that I was starting to breathe easier myself.

The calf let out a blat when Tilly pierced his ear with a tag; the big blond cow lunged to her feet, pulling at the rope to get to her baby. I slopped tincture of iodine over his navel.

"I need to do everything that has to be done right now. I don't expect I'll get another chance to get hold of him." Tilly handed me a pair of syringes and I injected selenium and vitamin ADE into the calf's hind leg. He struggled to a sitting position.

"Are we ready to let her have him?" asked Tilly.

She moved her bucket of supplies to the other side of the corral. We closed the gate to the holding pen, and I leaned over and fumbled with the lariat. The cow flipped her head at me in a belligerent fashion, then pulled back and struggled against the rope. I finally managed to release the metal latch, and the cow propelled backwards to crash into the far wall. Shaking her head defiantly, she took a quick run in my direction.

We retreated to the far end of the corral with our equipment. Tilly climbed over the wall first, and I handed everything to her. When we looked back at the new mother, her head was lowered; she was licking at her treasure.

"Looks like she's going to take him."

"She's a good mother," Tilly sighed. "I had no doubt of that."

We wandered lazily back up the trail to the fence. I had thrown the last of my things to the other side of the metal gate and was about to climb over myself when Tilly spoke up.

"You have to have a look at last year's baby before you leave."

She was already on her way back down the hill, and I followed. Stopping at an old building that could have once been the living quarters of the homestead, she grabbed a flake of hay and carried it to the fenced area at the back.

"Come, Bullie! Come, Bullie."

I watched in awe as the animal swaggered in our direction. His shoulders and hindquarters were simply massive. Tilly threw the hay into the rack at the corner of the shed, and Bullie grabbed a mouthful. He was munching contentedly as I stepped around the corner of the building.

"Man, he's big for a yearling."

Before Tilly could comment, the bull reacted. As if shot from a cannon, he tore across the pasture. Fifty yards away, he stopped and turned to face me. Raising and lowering his head, pawing with his front feet, he peered myopically in my direction and advanced a few steps towards me. A low rumble emitted from his throat as he stared me down.

Tilly flushed. "He's his mother's son, don't you think?"

Super Saturday

I was easing into the day with a piece of toast and peanut butter when I heard shuffling noises in the lab. I tramped down the stairs from my apartment. "What's up, Doris?"

She was busy folding surgery drapes. "The phone hasn't rung since I got here, and you don't have a thing on the book." She wrapped the package tightly and taped it closed. "Oh, don't you look snappy."

I was wearing one of the new shirts I'd just received by post from The Big and Tall Store in Vancouver. At six feet eleven, the only articles of clothing I could find to fit me in Creston were underwear and a belt.

"It feels good to wear something new for a change. With this job though, God only knows what it'll look like by the end of the day."

Saturday could be so unpredictable. We tried to keep it for people who couldn't get in throughout the week and, although we made a policy of only booking morning appointments, it often turned into a full day. I sat at my desk and mulled through the stack of patient records that were waiting for my notations. I had progressed as far as the current week when I found a page that stumped me.

"The Anderson dog, Doris...do you remember anything about him? The owner's name is Bill; the dog's name is Rex. You forgot to write anything on the card when he was brought in."

Doris sighed and left her post at the examination table. Scanning the daybook, she appeared puzzled. "I'm sorry, I don't remember any of the Andersons being in lately. Funny that it's not even on the day page."

She retrieved the big black binder that contained all the billings for the current month. "So what date am I looking for?" Her tone implied that she didn't expect an answer that would be of much assistance.

"Well, most of these cards were only a couple of weeks old, so I doubt it would be much further back than that."

I worked on the others while Doris searched for evidence of a visit from Rex.

"Here it is! And why am I surprised that it's in your handwriting? The bill's for an out-of-hours office call and for Panolog ointment. You saw him on March 12."

"Oh yeah, I remember! That was the guy from Penticton who was travelling through and had a dog with an infected ear."

Doris replaced the record book in the desk drawer and returned to her drapes with a smug look on her face. She had proven to be a capable and meticulous record-keeper; it wasn't often that I could catch her up on something she hadn't done correctly.

The telephone started ringing with a vengeance, and my record-keeping was quickly pushed to the back burner. I had just hung up the receiver when a buxom blonde woman came crashing through the door. She had a grouchy-looking dachshund tucked under her arm like a loaf of French bread.

"His toenail's been bleeding all morning, and I just can't get it to stop!" Her words spurted between short, choppy breaths. She motioned to the right front foot that was swaddled with a grubby-looking, blood-soaked rag.

I recognized the woman from a previous encounter and, although I couldn't remember her name, I knew she'd been in with a tabby cat that had been scratching incessantly at its ears. She wore no makeup; her short bleached hair was unkempt. The front of her white blouse and a large area of exposed bosom were covered with blood and dog hair. She was holding the animal's bandaged foot as far from her as possible. If she was concerned about her appearance, she made no apology.

As I approached, the old dog rolled back his lip to expose yellow, plaque-covered teeth. A low-pitched grumble sounded from the depths of his bowels. His owner rapped him sharply on the nose. "Jasper, be nice! Don't growl at the doctor like that!"

I quickly changed my mind about taking the dog from her arms. If the growl was not sufficient warning, the look in his feisty old eyes certainly was.

"I'll need you to give me a hand, Doris!" I found a three-foot length of gauze and formed a loop with a loose slip knot at the top. At my approach, the dog again rolled back his lip and turned his head so that he could watch me more carefully.

"Oh, hello Katherine," Doris said. "Is he not too happy to be visiting?"

"Jasper! You quit that!" Katherine hollered. "This dog's fine so long as you never have to do anything to him. He bites me too, whenever I try to handle him."

"Can you hold him just a little closer? I'll see if I can get a muzzle on him."

Katherine pulled him against her body, managing to get one hand near the base of his neck. Panic-stricken, he tried to bite her finger. While he was distracted, I slipped the loop over his nose and reefed it tight. He emitted a stifled yelp, then wheeled to bite me but, by that time, I had already tied a second knot and tightened it under his chin. With Jasper still wriggling like a fish on a line, I tied a final knot behind his head and cinched it down.

My voice was as calm as I could muster. "Settle down now, fella, we're not going to hurt you."

At that, he threw a good old-fashioned temper tantrum. Urinating and defecating all over Katherine's pants, he struggled frantically to break free of her grasp. I held the reluctant mutt closely against my body and headed for the examination room. Several turds plopped to the floor behind me.

"Now you know why his nails look like they do!" Katherine crumpled into a heap on the bench. "I took him to another vet to get them done when he was younger. Once when he was about a year old, the vet cut a nail too short and made him bleed. What a circus! After that, I could never control him; if we tried to do anything, he always put on this big scene! I haven't even had him to the vet in the last five years."

"Well, we'll see what we can do with him." I passed the dog to Doris. "If he doesn't behave, we'll just have to sedate him."

Jasper sat rigidly in Doris's arms, every muscle tight and ready to explode. I grabbed a pair of nail clippers and began snipping away at his back feet. He glared at me with passionate distaste. At each crunch of the clippers, his eyes flashed and his body flinched. When I finished trimming his back nails and moved to the front, he flared again. His front nails were so long that his toes were now deformed; both toes and nails had twisted until they were flat to the ground.

Scratching and flailing with front and hind feet, he struggled to be free of Doris's grasp. What little urine he had not already passed dribbled down the front of Doris's smock. The outburst ended as soon as it had begun and, within a few seconds, he was quiet. Focusing again on me, he resumed his glaring.

"That's a good boy." I finished trimming the left front foot and removed the tape that held on the bandage. "You just hold still for a few minutes more and the whole affair will be over."

Jasper demonstrated more temper when I grasped his sore foot, but settled down as soon as he realized I was in for the long haul. The middle claw had been torn free from the nail bed; now it was hanging by only a small bit of cuticle on the lower side. "He obviously hooked it on something," I muttered.

I grasped the nail just as Jasper pulled back, and it came off so easily that he never realized it was gone. Blood dripped liberally from its base, but slowed nicely when I put pressure on the toe.

After I trimmed the remaining nails and bandaged his foot, Doris carried him back to Katherine. "By God, that was slick!" she boomed. "They sure had your number, Jasper; I'd never have believed they could do anything without putting you to sleep!"

We had finished expressing anal glands on an old cocker spaniel and were waiting for a cat to arrive for vaccinations, when the Pridhams called. David's Jersey cow had calved the night before; when he went to bring her in for milking, she was reluctant to stand. Although she finally got up, her movements were so erratic he couldn't handle her.

Within a half hour, I had vaccinated the cat and was pulling off Highway 21 onto the dirt road that headed across the flats towards the old ferry landing. I turned left at the first driveway and pulled up in front of the sign advertising the Pridham Strawberry Farm.

David emerged from his trailer and met me as I climbed out of the car. He was of medium height and slender build. In his early twenties, he was a budding farmer, struggling to find a crop that could sustain him.

"I don't know what's up with her; she's staggering around like she's drunk!"

"Could you get me some warm water, David?" I handed him the stainless steel bucket. "Make it comfortably hot, but not so hot you can't stick your hand in it."

I slipped into my coveralls and pulled on my boots. When he returned with the bucket full to the brim, I was ready to go. Tossing a couple of bottles of calcium into the water to warm them, I grabbed my lariat and the container with my IV drip. David had already forged ahead across the pasture, so I ducked through the fence and hustled after him.

The cow was lying at the base of the dike with her head bent backwards and tucked beneath her hind leg. She seemed unaware

19

of our approach and didn't stir a muscle when David patted her on the back.

"She was like this when I found her the first time." He looked in disgust at the recumbent cow and ran a hand over his short-cropped hair. "I managed to get her up; she staggered around for about ten minutes, then she lay down again."

I pulled a thermometer from its case and inserted it in the cow's rectum. Grasping a horn, I lifted her delicate dish-faced head. Her eyes were closed to slits. I pried her right eye open and watched the pupil for its response to light; it constricted very slowly. I listened to first her chest, then her abdomen. Her heart rate was slower than normal but very regular, and her rumen sounds were barely evident. I checked the thermometer: 37.7, almost a degree below normal.

"It certainly looks like she has milk fever, David. I'll just put this rope on her, and we can give her a bottle of calcium."

I had slipped the noose of the lariat around her neck and was adjusting a loop about her muzzle, when she awakened from her trance. She swung her head forward and pushed up on her hind legs. With her rump in the air, she balanced briefly. Battling for momentum, she threw up her head to get her front feet under her, then lurched off across the pasture, dragging the rope behind her.

"That's what she was doing before!" David jogged after his charge in an attempt to head her off.

The animal was indeed travelling as if inebriated, moving her limbs in an irregular, highly uncoordinated fashion. David managed to grab the rope. As he planted his feet, the sudden jerk pulled the cow's head back and almost knocked her over. Struggling for balance, she ran along sideways for four or five shuffling steps, then splayed her legs and turned to face us. Her whole body was shaking; only by spreading her legs like a saw-horse was she able to remain standing.

We were out in the middle of the pasture. There was nothing in sight that we could use to anchor her. Although she was small and easier to handle than most bovines, she was still a cow; it was going to be far from easy for a man David's size to hold her still for the intravenous treatment.

As I approached with the water and administration kit, he and his cow were at a standoff; David was holding the rope, and the cow was leaning back on it. She didn't move as I attached the bottle of calcium to the intravenous drip set. Quickly, I blocked the jugular vein at the base of her neck, drove a needle into the rope-like structure, and watched blood spurt from the end to spill in an irregular trail beneath her. Tipping the bottle of calcium, I ran the air out of the tube and connected it to the needle.

As soon as I began administering medication, the cow lurched towards David, no longer resisting him. Hoping to hold her still, I wrapped my right arm around her neck, grabbed onto her left horn, and shuffled along with her as she zigzagged forward. The next ten minutes played out as a bizarre choreographed ballet, the cow playing the lead, David and I following as supporting dancers. I maintained my embrace of her head and she dragged me reluctantly along as I held the bottle at shoulder height.

The more calcium the cow received, the more strength she had to resist. The bottle was about two-thirds gone when she decided she'd had enough. Flipping her head, she broke free of my grasp and crumpled to the ground. Her nice little upturned horn managed to hook through my coveralls and catch the front of my shirt. There was a sickly tearing sound as she dropped, and I was yanked to my knees. Something told me I should have left that new shirt in the package.

The intravenous kit pulled apart from the needle, and both calcium and blood spewed onto the ground. Struggling to reconnect the tube, I passed the bottle to David and grabbed the cow by the horns. I wrestled her head towards her hind leg, then wrapped the lariat around it and pulled back to prevent her from getting up again. I slipped the tips of my stethoscope into my ears. Her heartbeat remained strong and regular, and the rest of the calcium soon disappeared into her vein.

While she was in this prone position, I deposited a second bottle of calcium under the skin, being careful to spread it around and only administer a small amount at each site.

"Make sure you remember where I've given these injections, David. Massage it in well and rub these areas two or three times a day for the next few days."

The cow was up and running on steady feet the moment we released the lariat. David was a much happier man, and I felt a glow of satisfaction. How I wished that all treatments could produce the immediate results that calcium did for milk fever.

Visions of a leisurely lunch were quickly dispelled when I opened my office door and was greeted by a waiting room full of people. Mr. McQueen sat stone-faced in the corner with his Siamese cat, Jake, clutched tightly to his chest. Sitting next to him was Mrs. Pulfer; her miniature poodle, Muffins, must have had diarrhea again. The gentleman with the German shepherd was new to me, but I noted with relief that he had a well-mannered dog and seemed to be in control of him.

Doris was talking to Randy Dortman, who was waiting calmly with a coffee in his hand.

"What happened to you?" Doris exclaimed, as she noted that the front of my coveralls was torn away. "Not your new shirt!"

"Yes, my new shirt! Guess it was meant to be a disposable—use it once, then throw it away...Hi Randy. How are things with you today?"

"Pretty good, really. Just have a problem with a calf at home and wanted to ask you a few questions."

"Sure, just let me get these things off, and I'll be right with you."

I threw my dirty bucket and empty bottles in the corner and quickly scrubbed, removing a trace of blood that I noticed on the heel of my left hand. I pulled off my torn coveralls and shook my head in disgust as I viewed my reflection in the mirror. My brand-new cotton shirt! The cow's horn must have hooked in the breast pocket, for it tore in such a manner as to nicely expose my right nipple and half of my chest. I decided against changing when I realized that I could cover the tear with the protective smock I wore during small animal appointments. The upper part of the shirt still looked fine. I took a quick look in the mirror and rushed out to get on with what was sure to be a very long day.

"So what seems to be the problem with the calf, Randy?"

He took a pull on his coffee mug. "Well, she's been doing poorly since birth. I thought she was maybe a couple of weeks early..."

EEEEEEEEEEEEEEEEeeeeeeeeeeeeeeeeee...

There was a terrible commotion across the street. Randy stopped in midsentence and craned his neck to look out the front window. I could hear a high-pitched screaming sound and people were hollering. The German shepherd in the waiting room stood up and strained against his leash, pulling towards the door. Muffins climbed further up Mrs. Pulfer's chest. Mr. McQueen had a definite look of concern on his face as Jake's claws dug deeper into his arm.

Randy and I moved in unison to the entrance. He threw the door open in time to see Verna Levett, with bundle in hand, dismount from the back of a pickup truck that was parked in front of the Creston Hotel. The squealing left little doubt as to what her burden was.

As if she were doing some casual shopping, Verna strolled to the corner and crossed the street towards my office. She was holding onto the hind feet of a forty-pound weaner pig.

EEEEEEEEEEeeeeeeeeeeeeeeee...EEEEEEEEEE...

Pumping his legs up and down like a trip-hammer, the pig screamed every inch of the way. All eyes on the street were focused in Verna's direction. Cars had stopped on both sides of her, and the drivers gaped in disbelief. Dressed in her work clothes and gum-boots, Verna looked like she had just stepped from the barn.

"Oh, my God," I muttered, as she strode into the clinic and extended the pig towards me.

"I went to castrate him this morning and noticed he had a hernia." She was as nonchalant as if she had just handed me a basket of tomatoes.

The pig's screeching changed in both pitch and intensity when I grabbed his legs and hurried towards the kennel room. The German shepherd was leaping against his leash, trying desperately to nip at the pig's dangling ears. Muffins had climbed over Mrs. Pulfer's shoulder and was heading for the planter on the shelf.

Mr. McQueen had lost his placid composure. The side of his neck was cut and bleeding from where the cat's claws had torn through his flesh. With one hand firmly on Jake's tail, he was struggling to grasp the scruff of his neck to pull him down from the wall. The Siamese persisted, determined to climb yet further up the black velvet wallpaper.

I quickly deposited the weaner pig in a kennel and ran back to assist in the waiting room. The German shepherd rushed up to me, nosing frantically at my hands to inhale the opportunity that had been denied him.

"I picked a hell of a day to decide to get Jake dewormed!" Mr. McQueen grumbled, trapping his cat under one arm and rubbing the wounds on the side of his neck.

"Why don't you go and take care of those scratches while we look after him?" I took the cat and handed him, still trembling, to Doris.

The German shepherd remained focused on the kennel room door. The pig's constant squealing had been replaced by a steady oink and a rattle as he rooted at the bottom of the kennel in an attempt to work himself free.

The remainder of the afternoon disappeared in record time and, whenever it looked as if we had caught up, another case materialized. It was six-thirty before Doris was able to sneak down the street to pick up a few sandwiches. We still had to fix the hernia on Verna's animal, and Mrs. Pulfer would be coming back soon to pick up Muffins.

Ten o'clock came and went. Verna had retrieved her still drowsy weaner pig. I was so thankful that the surgery had gone well, considering my dealings with Verna a year earlier. Although she was always pleasant enough, her no-nonsense air kept me off guard.

We were finally ready to call it a day when Paul McCartney phoned.

"Yes, Dr. Perrin, you remember me from the time you fixed that horse's leg out here in Yahk? I run the store here and have a real problem with people breaking in and helping themselves to my stock. The only thing that keeps them honest is my German shepherd, Vandal. He spends most nights in the store and raises a serious commotion if anyone comes near the windows."

"Does he have problems tonight, Paul?" I was tired and wondering where the conversation was leading.

"He sure does! I'm at the store right now and he's in terrible shape…I think someone must have poisoned him to get him out of the way. Can I bring him in?"

"Sure," I replied, seeing the remainder of the night drifting away. "The sooner you can get him here the better."

Doris had just finished bundling up the last of the surgery packs. "Do you want me to hang around for a while yet?" she asked.

"If you don't mind. That dog of McCartney's sounds like he's in pretty rough shape; I may need a hand to start an IV."

Three-quarters of an hour later, Paul pulled up in front of the office. He slowly emerged from his car, a look of defeat plainly etched on his brow.

"Well, the buggers beat me! I got as far as Kitchener, and I could see Vandal wasn't going to make it—he threw up all over the back of my car and then just quit breathing." He removed his base-ball cap and ran his hand fiercely through his thick, carrot-red hair.

I opened the back door. The old German shepherd was in-deed dead. His eyes were glazed, and his protruding tongue was a sickly grey. A good part of the back seat and the forepaws of the dog were covered with vomitus. Poking through the material on the seat, I could see nothing that indicated it was a poison of any kind.

"Could you do an autopsy for me?" Paul asked, as we stood looking down at the body of his friend. "If there's any possibility of catching who did this to him, I certainly would like to! I'll call the cops as soon as you know what it was."

"The problem's always proving who did the deed. Unless you actually saw them put out the bait, it's hard to prove that it was done intentionally. Let's do a post-mortem examination and see if we can determine a cause of death. If it was a result of poison, you can decide where to go from there."

"Well, what else could it be?" asked Paul defensively. "He's been in great shape up until today, and he ate his supper tonight at six."

"I'm not sure, but he looks very pale to me, and there are a variety of things that could cause that."

I went around to the other side door and pulled Vandal's corpse towards me in an attempt to leave as much of the vomitus as possible in the car. The dog was obviously getting on in years, but Paul was right; he was in good shape and hadn't been suffer-ing from something long-term.

I scooped the body into my arms and headed for the clinic. The dog's hind end and head dangled awkwardly. It never ceased to amaze me how much heavier a dead dog was than a live one. I'm sure that death nearly doubles their carrying weight.

"Do you want to take him home to bury him, Paul, or would you rather I cremated him?"

"Why don't you look after him," he muttered despondently. "I don't want to see him after you're done with him!"

It was obvious from the very beginning that there was a vascular disorder somewhere. In the light of the surgery, the mucous membranes were a terrible muddy grey colour. Something had claimed this dog's blood! Tapping one side of his tummy produced a wave that could be felt on the other side. For some reason, he had bled into his abdomen.

Doris was attentive at my elbow as I made my evaluation.

"Paul may have been right about Vandal being poisoned. He looks like he's bled out into his tummy, and warfarin poisoning's certainly a possibility."

Donning plastic gloves and palpation sleeves, I explored the oral cavity and examined the sclera of the eyes. There was no evidence of hemorrhage in either area. Although that didn't totally rule out poisoning, it moved it further down the list as a cause of the bleeding.

Rolling the old boy onto his back, I lifted while Doris placed the thoracic positioner under him to keep his body steady. I made an incision along the dog's midline and peeled back the skin, separating it from the layer of yellow fat. There was no evidence of hemorrhage in either the fat or in the subcutaneous tissues.

"This is looking less and less like a warfarin poisoning." I prepared to make an incision into the abdomen. "Better get the mop and some buckets ready, Doris," I grimaced. "Unless I miss my guess, we're going to have a lot of blood on the floor before long."

My words were prophetic. From the very first puncture of the abdominal wall, fluid flowed like a river onto the table. Doris ran hither and yon with ice cream buckets and gobs of paper towel, trying to corral the stream and keep it from reaching the floor. At first she seemed to be holding her own; most of the blood was either in a bucket or dammed beneath the dog with wads of soggy paper towel. But, when I extended the incision to allow room for my hand in the abdomen, she had to admit defeat. Blood flowed in all directions at once and spilled over the side of the table onto our shoes.

"Oh, my God," Doris moaned. "There's no way that I can keep up now!"

She was right. A gallon of blood had exited in a matter of seconds, and there was no way of capturing it. I went on with the post-mortem as if the sticky mess wasn't there; we'd just have to clean up later. I soon discovered where the leakage had come from.

"Will you look at that!" I lifted a monstrously deformed spleen from the abdomen. "Just look at all the lesions—this poor dog was riddled with cancer."

The spleen was little more than a huge tumour, and the liver wasn't much different. One of the larger masses had burst open like a ripe melon after a rain and had caused the dog to bleed internally.

"Why didn't they notice something sooner?" Doris stared at the hideous growths that protruded from the surface of both organs. "You'd think that the dog would've been feeling sick for a long time for the cancer to get this far!"

"Not necessarily. This looks like a type of cancer called a hemangiosarcoma. It involves the vascular system; the first notice-able signs of problems are often associated with bleeding into the abdomen."

There was no question that this was going to be a very gory affair from beginning to end. No matter where we moved or what we did, we spread more blood around the office. The main flow had been from the table to the street side of the surgery, and Doris was concentrating her effort on keeping it from oozing under the baseboards.

The place could easily have passed for a hall of horror. The dripping red mop, the bucket of crimson water, and our bloody shoes heightened the image. Doris had just dumped her bucket for the second time when I called her to help me fit the dog into a cadaver bag. I had sutured his abdomen to help contain the bowels, and was now ready to move the body to my vehicle.

"I don't know how we're going to get him in this bag without wearing more blood." I was in a quandary. The dog was soaked.

Doris held the sack open at the end of the table, while I lifted the body and pushed from the back end. Little by little, she pulled the bag over Vandal. With a final plunge, I slid him in fully and grasped hold of the sack so Doris wouldn't take the entire weight. Blood dripped from the dog's soggy tail and continued to run onto the floor and, inadvertently, onto the leg of my pants. I grabbed Doris's end of the burden and took off briskly to minimize the sanguine track that I left in my wake. I reached the back door and flung it open. Still at a half run, I stumbled down the stairs and deposited the dead dog in the back of the pickup truck.

What a mess! I looked at the trail of blood that ran up the stairs and over the floor of the clinic for as far as I could see. We were going to be here all night cleaning this up! I would have to douse the stairs with water to dissipate the blood before it had a chance to soak into the wood. Even the door was smeared, from the knob on down.

"Dave!" called Doris from inside. "I need a hand to move the surgery table so I can clean up underneath it."

She had removed most of the debris from the floor and, for the first time, I could see an end in sight. Rolling the surgery table towards the clean section of floor, I carefully avoided the large pool of blood that had accumulated underneath. With the dust pan, Doris scooped up the congealed mass and deposited it in a garbage bag.

"It sure would have been a lot simpler for you to have done this post-mortem outside somewhere!" Her voice was dripping with sarcasm.

"Yeah, wouldn't it? I'll keep that in mind for next time."

Doris inspected me with disgust. "Just look at you!"

I peeled off my smock. I hadn't realized that it had absorbed so much of the blood that had leaked out of the cadaver bag. "Would you look at that," I moaned, checking out my torn, stained shirt. "I guess that'll teach me to wear something brand new to work."

"I know what it's like," Doris said sympathetically. "I can't seem to keep my clothes looking decent for more than…"

Suddenly, Canyon Street was coloured with the flashing lights of an oncoming police car. The vehicle raced past the office and squealed around our corner.

"There's something going on in the alley, Doris!" I darted towards the back door, determined to get outside in time to see what could be happening in Creston to get the police so excited.

Doris dropped her mop and followed my vanishing shadow. It was difficult to slow down on the slippery, blood-soaked floor, and I was out of control when I reached the top landing.

"Halt! Halt!" The voice was shrill and full of anticipation. "Stand where you are!"

I was startled by the unexpected turn of events, but still mentally prepared for the run down the stairs. Below me, with a .38 revolver trained on my chest, was a young RCMP officer I had never seen before. My first impulse was to laugh, but then the cruiser that I'd seen out front smoked down the alley; the corporal jumped from behind the wheel while his car was still rolling. I knew this was no joke.

"Put the gun down!" The bulky corporal was bellowing at the top of his lungs. "He's the vet! He's the vet! Put the gun down!"

He reached the young officer in a few long strides and deflected the gun so it pointed to the ground. I was about ready to laugh again when I saw the looks on their faces. I turned towards Doris—she was ashen.

The young officer pulled off his hat. With his gun dangling aimlessly from his right hand, he staggered to the stairs and sat down. He took one look at the corporal and burst into tears.

"I almost shot him." His voice was barely above a whisper. "I was just doing a routine cruise down the alley. Saw that back door open…all that blood. I radioed in…I was going to check things out when that big son of a bitch ran out all tore up and covered with blood. I almost shot him…I almost shot him."

I didn't know what to say. I shivered. The chill I felt was more profound than the cool air warranted. The young officer sat in a crumpled heap, weeping softly, mumbling to himself. The corporal shook his head. His voice was deadpan.

"Well, I know what we'll be doing for the rest of the night. There's no end of paperwork when a gun's been drawn."

Slick

It had been a hard week. Deep in sleep, I woke to the sound of a drunk hollering on the street below. I stumbled to the window to see him shake his fist at a disembodied voice at the end of Canyon Street. Back in bed, I couldn't drift off again—another Friday night in the town of Creston. I lay for hours commiserating with myself about everything from Alex Shopa's aborting calves to Cindy, the yellow Lab that had died under anesthetic just a few short weeks before. Some memories didn't fade quickly; some may never fade at all.

I maneuvered to the bathroom with Lug following on my heels. He seemed disappointed when I had a pee and went back to bed. I closed my eyes, but my mind was whirling a hundred miles a minute. Finally, I got up, put on a Gordon Lightfoot album, and stretched out on the floor with my head on the huge overstuffed pillow that Ruth Veitch had given me for Christmas. Lug followed me and plunked down with his nose nestled on my leg.

I lay in the dark listening to the click, click, click of the fluorescent sign advertising the City Centre Motel, watching as it intermittently lit up the night outside my window. I envied Lug his peace of mind. I could hear the air flow in and out of his nostrils, see his chest rise and fall. Dogs had it made.

I grabbed a pen and notepad and started scratching thoughts. Why was it I so often felt that I had been pressed to serve on a rudderless ship? Although some days I got to play captain, more frequently I was just the collier who shovelled fiercely to get enough fuel into the fire to keep the pressure in the danger zone. I somehow had to get into the pilothouse, had to plot a course and at least decide which continent I was sailing to.

There were so many questions. Being a real, live country vet was not without its share of knocks. I loved the fact that I was providing a service and that I made a small difference in some people's lives. The better part of three weeks had passed since Gerald Phillips had called about one of those strange milk fevers, and at least as long since a cow had aborted on the Shopa farm. Had my recommendations made a difference, or were we just waiting for the other shoe to fall?

I looked at the chicken scratch on the notepad, then tossed it into the corner. I wanted to sleep. I was so tired—deep down tired—but I knew it was a waste of time to go back to bed. I grabbed the pad and once more started making notes. This time it took the form of a poem—a poem about sleep, or rather, the lack of it.

Just after seven, I started the car and pointed it towards West Creston. I didn't know why I always headed to Grampa's place when I was in a pensive mood like this, but there was something about it that was comforting. Maybe because the house was high on the mountain and offered a perspective that allowed me to look at my problems from a distance.

I parked at the bottom of the drive and strode up the hill to the log cabin. Lug raced ahead, sniffing out all the new smells and lifting his leg on each fruit tree he passed. I wandered to the far end of the verandah and straddled the rail. This had been my favourite place when I lived here and conducted my practice out of the old house. How many hours I had sat in this exact location watching the goings-on of the valley below me. Here, I was just an observer; here, I could stay above the fray.

I felt like a child again, free from the financial worries of the practice, free from the demands that were constantly being put upon me. If I worked hard on my father, gathered enough worms and dragonflies, I would maybe get to go fishing. I could almost hear the screen door slam, almost see my grandfather shuffle out onto the verandah and give the valley his morning inspection.

There was the faintest tinge of green eking its way into the muddy yellows and browns of the flatlands below. It wouldn't be long now before the grass would really take off. The trees would leaf out and blossom, and winter would be driven from the stage. It was just the other day that I had seen the first pussy willows. Where had that been?

The quiet purples of the surrounding mountains, the reflective ribbon of the Kootenay River meandering its way along the length of the valley. It was all so soothing. I watched a pair of calves tear across the neighbour's field. A nighthawk wooed; a cow bawled in the distance. A hawk sailed effortlessly above me. His wings fixed, he was held aloft by the wind alone. I wondered if he even noticed me.

No one had moved in after I had vacated the premises eight months earlier, and things had continued to revert to the wild. In my mind, the life that my grandparents had lived here had always been something romantic; they survived quite nicely without the amenities of running water and electricity. For them, the activities of the day were dictated more by the position of the sun than by the hands on a clock.

Along the path to the outhouse, brush and weeds had reclaimed what had once been a hard-packed thoroughfare. I stomped down the tall, dry remains of some bull thistle and rounded the clump of cedars that hid the wooden structure from the house. The ancient biffy had settled with the years. Its floor was several inches lower than ground level; its door hung askew. I laughed out loud as I thought of Riga, my brother-in-law—how he hated this simple facility. On our final trip here as a family, he had delayed using it as long as possible. He hated the spiders, hated the stench, hated the closed, dank confines of the little cubicle. I remembered the feeling of exhilaration as I sneaked up and lodged a pole against the door when he had finally forced himself to venture inside. I could hear him holler yet.

I suspected little had changed in Grampa's house since my departure. Peering through the kitchen window, I could make out the bucket that I'd set in the middle of the room to catch a leak. The sheet of drywall that was sagging so badly in the ceiling had finally given way.

I roamed the property for hours that morning, breathing in the memories and contemplating my future.

The remainder of the day was remarkably quiet. Other than the hospitalized critters, nothing demanded my attention. What a treat to have some time to myself. I clicked on the television to catch the news and was immediately overwhelmed by coverage of the evacuation of Saigon. The Americans were finally willing to admit defeat and put an end to the anguish of their own young men. Heart-rending footage of abandoned South Vietnamese soldiers left little doubt that their suffering was a long way from over.

I drifted off with the picture of a Vietnamese soldier clinging to the undercarriage of a helicopter firmly etched in my memory. Thank God I had been spared the horrors that those poor men had endured.

At midnight, the phone rang. Damn, it seemed that I had just closed my eyes. Flicking on the bedroom light, I plodded reluctantly to the phone.

"Hello," I croaked.

"Yes, Doctor, this is Mrs. Regier."

"Mrs. Regier. What can I do for you?"

"It's Slick. We're terribly worried about him. He's running all over the house—just won't settle down. I tell you, he's driving us crazy!"

"How? Do you think he's in pain?"

"No, he doesn't yelp or anything...But, he is very sick. The way he's acting, we're afraid he won't last much longer." Her voice quivered.

"Can you be more specific, Mrs. Regier? What's different about Slick that makes you think he's so ill?"

"He's just acting strange! He hasn't settled down all evening—won't sit on our laps, won't even look at us. I'm sure it's something serious. I had him in to see you a couple of weeks ago, but that was a waste of money. You couldn't find a thing wrong with him; now he's worse than ever."

I could feel my ears burning from a sudden rush of blood. The muscles of my jaw tightened reflexively, and I continued through gritted teeth. "Has the dog been outside? Could he have gotten into something rotten or picked up poison?"

"No, he hasn't been out all evening, and it's impossible for him to get into anything in the house. Besides, he's the same as he was the last time I brought him in!"

"Did he eat tonight?"

"Yes, he ate his supper."

"How long ago was that?"

"I told the sitter to feed him around seven—his food was all gone when we got home."

"Would he eat now?"

"He might."

"Well surely, if he would eat, he can't be all that sick. Is it possible you're overreacting a bit?"

"I am not overreacting, Dr. Perrin!" I shifted the phone from my ear as Mrs. Regier roared on. "Slick's a very sick little dog and I would like to have him seen...tonight."

I took a deep breath and counted slowly to myself. One...two...three...four...five. I exhaled.

"Okay, Mrs. Regier, why don't you bring Slick to the clinic." Fighting the urge to slam down the receiver, I hung it up carefully and deliberately.

The battle for the possession of my mind was on. The whole

time I was dressing and all the way down the stairs, I played the tape of reason, a message of consolation that I had recorded for just such occasions. Take deep breaths and relax. You're a public servant. It's in your own best interest to serve your clients well. Service. Service.

Bullcrap! My friend Gordon's favourite expression echoed from within the sleep-deprived recesses of my mind. That woman doesn't have an ounce of sense. If she did, she'd have booted the dog's arse outside and gone to sleep. Any person with a trace of consideration would have waited till morning to see what was up. But, countered the voice of reason, what if there actually is something wrong with the dog? You'll never forgive yourself if the dog is really sick and dies unattended.

The voices were still bickering back and forth when I heard the rap on the door. I reached it in a few strides and flung it open.

"Thank you for seeing us, Dr. Perrin."

Mrs. Regier's short, squat body was swaddled in a bulky woollen coat. Flashing green eyes peered out from beneath a red toque. A matching scarf encircled her neck. Perched in her arms was a long-haired, shaggy dog that looked like an overgrown Pekinese.

"Well there, Slick, you're looking chipper."

"He's brightened up now that we've been out in the cool air," Mrs. Regier countered defensively. "There's something drastically wrong, though…isn't there, Bill?"

The burly man behind her nodded his head glumly. "There's something not right with our boy."

Bill removed his cap, exposing a shiny, hairless crown. He stared down at the bundle in his wife's arms, raising and lowering bushy red eyebrows as he focused on the dog's quivering frame. Slick's buggy brown eyes stared into Bill's face as if pleading with him to take him back out on the street. He squirmed and crawled over Mrs. Regier's shoulder. Bill quickly stepped forward and scooped him up. "There's a boy. We'll get to the bottom of this. Settle down…Settle down."

He lifted Slick to his face and the dog's long, pink tongue lashed madly at Bill's cheek and bulbous nose. Mrs. Regier shot an accusing look at the trembling dog, as if put out that he had abandoned her, then began picking absently at the long black hairs that covered her white coat.

"Let's bring Slick into the examination room, Mr. Regier."

I headed through the clinic with the anxious couple on my heel. Grabbing a thermometer, I waited expectantly for Bill to put Slick on the table. The big man stood stock-still, holding the reluctant patient closely to his breast. His stance made it perfectly obvious that he was not about to subject his boy to the indignity of the cold, slippery surface of a stainless steel table. Drawing a deep breath, I maneuvered my way around Mrs. Regier and gently slid the thermometer into Slick's rectum.

"There's my boy," Bill chattered. "You're goin' to be just fine. Dad won't let 'im hurt you."

Slick shot a worried look towards Mrs. Regier as she stood back to give me more room. He flinched when the gas heater clicked on and a blast of hot air cascaded over us. Mrs. Regier removed her scarf, then absently undid the top four buttons of her coat. Not even for a second did she take her eyes from Slick.

"Is it bad?" she asked, as I removed the thermometer and wiped it with a paper towel.

"As a matter of fact, it's perfectly normal—38.5. Right where the textbook claims it should be."

Mrs. Regier and her husband exchanged worried glances as Slick struggled to climb yet higher up Bill's torso. A bead of sweat appeared magically on the bulky man's forehead, enlarged, and trickled slowly down his brow.

"It's okay, boy...It's okay. You're goin' to be just fine."

I ran my hands over Slick's trembling body, looking for anything that could be considered abnormal. His smooth, glossy hair coat ran freely under my fingertips. Nowhere could I find evidence of a blemish or scab. Plucking him from Bill's arms, I settled him on the tabletop.

"Hold him steady, will you, Bill?"

Bill stooped his massive frame to kneel next to the table. He held Slick's face against his cheek, then focused on my hands as they travelled from one site to the next in search of enlarged lymph nodes. His bushy eyebrows moved in concert with Slick's as they flicked rhythmically up and down.

"Has there been any change in his eating habits over the last while?"

"No," replied Mrs. Regier vacantly. "He still seems to be eating well."

"Has he ever stiffened as if he were having a seizure? Has he had sessions when he twitched or looked dazed or confused?"

Both heads wagged in unison and I continued my search in silence. Slick stared woefully at his master's face as I palpated his abdomen. Not a thing abnormal, not a loop of bowel out of place. I applied pressure over the base of the dog's spine, slowly working my way forward, searching for indication of back pain.

"Has he been able to climb stairs and jump up on things today?"

"He was on the bed and the sofa tonight, but as soon as we sat down, he got up and left," Bill replied in a morose tone.

Lifting Slick's head, I manipulated his neck first one way, then the other. "Does he ever drag his butt on the ground or act as if he's constipated?"

"I've seen him drag his bum before." Bill's voice was hesitant. "You remember, Helen, when he scooted across the rug in the entry room a couple of weeks ago?"

Mrs. Regier nodded in agreement. Her eyes widened as I smeared lubricant on my gloved index finger and slowly applied pressure against Slick's anal sphincter. Bill tightened his grip. Rivulets of sweat coalesced on his forehead to run in streams down his nose and flushed cheeks. He blinked as his eyes flooded. Mrs. Regier retired to the waiting room, her face an ashen contrast to the fiery red of her scarf and toque.

"There's a boy, Slick," I chimed. "We'll be just a moment."

Slick squirmed in Bill's grasp as he struggled to evade my marauding finger. Riding out his protest, I waited for his sphincter to relax, then trapped an anal gland between my finger and thumb. Slick whimpered as a watery, grey material ran from an orifice just inside the rectum and dripped onto the tabletop. I repeated the procedure on the opposite side, then slid Slick forward to protect him from being soiled by the puddle that had formed at his feet.

Bill's face skewed as he caught wind of the foul-smelling excrement. Moving Slick to arm's length, he lumbered to his feet. I continued my examination; the prostate, bladder, and bowel all felt normal. I grabbed some paper towel to clean up Slick's bum. I had sprayed down the hair on his rear end and cleaned off the table by the time Mrs. Regier returned.

"My Lord, what's that putrid smell?" Wrinkling her nose, she gave me a look of disgust and retraced her steps to the waiting room.

"Do you think that was his problem?" Bill was still holding the dog at a distance, even though Slick was using all his charms to evoke a cuddle.

"The glands were getting a bit full, but there was no evidence of infection." I slowly wagged my head. "I doubt that they are much cause for concern."

I held Slick's head in my hands and stared into his big brown eyes. He struggled to get out of my grasp, his eyes turning almost inside-out seeking the big man behind him. Finally, he settled down to stare grudgingly in my direction.

His eyes were bright, both pupils the same size. I rolled back the eyelids one at a time; the mucous membrane looked perfectly normal. Slick licked his lips nervously. I placed a finger in his mouth and pried open his overshot jaw. His teeth were pearly white, his gums healthy. I depressed his tongue. The lining of his throat was a healthy pink, his tonsils normal in size, buried nicely within their crypts.

"There we go, Slick. That wasn't so bad, was it?"

"What have you found?" Mrs. Regier had returned from her self-imposed exile.

"Nothing out of the ordinary, to be honest."

I could feel the woman's eyes boring into my back. "You're missing something, Doctor."

"Just be patient please, Mrs. Regier...Give me the opportunity to finish my examination."

I grabbed a stethoscope and lifted Slick into my arms. He shivered and looked desperately back and forth at the Regiers, as I carried him into the waiting room. I took a deep breath and tried to concentrate on listening to his chest.

Nothing about this whole evening made the slightest sense. At one in the morning, I was wandering around the office with a perfectly healthy dog in my arms trying to pacify a couple of neurotic owners. Why was it so tough to be successful at his racket? I was tempted to just give Slick a shot of saline and send these folks on their merry way. Maybe they'd be happy with that. Mrs. Regier was certainly not going to accept the fact that there was nothing wrong with her dog.

I yawned and shook my head, trying to stem the flow of negative self-talk. Concentrate. Concentrate. As Slick stopped struggling, the thump, thump of his heart finally settled to a steady lub-dub, lub-dub, lub-dub. I moved the stethoscope head further up and listened to the gentle ebb and flow of air from the dog's chest. Everything sounded disgustingly normal.

What in the world was I going to do with this trio? They had about exhausted my repertoire. I didn't want to invent something wrong with the dog, but Mrs. Regier really wanted me to discover an ailment.

I plunked on the bench in the waiting room with Slick on my lap, peered into his eyes, and gently ruffled his ears. I casually flipped each of them over and looked for signs of discolouration, irritation, or wax build-up. Slick had the healthiest ears in town.

I lowered him to the floor and let him go. He tore across the waiting room like a child running into the drifts at first snowfall. He whined excitedly and danced around the feet of his rather perplexed owners. At that moment, even they would have to admit he looked a long way from Death's door.

The Regiers stared mutely as I wandered to the kennel room. Sorting through a stack of cans, I grabbed one and pulled open the tab—nice smelly cat food called Turkey Feast. Ladling some into a stainless bowl, I set it on the floor. Mrs. Regier had already scooped Slick up, and he was busily washing her cheek.

"Would you mind putting him down, Mrs. Regier? Let's just see if he would be interested in food."

She gave her husband a look of resignation, then reluctantly lowered the dog to the floor. Slick stuck his nose in the bowl and ravenously devoured the offering. I dumped in the remainder of the can and watched with a strange feeling of satisfaction as he polished off the last of it.

Mrs. Regier settled on the waiting room bench and shook her head in disgust. "There's something wrong, I tell you. He's doing his best to make a liar out of me, but he's not well."

"Has there been anything unusual going on at home today, Mrs. Regier?"

"What do you mean by that?" she snapped defensively.

"I'm just wondering if anything has changed. Have you had company? Had a fight? Made any major changes to your routine? It may well be that Slick is just reacting to something that's going on in the household. Pets can pick up on stress and sometimes react in unpredictable ways."

It was a moment before either of them spoke. "Well, Bill was packing his suitcase this afternoon," Mrs. Regier offered hesitantly. She looked at her husband pensively. "Do you think it's possible, Bill? Do you think he could be upset that you're leaving?"

I could detect a glimmer of light in this dismally dark night and wasn't anxious to see it fade. "That could certainly explain

Slick's behaviour. I can't find a thing wrong with your dog physically. As a matter of fact, he's the picture of health. We could run some blood tests to rule out something exotic, but from what you've told me, I think that his problem may well be psychological."

"Is that probable?" Mrs. Regier looked skeptical. "Could it be that we have a neurotic dog? Maybe we should consider doing some blood tests."

"You have no idea, Mrs. Regier. It's ever so common that upheaval at home causes major changes in a pet's behaviour. Animals quite often amplify what's going on around them."

Bill shuffled to the bench and plopped down next to his wife. "You see, I work up north—three weeks in and a week out. Before I started packin' this afternoon, I sat down and had a long talk with Slick." His eyes were very sad as he continued. "I told him that I was goin' to have to leave again. I explained to him that I wasn't leavin' because I wanted to, that I had to work or there would be no place for us to live and nothin' for us to eat..."

"You think he got mad at you because of your little talk?" I was struggling to hide my skepticism.

"It gets worse from there," Mrs. Regier interjected. "After his talk with Slick, Bill wanted me to phone and cancel our plans so he could be with him on his last night home. We were going out to the Dionisos Restaurant with my sister and her husband. I phoned and told her we couldn't make it, but my brother-in-law phoned back and said they were coming to pick us up anyway because he wasn't going to be stood up over a dog. They just don't understand...We should have stayed home."

The Regiers exchanged forlorn looks. Bill closed his eyes and rested his head against the wall. His wife carried on. "We made arrangements for our next door neighbour to come over and baby-sit. Slick likes her and we figured it might be all right. They watched television. Slick loves that sort of thing—lots of noise and cars and fighting."

"I knew we should have stayed home, Dr. Perrin," Bill muttered. He had the most tormented look on his face; his eyes were watering. "We've put Slick through so much…It just wasn't fair of us. Now that I think back on it, it all makes sense. He just hates us for what we've done to him, and now he's punishin' us."

"I wouldn't feel too badly about that, Bill. I think it's up to Slick to adjust to your lifestyle and not the other way around. Maybe if you were to just let him work through his moods on his own, you'd be further ahead. When he's being antisocial and punishing you, put him outside by himself and see if he isn't happier when he comes back in…You're letting him run your life. Dogs in the wild have traditionally worked under a system of dominance in the pack and, right about now, Slick feels he's in the alpha position."

I had finally found a narrow trail through the minefield that Mrs. Regier and her culpable pet had laid for me. The last notations on Slick's hospital record were made just over three weeks before. Mrs. Regier had presented him with a vague history of his "not doing well," and I had been unable to come up with anything out of the ordinary.

"Mrs. Regier, when you brought Slick in last time, was Bill at home or was he away?"

"He was still in camp…But, come to think of it, that was the same day he talked to Slick on the phone."

"You're kiddin'," Bill interjected. "I wonder…"

"You…you talk to Slick on the phone, Bill?"

"Oh, yes. A couple of times a week, actually. I call up and chat with Helen for a bit. Then she sets the phone on the sofa, and Slick sits there and listens. When I'm done talkin', he leaves the phone and Helen knows that it's time to hang up."

I had no idea how to respond. It was Mrs. Regier who finally spoke.

"You know, Doctor, I think you may just be onto something. I would never have taken Slick for a neurotic dog, but the more I think about it…"

After a long discussion about the strange things that animals were capable of and a complete rundown of Slick's antics since he was a pup, I wrote out a statement for the Regiers. Bill pulled his coat on and herded his wife towards the exit. They were almost to the door when she broke away from him, put her hand on my forearm, and smiled warmly. "Thank you, Dr. Perrin, Slick is feeling so much better now."

Completely at ease in his caretaker's arms, the dog was the picture of contentment. The very tip of his long pink tongue stuck innocently over his protruding lower jaw; his eyes were closed. He looked for all the world to be in meditative bliss.

For a while that evening, I had felt that no matter how I handled Slick, I was going to come out looking like a quack. As it was, everyone seemed to be content. I slipped on a jacket and called Lug downstairs for a quick walk to the alley. I shivered; the cool air was refreshing. As my faithful companion snuffed around and lifted his leg at all his favourite spots, I stared up into the starlit night.

Life was filled with contrasting realities. Every time I closed my eyes, two pictures battled to predominate. How was it possible for them to co-exist? One was of Slick sitting on the couch listening to the telephone; the other was of that young soldier a world away hanging on to the only reality he had come to know. I sighed. Would I sleep tonight?

Eleanor

My morning had started early. It was just after eight when I picked my shirt off a straw bale and slipped my arms into the sleeves. The Caesarian at Shopas' farm had gone well. Shirley rushed in to clean up while Alex and I milked the heifer and gave the calf his first drink of colostrum. By the time we arrived in the house, the coffee pot was perking and bacon was sizzling in a large cast-iron frying pan.

Alex washed up at the kitchen sink as I braced my elbow on the top of the refrigerator and struggled to pull off my coveralls. Shirley gave me a funny smile, then waved me to the bathroom. Submerging my arms in warm water, I scrubbed away at blood that had crusted on my elbows. A shiver ran up my spine; it had been cool in the barn this morning, but the frigid conditions of winter were thankfully gone for another year.

I returned to the kitchen to find the wiry, sandy-haired man seated at the head of a well-used chrome table, busily rolling cigarettes. A can of Player's tobacco sat open before him. Stuffing his little machine with tobacco, he licked a paper and ejected a perfectly formed cigarette into a stack on the table. He packed the dozen rolled smokes into a metal container, then swiped some errant shreds of tobacco back into the can.

"Well, that surgery sure went slick. Can't say I like having to call you out here, but it feels better when I got something to show for it...was driving me nuts the way those calves came early

one after the other." He grimaced; his frown accentuated well-entrenched wrinkles. "You have no idea how tough it was to go out there every morning expecting another carcass—had such a gut ache, I couldn't eat for days."

Shirley nodded her head in agreement. "It's not as if poor Alex could afford to miss many meals; he has trouble holding his weight as it is."

We all chuckled. Taking a deep drag on his cigarette, Alex tipped his head back, stared at the ceiling, and exhaled a jet of smoke. "What a waste—feeding those damned critters and looking after 'em all that time for nothing. I was beginning to have visions of wandering in and giving the banker the keys."

I nodded my head in sympathy. "I can only imagine how it must have felt. Thank God for everyone's sake that the abortions seem to be over."

Alex reached an arm around his wife's waist. "May have to put the boss out to work soon."

"Well, there's an option," I interjected. "You're a fantastic help around critters, Shirley, and Doris and I have been talking about training a new assistant at the office. Maybe you should give it some thought."

Shirley smiled and turned to her husband. The couple traded a knowing look. Alex took a final drag on the butt he'd been playing with and exhaled. Retrieving one of the neatly rolled cigarettes from the case in his vest pocket, he popped it in his mouth and delicately held the tiny morsel of the dying butt to light the new one. After a few quick puffs, he dropped the butt into the ashtray and ground it out.

Shirley meticulously fished out bacon strips one by one, then cracked a pair of eggs into the sizzling pan. "How do you like yours, Dave?"

"Sunny-side up, if you don't mind." My mouth watered at the prospect of my favourite breakfast.

"Do you know anything about Eleanor Blair, Dave?" Alex

stared inquisitively at me through a haze of smoke. "You must have had something to do with her, what with all the critters she has."

I smiled. "Yeah, I see a lot of her…Why?"

"She called me again this morning; wants ten more bales of my best hay." Alex squinted as smoke from his cigarette slowly drifted into his eyes. "I've been supplying her a few bales at a time since last fall. It's a pain in the arse, but what can I do? I feel sorry for her…I know she only takes what she can pay for. Hate the thought of her not having grub for those old plugs of hers."

Shirley handed me a plate with my bacon and eggs and cracked two more eggs into the pan for Alex. I poked my toast through a yoke.

"That sounds like Eleanor. She hates not being able to pay her way. How she makes ends meet to look after all those critters and feed herself is beyond me."

"She strikes me as a pretty smart woman," Alex observed. "She's not above using a few four-letter words, but she talks as if she knows the Queen's English."

"That she does. Eleanor's father was from a very wealthy and influential family in Britain. By the sounds of it, he had quite a little grubstake when he arrived in Canada. I think Eleanor was born here, but they sent her to finishing school in England. You should see her when she gets one of those old nags of hers all fitted out with her English saddle and riding habit. She looks like something right out of the movies."

"Really?" Shirley plunked Alex's breakfast on the table and cracked an egg into the pan for herself. "Who would have thought she came from such a background? I've never seen her in anything but old clothes and rubber boots."

"Dress Eleanor up in fancy duds, and she could pass for royalty—thing is, she'd rather have a couple bags of cat food and a few bales of hay for her horses than a new coat."

Alex peered at me over his coffee cup. He was showing more

interest in the conversation than he was in his breakfast. "She seems to be more at home with critters than with people. Does she have any family here?"

"Not that I'm aware of. Her father died when she was quite young, and her mother passed away somewhere back in the sixties. She may well have relatives in the old country, though."

Shirley slid her plate onto the table and sat down next to Alex. "How does she make do—does she work out at all?"

"I know she tried to become self-employed with her horses. She took them to Kootenay Lake to rent them out for treks into the mountains, but it cost her more than she earned. She takes in a few dollars from riding lessons, but she's really surviving from one welfare cheque to the next…I don't know whether she's old enough to collect old age pension or not, but her health isn't the greatest. She's had a few run-ins with cancer over the years—lost a breast, a lung, and part of her nose."

Shirley gave Alex a knowing look. "You guys and your smoking. I keep bugging Alex about cutting back, but you can see how much good it does me."

Alex shrugged and pushed back his empty plate. Digging in his shirt pocket for his cigarettes, he flipped one out and lit up. "There's nothing like relaxing and enjoying a good smoke after breakfast."

"Or before lunch, or after supper, or before you go to bed," Shirley quipped.

Alex shrugged and gave her a meek smile in reply. He was intent on changing the subject. "Saw one of Eleanor's paintings in the Fall Fair last year. Was a picture of a big cougar, I think…She's pretty good at doing critters."

"She's actually a brilliant woman—just has some trouble fitting into a mould."

"She'd fit right in with a lot of those hippies down the lake."

"Oh Alex," chided Shirley, "you know that anyone who acts a bit different or has long hair is a hippie to you. That's the first thing you said when you saw Dave had long hair."

Alex's ears were suddenly crimson. He gave Shirley a pleading look.

"More coffee, Dave?"

"Thank you, Shirley. Maybe one more shot before I hit the road."

"You're suddenly quiet."

"Sorry, just drifting a bit."

Alex gave me a discerning look. "We didn't hurt your feelings about that hippie thing?"

I smiled. "No, not at all."

Alex glanced at his wife with impish intent. "Seeing as we're telling stories out of school, what do you think the last thing my better half was doing before we left the house at four this morning?"

Shirley flushed in anticipation as Alex broke into a broad smile.

"She was standing on a chair dusting the top of the fridge. When I asked her what the hell she was doing dusting at that time of day, she said, 'Just watch. The first thing Dave'll do when he comes in for coffee is lean on my fridge and pull off his coveralls— just because we can't see any dust from down there doesn't mean he won't see it from up here.'"

They were still laughing when I headed out the door. "Be sure and give me a call, Shirley, if you're interested in that job."

I drove back to town on the Lower Wynndel Road. The talk of Eleanor had raised memories of our first meeting at the Herchmer home in Canyon. She'd made such an impression on me that I could see the event in minute detail.

Chris introduced her to me. "Dave, I want you to meet a dear friend of mine, Eleanor Blair."

The woman got up from her chair as if she were a debutante at a ball. Her movements spoke of culture and grace; her posture was straight and poised. She tossed her head and, in the most deliberate fashion, whipped a lock of grey hair from her forehead. She extended her hand as if she were a member of royalty being introduced to a king.

"Dr. Perrin." Her voice was far deeper and richer than I'd expected. "We're so happy you've decided to come to Creston. We certainly need someone like you here. I have to tell you that, so far, we've heard only the best of reports about you. In a town like Creston, that's quite something!"

"Well, thank you," I replied bashfully. "I do try hard to do what's best for my patients." I squirmed uncomfortably for a moment, then turned to Chris. "You mentioned on the phone that your dog has been having skin problems."

"Yes, Kid's chewed at himself till he's absolutely raw. He was making such a ruckus last night that we had to put him down in the basement—none of us could get any sleep. He whines and scratches and chews until he's worked himself into an absolute frenzy. This morning, there were clumps of hair all over the house."

Eleanor and I followed Chris to the basement. We were greeted by a huge dog. His exuberant nature and long red hair suggested setter lineage, but his deep chest and heavy bone structure were testament to a much hardier breed. The dog bounded immediately to the two women. After being acknowledged, he rushed up to me and thrust his nose under my hand in a demand for recognition.

"Hello, Kid." I rubbed his shaggy head. "I'm glad to meet you, too."

Kneeling beside him, I ran my hand down his neck to an area behind his right front shoulder where the coat was moist and clumped. As soon as I parted the hair, he winced, plunked himself down, and began chewing madly.

"It's as if he can't control himself anymore," moaned Chris, frowning. "He digs at himself like that constantly!"

"It's no wonder." I gently straightened his head and levered him onto his side. "Just look at what he's done to himself. See if you can hold his head down so I can get a better look at what's going on."

I surveyed the damage. A large portion of hair had been abraded from an area half the size of my hand. The skin was irritated, bleeding, and covered with clumps of a whitish discharge. The surrounding perimeter was inflamed and speckled with raw patches. Over the remainder of his body, I could find nothing but a glossy hair coat and clean, healthy skin. There was no evidence of fleas or other external parasites.

"This looks like what we call a hot spot. They occur most often in the warm months of the year…Seem most likely when the dog is bored and has nothing better to do with himself than to sit and lick. Once the hair's constantly wet from chewing, it makes an ideal growth medium for bacteria, and the infection spreads in all directions like a forest fire."

"Well, that story certainly fits Kid's circumstances," Chris interjected. "I just started working last month, and he's not the least bit happy about being home by himself. He gets so lonely without someone around to talk to him. He's spoiled when we're home—constantly at us to let him outside every time he figures he needs to check things out."

The two women watched attentively as I worked on the dog. Although Eleanor said very little, I got the impression she was carefully evaluating my performance. I watched her face as I lathered the soap and scrubbed at the pus and debris. She was keenly interested in what was going on, not once taking her eyes off the action.

Kid groaned throughout the entire treatment. Eleanor stroked his head, cooing at him constantly. Her eyebrows went up when I slipped a double-edged razor from the packet and began to scrape the hair from the surface of the wound. She watched in amazement as the hair accumulated in a mound on the basement floor, leaving smooth, cleanly shaven skin.

Once or twice, Kid struggled to get his feet under him. Each time, Eleanor rode out his complaint, then returned to her gentle stroking. She never raised her voice. She showed no emotion when I injected antibiotics and steroids and applied an ointment to the raw and abraded area. She made no comment when I clipped the nails on his right hind foot and bandaged it to keep him from mutilating the lesion further. She offered to help Chris look after the dog over the upcoming week.

It wasn't until I had carved the bottom from a blue plastic scrub pail and slipped it over Kid's head that I noted the first inklings of Eleanor's disapproval. Her forehead was suddenly deeply etched with wrinkles and her mouth was pursed as she struggled to keep quiet. I had finished tying the bucket to Kid's collar when she stood up and walked away. Grabbing a cigarette from a pack in her pocket, she lit it, took a deep drag, and turned her back on us like a sulking child. I glanced towards Chris with a question on my face, but got a shrug and a meek smile in return.

Kid looked from one of us to the next, sure that the bucket had to be some sort of joke. When no one moved to free him from his predicament, he pawed at the hood with first one foot, then the other. The collar held firm and he put both front feet on the back of the bucket, pulling with all his might and howling for added effect.

"You'll only need this for a couple of days, Kid." I was trying to reassure Eleanor more than the dog. "It's the easiest way for you to leave the wound alone long enough for it to heal."

After several attempts to pull the bucket from his head, and a considerable amount of whining, Kid dragged himself to the furthest corner of the basement. Totally dejected, he collapsed on the floor, glaring straight ahead, his dark brown eyes pools of gloom.

"Oh, you've humiliated him!" snapped Eleanor. Sparks emanated from her eyes. "Can't you see that he has pride? He's offended by that contraption."

I smiled at the memory now, but I could recall just how taken aback I was by the woman's sudden change in demeanour, how I tried every means to justify the hood. To Eleanor, Kid's dignity was far more important than the feelings of some wet-behind-the-ears youngster who happened to have a degree.

I dealt with Eleanor frequently over the ensuing months as she brought a stream of cats to my doorstep for treatment. There were cats with broken legs, cats that had difficulty queening, cats with diarrhea, cats sneezing, cats aborting, cats that were starving, and cats wasting from diseases like feline infectious leukemia, and feline immunodeficiency virus—disease entities that were not even recognized until years later.

Eleanor's whole life revolved around her animals—she ate with them, she slept with them. She could not turn an animal away; as a result, any injured or hungry stray that turned up in the neighbourhood eventually made its way to her doorstep. Once granted sanctuary within her walls, any creature that could survive exposure to the diseases that were propagated by the overcrowded conditions was guaranteed good care until its final breath was drawn.

On many occasions, I recommended euthanasia for conditions like pyothorax, where the cat's chest was full of pus and the animal was severely debilitated. Without exception, Eleanor forestalled the inevitable and justified an alternate action. "Let's just see what happens if we treat him with antibiotics for a few weeks first," or "Why don't we just drain the pus out and see how he'll do?" or "Why don't we force-feed him with Nutri-cal? It worked so well with Timothy."

There was never any sense in arguing with her. She respected my opinion and knew that I was not quick to be pessimistic, that when I recommended euthanasia, I was usually right. But with Eleanor, where there was breath, there was hope; where there was even the tiniest hope, she would persist beyond all reason.

Just recently, I had seen a postcard that someone had brought out featuring a dilapidated old house and a wildly overgrown apple tree laden with blossoms. It took me a moment to realize that it depicted Eleanor's Canyon home. How much more picturesque it appeared on the postcard than it did on the many trips I made to her doorstep to treat one of her critters.

A one-level clapboard building that was erected at the turn of the century, her home had fallen into a terrible state of disrepair. The roof leaked badly and sagged in the middle as rafters rotted and the timbers of the foundation became one with the earth beneath them. An old wooden verandah featuring planks of varying levels led up to the front door. The railing had long since disappeared and may well have been used elsewhere on the property to prop up a section of fallen fence. The greying cedar-panelled door hung askew, fastened with a piece of baler twine strung between two nails. When it was tied, it was obvious that Eleanor was outside; when it was not, it was likely she was at home.

Initially, Eleanor had Chris drive her to town for each little crisis. Later, my examinations were done on her verandah while she clutched the latest invalid to her chest. Numerous times, the cats she had me treat were completely wild, and she was only capable of restraining them because of their debilitation. Often, she would be sliced to ribbons by their claws and left bleeding from their bites. I can never remember her letting go until I had finished my examination and started a treatment.

The first time I was allowed inside her domain was a memorable event. It had been a bitterly cold night towards the end of November, and we were all hoping it would warm up and start to snow. Farmers were already predicting doom and gloom: without a snow pack for insulation, the alfalfa plants would freeze out and, with this prolonged cold, orchardists would soon give up on next year's soft fruit crop.

It was dark when I arrived, but I could see my way to the door in the long rectangle of light extending from a curtainless window. A nippy wind was blowing from the east; I shivered as the cold seeped through my clothing. I could see Eleanor moving about in the house as I approached, so I carefully made my way across the verandah and knocked on the door.

"Who's there?" Her voice was demanding—husky and gruff.

"It's Dave!" I hollered, my teeth chattering.

I heard a grating sound against the door. It swung inward, scraping along the floor as it opened. I was hit by a wave of heat accompanied by an unimaginable potent odour.

Eleanor hesitated for a moment as she tried to think of an alternative to allowing me in. Finally, she stepped back with a look of resignation. "Come in."

I took a deep breath of cool air, then stepped over the threshold. This was a moment that I had been anticipating for some time. Chris had said to me months ago, "You'll know you have Eleanor's confidence when she lets you into her house." There was no way that a person could be prepared in advance for that step. How could anyone anticipate the sweltering dry heat, the acrid, rank odour of cat urine and feces, the clutter that covered every square inch of the room, or the sight of cats scurrying in every direction to hide from the invasion of a stranger? I had stepped into Eleanor's world, and what a world it was!

She swung the door closed with a sense of urgency. Pressing her shoulder against it, she slid a butter knife between the door and the jamb to keep it closed.

"This damned cold weather! When the wind picks up, that old stove just drinks the oil. I went out and measured the barrel this afternoon…I'm praying I have enough left to last until they fill me up tomorrow."

She picked up a pack of Player's Light from amid the clutter on the counter, grabbed a cigarette, and lit it from the smouldering remains of a dying butt. "This weather's just so hard on everything. The horses have to eat more to keep up, the cats won't go outside for anything, and that stove just never shuts off."

I was still having too much difficulty moving air to reply. I had tried several times to draw in a breath. Each time, I aborted the effort halfway through. My taste buds and lungs wanted nothing to do with it.

Eleanor's complaining tone softened. "I told you last week that someone had dropped three kittens out at my gate in the middle of that snowstorm...Septamus! Septamus, get out of there!"

A massive orange cat had jumped up on the table and climbed inside the almost empty bag of Purina Cat Chow. Eleanor maneuvered around a towering stack of magazines to get to him. His face bore a look of contempt as he grudgingly stepped out onto the table. He swallowed a few kernels of the food whole and jumped to the floor ahead of Eleanor's advance. Landing next to a sickly looking grey tom, he boxed him soundly on the side of the head with a huge paw then chased after him, hissing as he went.

"You haven't met Septamus yet." Eleanor extended her hand to present him, then haphazardly rolled up the top of the cat chow bag. "He doesn't hang around here much, except when it gets really cold outside. He's too busy spreading his genes around the Canyon area. I called him Septamus because he has seven perfectly formed claws on each of his front feet."

She bent down to the base of the stove and picked up a small carton covered by a frayed green towel. She exposed a shoebox filled with pieces of an old sweater. Within those folds of tattered wool was the saddest excuse for a cat that I can remember seeing. "I'm really worried about this kitten," she muttered.

The tiny creature that Eleanor held in her palm was far too young to be taken from his mother. Although he had survived the last few days without food, the cold weather had drained what little reserves he had. His bones were prominent as a result of the wasting of surrounding muscle; his face was haggard. His eyes were sunken into his skull, his tail crusted with pasty stool. Huddling in Eleanor's hand, he was barely able to support himself in an upright position.

"I'd love to get my hands on the person who left them here!"

she growled. "People dump animals at my gate without giving it a second thought. I brought the other three into the house, but I obviously missed this one." Her eyes were fiery. "This morning I went out to feed the horses and pulled a bale of hay down—out he tumbled. I thought he was dead, but when I picked him up he gasped. I rushed him in here next to the stove. As you can see, he's improved a bit, but I still can't get him to eat anything."

Eleanor passed the limp little creature to me. I looked around the room at all the eyes that were staring at me and wondered what sort of favour I would be doing this kitten to save him. Septamus had jumped back onto the table and was working at tearing a hole in the bottom of the cat food bag. Three emaciated grey cats huddled in the corner, keeping an eye on me without losing sight of Septamus. They sneezed incessantly, pus draining from their eyes and nostrils.

The long-haired queen that I had seen only last month and spayed with a litter of dead and rotting kittens inside her was happily sleeping on the pillow of Eleanor's bed. Two more nondescript shorthairs were curled up on the foot of it. The box with the remaining three rescued kittens was pushed up against the wall; periodically, I could hear their toenails scratch down the cardboard as they made feeble attempts to escape.

I wrapped the poor creature in the remnants of the sweater and took him back to the office with me. After several days of injecting fluids under his skin and feeding him with a stomach tube, the kitten began to take formula from a syringe. Eleanor eventually took him home and nursed him back to health. By the end of a month, we'd found homes for the other three foundlings, but I was never able to convince Eleanor to part with the one she had nursed back from the brink.

I wasn't surprised when I got back from Shopas that morning and saw a note on the book to call Eleanor. A queen that she hadn't seen for several months had shown up this morning and was in the process of aborting. She thought they had all been delivered but wasn't sure. Was there any possibility that I could stop by if I was in the neighbourhood?

Most veterinarians would have viewed Eleanor as a nightmare—with her menagerie of sickly animals and her decided lack of funds. As it turned out, she became one of my closest friends.

The Farm

"Don't be ridiculous." I gave Gord an incredulous look as we stopped at the newly installed light on Canyon Street. "I'm just able to keep my head above water now. How could I possibly consider buying property?"

We had devoured a pair of clubhouse sandwiches and a couple of plates of fries at the Depot Restaurant. All through the meal, Gordon had harped on my buying a piece of property, on doing something about building equity. His point of view made sense but, right now, I was strapped. Every cent that came through the door seemed to go back into either a new piece of equipment or another shipment of drugs.

The light turned green and we crossed the street in silence. The moment his foot hit the curb on the other side, Gord came to an abrupt halt and spun to confront me. His face was red with passion, his jaw set and resolute.

"If you wait until you have money," he huffed, waving his hands in front of him, "you'll never have a bloody thing."

I opened my mouth to respond, but could feel myself wilting under his determined glare.

"I'm going to keep my eye out for something that'll suit you. Maybe we can get you a piece of property that can make its own payments." I smiled glumly, pondering how I could ever afford more than a doghouse, and watched my portly buddy retreat up the street in the direction of his office.

Gordon had such a different way of looking at things. I was a hoarder, a dig-a-hole-in-the-back-yard-and-bury-the-can type of guy. Gord was something else. A dreamer, an innovator, he was continually hatching new schemes for putting a rental unit here or a few apartments up there. He had a folder in his file cabinet where he kept doodles on various buildings in town. There weren't many properties that he hadn't deliberated about buying, few that he couldn't produce sketches of if given a few minutes. To him, the entire town was just one endless collection of opportunities.

I wandered down the street towards the clinic. Gord was right, as usual. It didn't make sense to keep paying rent for the rundown facility I was in if I could find a suitable building to buy. We had the place fixed up to the point where it was beyond humiliation and, although I had given consideration to buying it, one trip into the basement of the sagging old relic had cured that idea. The location was fantastic, but the building as it stood was a liability.

I looked at each property I walked past with new interest. Would any of them have possibilities? Most didn't have enough parking, and I really needed somewhere with lots of room to exercise hospitalized patients and work on horses, too. I wondered what Al Ingham was planning for that empty lot.

"Oh good, you're back." Doris rushed up to me, daybook in hand. "I was just ready to start calling around looking for you. You've got a call to Erickson. Sorina Maletta has a sick horse."

"What's up?"

"She says she found her filly lying on its side groaning—the horse keeps trying to roll."

"Sounds like colic. Call her back and make sure she gets the critter on its feet. Tell her to keep walking it until I get there…Come on, Lug."

Driving along the Erickson back road, I couldn't think of a more beautiful place to be. What a special moment! Mulling over lines of a poem that I had written years before, I struggled to retrieve bits and pieces of it. Why was it that other people could recite reams of someone else's poetry, and I could never remember more than a few lines of my own?

What difference did it make anyway? How could any mortal properly describe the beauty around me? Over the past weeks, the blossoms of the apricot, peach, and cherry trees had each had their moments to decorate bare limbs and flaunt their beauty. They had been the first, irrevocable evidence that spring was finally here. Now, although faint traces of colour were still detectable, flower petals had fallen and the limbs were taking on a greenish hue.

Today, elegant McIntosh and Delicious trees were strutting their stuff. I rolled down the window and took a deep breath. How could words ever do justice to that delicate smell?

I slowed down as I passed the Veitch driveway, glancing at the directions I'd written down—2915 was just up the road. I turned off onto a narrow drive that was bordered on both sides by mature apple orchards. Massive trees with tortuous limbs were laden with huge white blossoms. The roadway parted to circle an ancient house that was taller than it was wide. Its red brick siding was accented by a profusion of reds, yellows, and purples from the tulips, daffodils, and hyacinths that proliferated at its base. I pulled up to the right of the house and got out beneath a massive weeping willow tree.

A barking dog welcomed me. He was a round, white poodle with short legs and thinning hair coat. Yipping shrilly, he advanced to my leg and took a sniff of my shoe. Lug growled, then barked aggressively, adding his voice to the cacophony. As he strained against the partially open door to get out, the poodle ran, still yelping, into the orchard.

"Enough!" I hollered.

The poodle stopped at the trees and looked hesitantly in our direction. A large tabby cat wandered from the house to rub against my leg. I scratched his ears and ran my hand over his back.

"Over here!"

I took a moment to orient myself to the direction of the voice and headed into the orchard.

"We're here."

I could see them making their way towards me down one of the mowed lanes. The woman was slender with short dark hair. On her heel was a palomino mare.

"I've been walking her like Doris said. She's fine when we're moving but, as soon as we stop, she tightens up and looks like she's going to roll." The woman stopped in front of me and extended her hand. "I'm Sorina Maletta. This is Farra."

I shook her hand. "Glad to meet you...Dave Perrin."

"I'm pretty worried about this little girl." Sorina turned to face the golden-yellow filly. The horse was a delicate creature, but muscular, well put together. She stood, flanks tucked up, nostrils flared, ears laid back, breathing in a rapid, irregular fashion. I ran my hand over a neck that was soaked with sweat; she shivered almost convulsively and closed her eyes.

I located the mandibular artery as it crossed the angle of the jaw. Her pulse was strong, but more rapid than normal. I looked at my watch, held my breath, and counted—almost one per second. The filly pulled back on the halter shank, and her flanks tightened visibly—her hocks began to flex, her body to sink.

"Yah! Stay up, girl! Walk on…Walk on!"

I slapped her briskly on the rump as Sorina pulled on the lead rope. The filly balked, then slunk forward in a crouched position. By the time we reached the end of the row, she was moving almost at a normal clip.

"Hold it a sec." I grabbed the filly's tail and slid a thermometer into her rectum. "Okay." I fell into step behind them as they moved off up the orchard row to the base of the hill. A gentle breeze blew towards us carrying the delicate yet powerful scent of apple blossoms. The aroma was tainted by the sweet smell of smoke drifting from a pile of prunings that smouldered at the top of the hill.

"Has she had problems with colic before?"

"Not that I'm aware of, but we've only had her a few months. I bought her from a fellow in Cranbrook."

"She sure looks Arab. I don't ever recall seeing a palomino Arab before."

"She's Arab, all right. We bought the filly with the hope of breeding her and getting some palomino foals."

I quickly checked the thermometer—37.7. Pretty much normal. I had a listen with my stethoscope. Her left side was alive with high-pitched squeaks and rumblings, as fluid and gas moved through her bowels. I thumped back and forth with my finger in search of the telltale ping of a twisted gut and was happy not to find it. I ran around to the right side and continued my search. Long tortuous gurgling sounds followed in rapid succession. At the end of one particularly prolonged grumble, her abdomen tightened and her knees began to buckle.

"No you don't, Farra!" I brought my hand down hard on her rump. "Away you go, girl. Away you go."

Sorina pulled valiantly on the lead shank and the filly moved haltingly ahead. "What do you think?" she gasped.

"It looks like a spastic colic. Sometimes it's a result of nerves, sometimes because of something that upsets the gut. When was the last time you dewormed her? What type of feed do you have her on?"

"She's picking at new grass and getting the same grassy hay she's been on since we got her."

The filly shuffled forward in a crouched fashion, as if she were still half thinking of trying to throw herself. I brought my hand forcefully down with another swat on the rump.

"Keep going, girl! Yah!"

As we approached the house, Farra was again moving almost freely.

"We haven't dewormed her since we bought her," Sorina puffed. "Could that be her problem?"

"Certainly a possibility. Let's see what happens once I've given her a shot."

Sorina followed the gravelled lane around the perimeter of the house. When we got to my car, I took leave of them. "You keep her moving while I draw up some Demerol."

By the time I was ready, Sorina was making her second trip around the drive. She passed by with the filly plodding resolutely at her heel. In procession behind them trotted a huge white hen, the white poodle, and the grey tabby. Sorina stopped in front of me. Blocking the vein on Farra's neck, I wiped down her jugular furrow with an alcohol swab and plunged the needle into the vessel. I drew back until a jet of blood shot into the clear, watery liquid, then injected and withdrew.

"Okay, let's keep her moving."

Within a half hour, the antispasmodic effect of the Demerol had kicked in; Farra was a different horse. Her hair coat was crusted together by the sweat that had dried, but her body was relaxed, her eyes bright. Sorina was being jerked back and forth by the lead shank, as the filly munched the grass at the edge of the drive.

"She has an interesting history," her owner offered. "This filly comes from a line of horses that was bred by Prince Edward. At some point after abdicating the throne, he bought a ranch in Alberta just out of Calgary, where he worked at establishing a line of palomino Arabs. He crossed purebred Arabs with Welsh palomino ponies because he felt the colour was most dominant with them. He seemed to be making progress too, so I don't know why he gave up. When he died, his wife sold all the horses without papers. It was apparently what he had requested. A lady from Castlegar bought the grandmother of this mare from the duchess. She was carrying Farra's mother at the time."

"Oh my, Farra, I've never been so close to royalty before."

Sorina smiled. "We love this filly but really wanted her mother...no way the owner would part with her. She was bigger than Farra, a beautiful mare."

I left the Malettas' farm with Farra grazing greedily on the grass along the edge of the orchard. It was difficult to head back to work. After a taste of fresh air, the thought of spending the remainder of the day in the clinic was a bit hard to wrap my mind around.

Four people sat patiently waiting for me when I got to the office. I was surprised to see that one of them was my father's cousin, Marshall. Sitting quietly in the corner, he looked up at me timidly and smiled.

I rushed to the back and slipped on a smock. "What's up with Marshall, Doris?"

"Your cousin, you mean…He wouldn't say, just that he needed to talk to you." Doris looked at me with her matronly expression. "You know that he's drunk?"

"I sort of gathered that. He's had a problem with booze, but as far as I know, he's been dry for quite a while. Dad said he was cooking up north in a lumber camp."

Doris frowned. "Well, I'm afraid he fell off the wagon. We better get Mrs. Campbell in here first—she's a real teetotaller, and she's moved about as far away from him as she can get."

"Can't blame her. The waiting room smells like a brewery."

I worked my way through my appointments. When I had a moment to speak with Marshall, I sat down next to him. His eyes were closed and his head rested against the wall.

"Marsh."

He peered at me as if through a thick fog. Sitting close to him, I realized how much he reeked of liquor—poor Mrs. Campbell. I suspect that, at that moment, Marsh existed at the centre of a huge vortex while the entire world revolved faster and faster around him. How well I could recall the desire to just stick out a leg and make things stand still.

"What can we do for you, Marsh?"

He focused carefully on my face. "I'm a little bit broke, Dave," he mumbled. "Could you help me out?"

"Where are you living?

"Home."

"Out in West Creston?"

He nodded. His eyes slowly closed again.

"Do you need a ride home?"

"Could you buy me a beer?"

"I think you've had about enough for a while. I'll call you a taxi."

By the time Bill's cab arrived, Marsh was sound asleep. We roused him and herded him into the back seat. I paid Bill for his fare and he left with his troubled cargo.

"If there's one thing that I can't stand it's a drunk," said Doris.

"Yeah, but I kind of feel for the guy."

We were changing the intravenous bag on a hospitalized cat when the door opened and in walked Gordon.

"Are you ready for a drive, Doctauri?"

"I am finished. What did you have in mind?"

"Nice day...just wanted to go for a drive." Gordon had the impish smirk on his face that always gave him away; for a salesman, he was a terrible liar.

"What are you up to?"

"Never you mind. Just come along."

Gordon drove away from town, down the Archibald hill, and turned south towards the border.

"Where in the world are you taking me?"

"It's a beautiful day. I told you we're going for a drive."

"I know what you told me, but I know you, too—you have something up your sleeve."

Gordon poked along, for all the world like he was on a Sunday outing. Turning at the Indian Reserve, he dawdled past the golf course and up onto the hill overlooking the community of Lister.

"Isn't that a view?" It was a comment I could have imagined his using on a prospective prairie client. He still displayed his mischievous grin.

"Sure is a picture today," I agreed, looking out at the valley that unfolded below us. The intense green alfalfa, screaming yellow dandelions, and lustrous white saskatoon bushes formed a dazzling spring mosaic. This valley truly amazed me. No matter where you happened to be in it, the view was utterly spectacular.

We had driven almost a mile south on Canyon Lister Road when Gordon piped up. "Have you ever done any work for George Sikora?"

"Nope."

"A guy by the name of Patriquin?"

"Nope."

"That's Patriquin's place up ahead. He bought a hundred and thirteen acres from George Sikora this time last year. He had sold off a hotel somewhere and decided to try his hand at country living. Didn't take him long to decide he wasn't a farmer. He just bought another hotel in Grand Forks."

"Are you telling me something?"

"He has someone dealing on the thirty-three acres with the buildings and wants to sell the other eighty acres separately. He came in to see me at the office this afternoon…doesn't want to list it, but told me he'd take fifty thousand for it."

"Come on, Gord, where am I going to get fifty thousand?"

Gordon drove past the driveway to the farm buildings, then slowed to a crawl. "The eighty acres starts right here at the trees."

He idled along the highway, craning his neck and pointing. "This is a beautiful chunk of property—lots of prime timber and fifty acres of good hay land. It'll give you a tax deduction, and the hay from it should help make the payment."

"I've got a news flash for you, Gord. A tax deduction right now is the least of my worries. I'm so busy buying things for the office, it'll be years before I have income to tax."

"Let's get out and have a look." We had driven past the woodlot and were meandering along next to a large meadow. He pulled his car through an open barbed-wire gate south of the trees and parked in the hayfield. I stepped outside and took a deep breath. The thought of having a place like this in the country had been with me since I was old enough to start dreaming about what I wanted in life.

"The fields are in need of some work, but it sure is a gorgeous piece of land." Gordon was right beside me, but he may as well have been on a different planet. I walked the land as if I already owned it. We strolled into a draw and hopped over a little creek. I looked around me as if in a dream. The rolling fields, the tree-covered knoll, the massive face of Mt. Hall that towered above the valley floor all seemed just too picturesque.

Could I really swing a deal for that kind of money when I had nothing tangible of my own for collateral? It wasn't practical, but somehow I couldn't shake the feeling that this property was destined to be mine. For some undefined reason, I already felt a bond with the ground beneath my feet.

I could see where I wanted a fence, where the horses would run. I could bring Snookie and Beauty over here from Casino, and they could finally run on property of my own, have all the grass they could possibly eat. I could get my own cows—have somewhere to take the wrecks that dairy farmers didn't want to be bothered with.

I looked back towards the woodlot. I could see my house sitting there in that clump of trees. It would be rustic. Log? Stone? Cedar siding? Yes, that would be the spot. Or how about over there where it would be closer to the road with far less snow to fight in the winter. Yes, that would be the place. No sense in such a long driveway. But think of how quiet it would be way back in the trees—no highway noise, absolute privacy.

"You won't have long to think about this one." Gordon jolted me to reality. "Patriquin told me he was going to take the first offer of fifty grand…not to make him any crap offers. I think he meant it. He doesn't sound like the type of guy who likes playing games."

"Oh man, Gord." We were standing in the centre of the fifty-acre field. I gazed around me and a shiver ran up my spine. How could I even be entertaining thoughts of owning this land? I had nothing for collateral other than a few bottles of penicillin and a calf-puller. In an argument with the banker, I would probably find that I didn't even own those.

"I think we should take him an offer tonight if you're interested. It won't stay on the market long at that price. Everyone's looking for something like this. I know I could buy it and flip it for a profit, but this is the one you should own."

"But I need to be realistic, Gord. Where am I going to come up with that kind of money?"

"From the bank! Where do you think I got the money to buy my properties? I wasn't born with a silver spoon in my mouth, and it's not all that long since we went bust up in Cranbrook. We'll call Guy from the Federal Business Development Bank and set up an appointment."

I shook my head. This had to be a dream; everything was happening so quickly. Twenty minutes ago, I hadn't the slightest notion of buying property, and now I was on my way to make an offer.

I had been in a trance the whole way back to town and hadn't eaten a thing for supper. Just the thought of going into hock for that kind of money left me with a big open pit right where I needed some strength. From the clinic, I had called Casino and talked to my father about the possibility of borrowing enough for a down payment. He actually sounded excited about the prospect. After all, he had always been a farmer at heart.

I stopped at Sorina's on the way back to meet Gordon. I needed to feel grounded, to deal with something I understood. The Malettas were in the back yard seated around a solid wooden picnic table. The grill still smouldered, and the sweet smell of chicken and barbecue sauce was heavy in the air. Farra grazed contentedly on the back lawn a few yards away. The dog, which had been begging at the family's feet, came running to the car to announce my presence. The big white chicken perched like an ornament on the picnic table bench.

"Jeeters, enough! It's only Dr. Perrin." The dog fell silent at Sorina's admonishment.

"Sorry to interrupt supper. Just thought I'd stop and see how Farra was doing."

"She's just fine. It's like there was never a thing wrong with her. Would you like a chicken burger? We're just eating."

"No thanks, just finished eating myself," I lied. My stomach was queasy; I wasn't the least bit hungry. I smiled in fascination as the huge bird waddled her way along the seat and hopped onto the knee of the stocky, dark fellow who sat at the end of the bench. He gave her a piece of meat and dropped her to the lawn as he stood to introduce himself.

"I'm Gene Maletta."

"Glad to meet you, Gene." We shook hands. He had a firm grip and a no-nonsense air about him. "That's quite the pet you have there." I motioned to the hen that still loitered at his heel.

"Gretta." He smiled. "Yes, she sure is. She was part of a flock of meat birds that we raised a few years ago. She imprinted on us from the very start and constantly followed us around."

"We're having her favourite meal tonight," Sorina interjected. "Barbecued chicken and green salad. She always sits with Gene because she likes French dressing. She won't even touch my salad—doesn't like Italian."

Chuckling, I wandered over to Farra. She was intent on mowing every last blade of grass and didn't even lift her head as I ran my hand over her flank.

"She looks to be out of the woods. I'd keep her close like this for the rest of the evening and come out to check her before you go to bed."

While the hen was again insinuating herself between Gene and his dinner, I left to meet Gordon. He was waiting expectantly as I turned into his driveway. Within moments, we were headed towards Lister in his big brown station wagon.

"I don't understand, Gord. Why are we making an offer tonight when I'm not sure I can even borrow the money?" He turned down the long gravelled driveway that led to the two-storied house with asphalt siding on Patriquin's farm.

"We need to tie it up as soon as possible. The deal you signed is subject to financing, so if it doesn't come through, then you haven't lost a thing. It's set up to close on the first of June, so that gives us time to see what you can do with the bank."

Mr. Patriquin met us at the door. He was a jovial-looking man in his middle fifties with receding hair, flushed cheeks, and a predominant belly. "Well, that didn't take long." He stood back and waved us in with a smile. "I must not be asking enough."

He escorted us into a cramped living room cluttered with boxes. "Have a seat, if you can find a place to perch. As you can see, we're in the throes of moving on."

Gordon and I settled on a sofa at the far end of the room. Mr. Patriquin shuffled through some papers in the kitchen and made a few notations on the back of an envelope. Dragging a chair with him, he sat across the coffee table from us. Gordon handed him the offer that we had filled out at his office. Mr. Patriquin turned his envelope upside down on the table.

A trace of a smile crossed his face as he read. He perused the offer thoroughly, then grabbed Gordon's pen, signed the paper, and handed it back.

"I have to admit, you surprise me. I thought you were going to make me a crap offer…This would have been my answer." He smiled at me and turned over the envelope—$55,000 was scrawled across it. "I'd have never sold this property for fifty grand if I hadn't already bought that hotel in Grand Forks. The deal closes the first of June. We're heading there this weekend to see what we can find for a house. The wife isn't big on living at the hotel."

I stared at the agreement that now lay on the coffee table. Had I really done this? Was this gorgeous chunk of land truly mine? I gazed out the window. On the other side of that barbed-wire fence were those majestic trees, those rolling knolls that were now my domain.

"You don't look like the type of guy to turn down a drink." Mr. Patriquin looked Gordon in the eye, then got up and shuffled to the cupboard. "What'll it be?"

"You got any scotch?" Gordon's tone was hopeful.

"Teacher's or Glenfiddich?"

A smile spread across Gordon's face. "A man after my own heart. Glenfiddich."

Mr. Patriquin turned to face me. "What about you?"

"Beer'll be fine for me."

He cracked a Kokanee and handed it to me, fired ice cubes into two glasses, and poured four fingers of scotch into each one. Gordon smiled. "I like the way you pour a drink."

Mr. Patriquin raised his glass. "Here's to you."

Gord raised his glass and winked at me. "Here's to the new Lister land baron."

Shirley's First Day

Shirley was nervous. "This is all so much different from out on the farm."

"The principle's the same," I assured her. "Just hold the critters still and keep things as clean as possible."

Shirley looked askance at the cat in Doris's grasp as it peered at her through half-closed eyes. Doris stroked the queen's head, scratched her behind the ears, and manipulated her through the opening of the cat bag. Fastening the Velcro tab around the cat's neck, she zipped the bag, leaving nothing exposed but her head.

"See how easy that was? The cat's already tranquillized, so there's usually not much fuss." I was sure that once Shirley overcame her butterflies, she'd be quick to pick up on the job; easier to get a farm girl over her reluctance to handle cats than to get a cat lover used to the sight of blood.

The telephone rang and Doris passed the bagged patient to her reluctant prodigy. I turned on the oxygen and nitrous oxide tanks and adjusted the flow valves to the anesthetic machine. "See where the gas levels are now? That's where we'll want to keep them until she's asleep…Once she's under anesthetic, we'll cut the nitrous till it's the same as the oxygen."

Shirley nodded as I slid the nose cone over the cat's face and held the plastic enclosure tight with my hand. The cat remained motionless for a few seconds then reluctantly took a deep breath. "This is the knob to control the halothane; after she's used to

breathing into the mask, we'll turn it up." I pointed to a box on the shelf. "You'll need to put on a cap and mask."

Shirley donned a cap, efficiently poked her long curly locks beneath the green linen, and fastened it behind her head. "A lot of good it did me to spend all that time in front of the mirror this morning." She had the top of the mask tied and was struggling behind her head with the lower strings. "Oh Dave, do I have to? It feels weird breathing through this."

"You'll get used to it."

Finally ready, she confronted me; her intense blue eyes squinted through a narrow slit left between the green serge and white linen. "How can you stand wearing this stuff?"

"It's just part of the turf—don't want anything falling onto the surgery site."

We clipped and shaved the cat's abdomen in preparation for the spay. As I scrubbed, Doris took over instructing our new assistant. Bending closely over the cat, she picked a hair from the margin of the prepared area. "Dave's a real fanatic about hairs…I swear he can spot one from across the room. He…Oh, my God!" Doris rushed to grab Shirley's arm. "Dave!"

Seconds before Shirley's knees buckled, I wrapped my arms around her waist and lowered her onto the stool.

"Oh, man," she groaned. "What's going on? This has never happened before."

"Just keep your head down for a few more minutes." Doris plastered a wet towel on the back of Shirley's neck. "It's probably just the thought of what's about to happen that's gotten you going."

"I can't believe it's me fainting. I could understand if it was Alex. He hates watching surgery. He can't believe how I love getting my hands in there when you do a Caesarian."

"Sit here…Do some deep breathing until you feel better. It's probably a combination of the strange smells and that mask over your face."

"A lot of good I turned out to be…passing out on you in the middle of surgery."

"Just watch what Doris is up to and get a feeling for what we'll need you to do."

By the time I had the stump of the uterus ligated and was closing the cat's abdomen, Shirley had perked up. She seemed to be getting her sea legs and assisted with two cat neuters without looking the least bit queasy. I left for lunch while Doris was demonstrating how to package the linen and instruments that we used with every surgery.

When I returned to the office, Doris had gone to the bank but was due back any minute. I noticed that Shirley was looking more comfortable. She was attacking a set of drapes with the lint brush.

The door burst open and a handsome, well-groomed man in his early thirties rushed into the waiting room and slammed the door behind him. A mournful meowing emanated from the good-sized box that he clutched to his chest.

"Damn it, Cleo! Can't you make things easy just once in your life?" Plunking himself down on the waiting room bench, he poked a black paw back into the box and tightened the plastic rope that secured the lid. He turned to Shirley. "I'm Dr. Chambers. Cleo's your one-thirty appointment."

Shirley gravitated reluctantly towards the waiting room with a clipboard and a client record card. Referring to another chart that Doris had filled out earlier in the morning, she nervously questioned her first client. "Has she…" There was a sudden flurry of activity inside the box. Shirley stared in awe as lower canine teeth poked through one of the air holes in the side of the box and tore a chunk out of the cardboard. There was a long, plaintive meow. My new receptionist eyed the box nervously, then smiled at the owner. "Is she as mean as she sounds?"

"She has a mind of her own, I can tell you; she's not what I'd call vicious, but she's big on making a statement. She's used to having things all her own way. I can't say I blame her about not liking this box, though. The last time she was confined was when we drove up from the coast—ten hours is a long time."

I had been watching Shirley struggle long enough. It was time to bail her out. "Hello, Dr. Chambers. I'm Dave Perrin...Is Cleo due for some vaccinations?"

"She's overdue if the truth be known, by almost a year." Straightening his suit jacket, he loosened his tie and sighed. "We kept getting reminders from our old vet, but my wife refused to take her, and I was busy trying to finish off my residency. It seems she created a bit of a scene the last time Gloria took her in. She swore if I didn't do it, Cleo would just have to take her chances with whatever she might catch. We seem to have a lot of cats in the new neighbourhood, so I thought I better get her in right away."

I smiled. "So she can be a bit of a handful then? In this business, to be forewarned is to be forearmed. Let's bring her into the exam room."

Shirley gave me a pleading look. "Shouldn't we wait for Doris? She said she'd be right back."

"I'm sure you'll do just fine, Shirley. You wait and see."

Dr. Chambers plunked his burden unceremoniously on the examination table and started undoing the rope. Shirley stood behind me, comforted by the fact that there was another body between her and the source of all those mournful wails.

"I'm embarrassed to be the one to bring Cleo in," the doctor chimed. "If she were my patient, I'd send her home on a diet and insist she join an aerobics class. She's just the most persistent creature when it comes to food; if we don't fill her dish up whenever she wants, she nags us until we do."

Dropping the lid to the floor, he quickly grabbed the cat before she escaped. "There's a girl, Cleo. Settle down now."

The rotund feline was not exactly the awe-inspiring panther that Shirley had been dreading. She was well endowed with fat, but had the bone structure of a rather delicate cat. Her coat was coal black except for the tiniest dash of white between her nostrils.

Dr. Chambers settled Cleo on the table, noting in disgust the hair that was clinging to the arm of his suit jacket. "I'm going to be shedding as much as you by the time we're done, Cleo."

"There's a girl," I murmured, stroking her gently. "You're going to be just fine."

Cleo looked inquisitively around the room. Her coat was shiny and sleek, her eyes bright and still fully dilated from her stint in the dark.

"Is she mainly an inside cat?"

"Almost exclusively until now. She was a city girl until we came to Creston. Now that we've moved to an acreage, she's been venturing into the back yard from time to time. She caught her first mouse. Ran into another cat out there the other day…You would've thought she was dying the way she screeched at the sight of him."

I listened to the cat's racing heartbeat. "Has she had any problems that you're concerned about?"

"Not really, other than her being so overweight. She doesn't usually shed like this at home." He picked a clump from the front of his suit and let it drift into the wastebasket.

"That's likely a result of the stress of her confinement. Cats tend to drop a lot of hair when they're upset."

"Let me hold her for you," Shirley volunteered. I had noticed her slowly build the courage to offer. "Your suit's going to be an awful mess otherwise."

I ran my hands over the cat's body, feeling for any unusual lumps or bumps. Ruffling the hair on the top of her head, I bent closer to have a look in her ears. They were clean and shiny for as deep in as I could see.

Smearing some lubricant on a thermometer, I lifted her tail and gently pushed forward into her rectum. There was a low-pitched rumble in the back of the cat's throat. Shirley's pupils dilated.

Dr. Chambers smiled. "She's not big on having her tail fiddled with. As a matter of fact, she's not fussy about any kind of handling unless she initiates it."

I could see Shirley's muscles tighten as the vibration reverberated throughout the cat's body. I knew she'd be much more comfortable if she had her hands on a bull that was huffing and rattling in a chute before her.

"There's a girl, Cleo," I crooned. "We're not going to hurt you." The cat's eyes were wells of gloom. Her tail twitched convulsively; her body was rigid, every muscle tight. I gave Shirley a nod of encouragement. She attempted a meek smile in return.

The door opened as I was reading the thermometer, and I motioned for Shirley to see who was there. A wave of relief swept her face as Doris crashed into the room with her usual enthusiasm. She threw on a smock and came to my assistance. "Poor Shirley," she whispered. "Your cousin is out there again, and he looks really hammered."

"Oh God, not again."

Cleo's temperature was normal. She grumbled momentarily when the vaccination needle pierced her skin, then looked around to see what had bitten her. I fastened the Velcro of the cat bag behind her neck. Her eyes smouldered and her song got louder as I manipulated her fat body into the bag and struggled to do up the zipper.

"You look like an old lady in a corset, Cleo." The doctor laughed as I let go of her and she rolled onto her side like an over-inflated beach ball. I pried open her mouth for a better look at her teeth.

"See how the tartar has built up like a fossil, how raw and inflamed the gums have become?" I worked the blade of my scraper under the concretion and flicked it off.

"Well, look at that." Dr. Chambers picked up the material and rolled it around between his fingertips. "And the tooth's as clean as can be underneath."

Shirley tiptoed into the exam room. "What do you want me to do with him?" she whispered to Doris.

"He's not *my* cousin," Doris replied with a wicked little smile.

I worked my way around Cleo's mouth, digging here and scraping there. "No one's ever been able to do this with you before, Cleo," chimed the doctor. "I think you've finally met your match."

The cat sputtered and hissed. On several occasions, she freed her head from my grip and bit down on the scaler. Shirley watched the procedure with amazement. "You'd never catch me sticking my fingers in there. I'm not sure I'm cut out for this job. I used to think I knew what a vet did for a living; now I'm not sure. A morning here has completely changed my perspective."

Dr. Chambers chuckled. "I guess that could be said for all of us. There are days you wouldn't believe what goes on in my office either."

We heard a crash in the waiting room; Shirley rolled her eyes. "What am I supposed to do?"

I stopped my scaling. "Tell Marsh I'll talk to him in a moment."

Dr. Chamber's smile was threatening to crack his face in two. "You have such an interesting practice."

I unzipped the cat bag and Cleo stepped onto the table, huddling next to her owner. "Well, that does it for this year, old girl." I headed to the front, working my wallet out of my pocket. As much as I wanted to get Marshall out of my office, I wasn't about to become his financier.

"Hello Marsh."

"Hi Dave. Do you think you can help me out?"

"Running a little short of cash, are you?"

He smiled and scratched his head. "That bugger Shean cut me off again…Told him I was headed back to the camp soon, but he says no more credit."

Suddenly, Shirley shrieked and all hell broke loose on the other side of the curtain. I pulled a five-dollar bill from my wallet and fired it in Marsh's direction.

Cleo yowled and her handlers cried in unison, "Oh my God, Cleo!" I rushed to the back. Shirley's arm was bleeding from three long rake marks. The tabletop was smeared with stool, and urine dripped from Dr. Chamber's tie. Like the black cat from hell in a horror movie, Cleo was spread-eagled across Doris's face, firmly gripping the terrified woman's nose in her mouth. The claws of each front paw dug into the flesh of Doris's cheeks. Cleo's hind legs scratched frantically at her blouse as if in a life and death struggle.

"Don't pull, Doris! Don't pull." I could see she wanted to fling the cat across the room. Her eyes crossed as she stared in horror at the black demon that was savaging her face. I disentangled the hind claws from Doris's blouse and ensured that Shirley had a grip on both feet. "Hold tight—don't let go."

Dr. Chambers held onto Cleo's scruff, taking as much weight as possible from the traumatized tissues. I grabbed a front paw and began freeing the claws one by one from Doris's flesh. Cleo screeched and another jet of urine sprayed across Dr. Chamber's tie and white shirt; a turd slowly extruded from the cat's bum.

"Oh Cleeoo..." Dr. Chamber's face was the colour of a well-ripened tomato. His fury was growing by the second.

"Get her off!" Doris wailed.

Blobs of blood formed where each nail had lodged in her cheek. "Hold this foot," I instructed. "And don't pull!"

Doris reached up to grasp the cat's forearm, and I extricated the claws from her other cheek. Gripping Doris's nose as if it were the head of a squirrel, Cleo growled nonstop. I had the second paw free. "Hold this one with your other hand."

Doris clutched it firmly. Tears formed in the corners of her eyes, trickled beneath her glasses and down her cheeks. I grabbed Cleo's head and struggled to get a hold on the skin of her lower jaw. I applied more pressure. Another turd protruded and plopped onto the table. She howled and wriggled against my efforts. I could feel her flex her jaw muscles as if intent on making the kill. I worked my fingers into the corner of her mouth, squeezed, and plugged her nose with the tip of a finger. She opened her mouth as if to try for a better grip, and we pulled her free. Doris flopped back against the wall.

Dr. Chambers, Shirley, and I moved in unison to deposit the enraged critter in the carton. I held her by the scruff as her owner secured the lid. Cleo was finally silent. Everyone turned to Doris. Blood was trickling down both cheeks; round blobs of red decorated both sides of her nose like ornaments.

"Oh, my God! I thought she was going to tear my nose off." Her voice trembled. She gently prodded with her fingertips and stared downward in a cross-eyed fashion. "Is it bad?"

"Let's get you to the sink and clean you up," said Dr. Chambers. "It sure could have been a lot worse." He carefully patted the wounds with a gauze sponge. "Thank God you didn't try to tear her off. There's nothing here that needs stitches. How long has it been since you had a tetanus shot?"

Doris was trying to focus. "I can't remember."

The doctor smiled. "Working here, you better get one."

By the time Doris and Shirley were processed as emergency outpatients at the hospital, they were both subdued. We managed to get through the remaining appointments without mishap. Doris kept examining her face in the mirror; Shirley massaged her arm constantly. "Should have gotten you to give me that darn shot. It hurts like the dickens."

I gave them a pathetic smile. "You girls have had a rip-roaring day—couldn't have packed in much more fun if we tried."

Doris sent me the look that said, "Right, moron," and headed for the door. I addressed her blonde sidekick, who appeared a mite weary. "Well, Shirley—what do you think? Have you found your new niche in life?"

Life Lessons

"The clutch, John! For God's sake, use the clutch!"

I cringed as a horrid grinding sound emanated from the gear-box. My poor Volkswagen had been screaming along for a hundred yards in first gear. It had survived one accident, and I was hoping it wasn't about to experience another. This four-mile drive to my farm was proving to be an exercise in endurance. "Put your foot on the clutch before you try to change gears."

The car veered towards the ditch, and I grabbed frantically for the wheel. "AAhhhhh!" John's brother, Brian, feigned a look of horror, then ducked behind the seat with his hands over his head.

"Keep your eyes on the road, John. You have to learn to change gears without looking at your hands."

John had been sixteen for several weeks already and was mortified that he still didn't have his driver's licence. He had worked like a hound all spring packing groceries after school at the Super-Valu and purchased a car a month ago. Since that time, the ugly little Fiat had perched in Martha's yard, teasing the boy. Every night he went home, fired the car up, and sat in it, listening to the radio.

Last week he had become convinced that he had been taken, that in fact, he had bought a lemon. After spending the entire afternoon in the driver's seat, lurching around the field next to Martha's house, he found himself in a real predicament. He'd been driving too fast and not paying attention to where he was going.

He jammed on the brakes and slid to a stop just before running over Martha's flower bed; another six inches would have put the front wheel on top of one of her award-winning begonias.

He struggled for an hour to get that car in reverse. No matter how he twisted his mouth, no matter how many times he tried to follow the pattern on the top of the stick, the car would only lunge forward. He shut the key off with the wheel perched definitively on the prize plant. It was only after his first lesson in my car—when I had shown him how to maneuver the stick down and to the right—that he saw the light and realized his own little chariot might also have a reverse gear.

The boys had been a major joy in my life during the past few months. Their zest for living was infectious, and their refusal to accept hard times was an inspiration. After their mother abandoned them, they were placed in a receiving home in Riverview run by a grandmotherly sort in her early sixties. Martha Rabel made the boys feel at home from the very first moment she led them upstairs to their room and tucked them into bed. They had been distressed when their mother left town without saying good-bye, but they never seemed to dwell on it. They simply dug into their new lives with a passion and accepted each and every improvement in their daily routine with enthusiasm.

John was determined from the beginning not to do without and was proving very capable of earning his own way. He was constantly coming up with odd jobs and would earn a few more bucks today to put towards his car insurance. The boys had been helping me since I'd purchased the farm; over the past month, we had made tremendous progress in cleaning things up. The site where I wanted to build the house had taken on the air of a park; the plan for today was to chop out the last of the underbrush and burn the old stumps and rotten windfalls that we had stacked on previous trips.

"Just pull over under that big pine tree, John. Gear down...Apply the brake slowly...Don't forget the clutch." John crammed the stick shift into second. The tires squealed, the engine screamed in protest, and we slowed mercifully. Finally, he jammed in the clutch, braked, and brought us to a stop at the side of the road. I smiled meekly at the boy and breathed a big sigh of relief. I now had an inkling of how my father felt when he was teaching me—a better understanding of why he had bellowed at me when I crashed his old Willies Jeep into the gas barrels at the front of the garage. I could still remember how foolish I felt when he reminded me the clutch was there for a purpose.

"Well, we got here in one piece." Brian was the master of the understatement. He grabbed his jacket and threw open the car door. John's face was flushed; beads of sweat had formed on his brow and some of his long curly locks were glued to his forehead.

Brian was already on his way to the brush pile. "Can I start the fire?" he yelled. I was still empathizing with Father. Being put into the position of the teacher made me realize how much like Dad I had really become. I was always critical of his short fuse; found it difficult to understand why he was so hard to please. Being around the boys made me realize how much I, myself, had to change.

"Okay, Brian, you boys light the big pile in the middle. Get the paper and matches from the car and start it so that the wind is blowing into it." I would rather have done it myself, but this would be a good time to start making some adjustments in my normal behaviour.

"When did you get that fancy jacket, John?" I admired the new jean jacket with its gleaming brass buttons. The boys were beginning to accumulate some nice clothing and John, in particular, seemed delighted to have things that originated from somewhere other than the Calgary Salvation Army Thrift Store.

"Just got it yesterday. Bought it with the money we got from working here."

"Looks pretty snazzy to be wearing for this kind of work. Make sure you don't tear it or burn a hole in it."

Leaving the boys to start the fire, I grabbed the shovel and axe

90

and attacked a clump of hawthorns. This ground would someday be my front yard; there was simply no place for one of these spiny creatures to be featured in it.

I stopped to suck my forefinger; a hawthorn spine had driven deeply into the flesh. I had worried away at the peripheral roots on one side and was chopping at the main root. I made the mistake of grabbing the stem to pull it over—those spines were so unforgiving. Sweat trickled into my eyes; I wiped my forehead on my shirtsleeve. It was good to get out here doing manual labour. There was something about getting my hands in the dirt that made me feel whole.

The occasional puff of smoke drifted from the far side of the woodpile, but I wasn't paying any attention to the boys. The last sighting had been ten minutes earlier when Brian trekked to the car and returned with more paper. I took a few final whacks at the taproot, then straightened my back with a sigh. I was ready for a breather.

"How're you boys making out?"

I was greeted with silence. John lay on his belly, his face red from blowing on a few embers that smouldered beneath an old cedar fence post. He smiled and sat up, out of breath. "We're not doin' too good."

"That's because you're thinking too big. Start a small fire first, then feed it till it has enough heat to start the rest of it going." I retrieved my axe, yanked the smoking post from the bottom of the pile, and split several long slender pieces from the side of it.

"Where's the paper?"

Brian looked at me sheepishly. "It's all gone."

"The matches?"

The boys exchanged looks. John timidly extended his hand with the bedraggled remnants of a book of matches. Three rather limp specimens were left. "Where are the rest? There were four or five packs."

"That's it." John remained stretched out on the ground next to the pile. The new jean jacket was already looking used.

I shook my head in amazement, motioning towards a clump of birch trees. "Come over here for a moment." I peeled ragged strips of bark from the base of the tree. "See how dry and fine this stuff is? It's nature's newspaper. Gather me a bunch of this from the other trees."

Five minutes later, they had accumulated a sizable mound of bark. Selecting a few of the finer pieces, I lit a match underneath them. Dark streams of smoke curled from the pile and flames licked upward.

"Why did you start it out here? How are you going to get the stack to burn?" Brian looked skeptical as I added more bark to the fire, then threw on some of the cedar kindling.

"We'll just start an intense little fire over here and keep it going. We won't have to worry about the rest." I added the remainder of the split cedar to the fire, then threw on dry branches collected from beneath trees. Before long, the fire was roaring and flames were licking at the edge of the pile.

"You better watch you don't burn a hole in that new jacket of yours, John. Maybe you should take it off?"

I returned to my struggle with the hawthorn. John and Brian were now stripped to their shirtsleeves, dragging deadfalls and old tree branches to the fire. It was a roaring blaze now, and I could feel its heat even from where I was working. I continued to dig around the periphery of the pesky clump of trees, seeking errant roots and cutting them with the axe. It was a feeling of personal victory when I severed the final root and dragged the massive cluster to the fire.

Working on my own land reminded me of my battle to clear our spare lot in Casino. As a youngster, I had dreamed of having my own pony. Like so many other things in those days, a pony was a luxury and Father's budget was stretched to the extreme to cover even the barest of essentials. For years, as Dad built the house and added on, it wasn't even possible to think the dream out loud.

I nagged at my poor mother for years about wanting a horse but never had the courage to bring it up with Father. When I was twelve, I finally mentioned it to him. I can still see his expression as he lowered the newspaper he had been engrossed in. I went on about how nice it would be for him to have a horse to ride to his favourite hunting spots—how it would save so much work when he had to pack out his deer. He sat poker-faced, listening to my lame sales pitch. There was an awkward silence as he stared at me, and seemingly through me.

He smoothed out the pages of the *Trail Times* as if it were a valuable legal document, then carefully refolded it. "When I was your age, I was out working on the family farm. Every night after school and every day of the summer, Dad had us clearing brush and picking rocks. I got to ride horses, but only because I was pulling stumps and dragging stone-boats. Don't you think it's high time you started doing more around here?"

I stood in silence, staring into my father's discerning grey-blue eyes. "How about if I clear the lot next door and plant some grass for pasture? Could I get a horse then?"

He looked at me for several moments, then uttered the words that he so often said to put me off. "We'll see." He slowly unfolded the newspaper and returned to the middle pages. I'm sure he had no intention of ever having to follow through with that promise, but he underestimated how determined I was. He wasn't all that impressed when I began whacking away with the axe that very afternoon. After several months of continuous activity though, as the cleared area grew and the brush piles got higher, he began to take it seriously.

Every night after school, I was out with the axe and swede saw. Birch and poplar that were big enough, I cut to length for fireplace wood. Stacks accumulated and people bought my wood by pick-up loads. When I had saved a good portion of the purchase price of my first horse, Dad finally broke down and helped me buy her. Her name was Beauty, a fat old black horse that was more than a tad lazy. But, for the next few years, we were inseparable.

I took my first outside job during the summer break between grades ten and eleven, with the idea of getting enough money to pay for Beauty's winter hay. With a school friend from Trail, I ventured to the Okanagan to pick fruit. Much to Father's chagrin, I traded the entire summer's pay to the daughter of the orchardist in exchange for a sorrel gelding by the name of Snookie. He was a cross between a Thoroughbred and a Tennessee walker, the horse of my dreams. He was tall enough to carry the long-legged kid that I had become, and he could sure cover the ground. Both horses were in Casino still; Pop treated them as pets and, once in a while, actually used Beauty for hunting.

I couldn't wait to bring them to Lister. To actually have my critters munching on grass that grew on my own farm. Just a bit of fence to stretch and a few hours of cleaning up junk and it would be safe for them. Patriquin had been lax with his waste baler twine, and the majority of the strings lay wherever a bale of hay had been fed.

I watched the flames lick at the leaves of the hawthorn, listened as the burning limbs produced high-pitched crackling and hissing sounds. It was time for a change of pace. "Okay guys, let's gather up all the junk that we can find around the pasture."

Spacing ourselves about twenty feet apart, we crisscrossed the twenty-acre woodlot, gathering errant strings and piling up mounds of discarded trash. Two hours later, we finished the chore and were eager to feed the dwindling fire with our armloads of scrap.

John struggled along with several empty beer bottles in his right hand, a pickle jar in his left, and a mess of twine piled in his arms. Setting the bottles down next to the car, he flung the tangled mass into the fire.

"Oh nooo!" he wailed.

I threw in my garbage, kicking unburned portions of brush into the circle of hot ash. "What's up, John?"

"My jacket." He stood staring down at his feet. A large circle of grey ash remained in the centre of an area where the surrounding pine needles and groundcover debris had burned. In the midst were six tarnished brass buttons—all that remained of John's spiffy new denim jacket.

D & G Enterprises

"It's time to slow down, Dave. This struggling around in the middle of the night is just getting to be more than I want to do."

Fred sounded tired. We had just finished washing up and seating ourselves at the MacKays' kitchen table. Bea plunked a mug in front of me and filled it with steaming coffee. "Help yourself to a sandwich there, Dave. You must be about all in after that calving. Poor guy…you've been running constantly all spring."

"It has been a steady go, Bea, but it's slowed down the last few weeks…I've been able to sleep through three nights in a row."

"You like cream and sugar with your coffee, don't you?"

"You bet."

She went to the fridge and returned with the treat that I'd been waiting for. Nowhere else had I ever seen such cream. Only here at the MacKays did the spoon stand straight up in the cream pitcher. I was still not a coffee lover; to me the joy of the drink was in the goodies I could add. I shovelled in some sugar and scooped a spoonful of cream from the pitcher.

"What will you do, Fred? Will you cut back on the number of cows you run?"

"I'm goin' to cut 'em in half—keep what I can pasture at home. No more haulin' cows all over the country lookin' for grass. No more traipsin' all over the valley with my machinery tryin' to put up enough hay for the winter. I'm goin' to sell my John Deere tractor and buy one of those little Fords. I'll keep a few of the younger cows and get rid of all the older ones, all of the late calvers."

I watched my coffee in fascination as the dollop of cream melted into a slick of shimmering oil. Until recently, I had no idea that cream could get this thick. Only Bea, with her Jersey cow and a cream separator at its maximum setting, could produce such a decadent treat.

"Eat up, Dave. A man your size needs to keep up his strength. Land sakes—you don't eat enough to keep a bird alive."

I reached for a sandwich, then sipped my coffee. I savoured the flavour and stirred in another generous scoop of cream.

"I see that old Jersey of yours is still cranking out the goods."

"You bet she is," Fred answered. "Don't know what we'd do without her, what with this bein' berry season and all."

"You make sure you save enough room for a big bowl of strawberries and cream there, Dave." Bea set a bowl of the luscious fruit in the centre of the table. She sprinkled a cup of brown sugar over the huge berries, then grabbed some bowls from the counter. "Yes, it's time to slow down a bit." Bea looked lovingly at Fred, then pulled out a chair and sat next to him. "Be nice to just enjoy the seasons out here and not dread all the work that comes with them. Don't know what we'd do without some cows around here though. I'd sure miss the calves…just love watching those babies running across the pasture with their tails in the air."

"I know what you mean." I took another swig from my cup. Now, this was coffee—sweet, and so rich I felt guilty drinking it.

"What sort of tractor you selling, Fred?" My mind was whirling. I needed a tractor, and Gord and I had talked about buying a few cattle. After all, we both had hay land and, in this country, there were always some bales that were less than top quality. It only made sense to feed a few head of our own.

"It's a 710 John Deere—fifty-some horsepower." Fred popped the last bite of sandwich in his mouth and ladled some strawberries into a bowl, taking care to get as much sugar as possible. He smothered them in cream.

"Bin a good tractor, but I won't be needin' anything that big from now on. That little Ford'll be more maneuverable out here on the hillside and will still be big enough to run my baler." He took a spoonful of strawberries, savoured them in silence, then gave me a knowing look. "Not interested in the tractor, are you? Could sell it to you for four grand. That's what they're goin' to give me on trade."

"Well, I have sort of been thinking about picking one up…now that I have the farm and all."

"Pete's sake, Dave." Bea nursed her coffee. "Don't you have enough to keep you busy without thinking about farming on top of it?"

"You're probably right, but there's something about having your own place and making your own mistakes that keeps a guy going. We'll have a look at that tractor before I hit the road, Fred."

Less than a week later, I climbed onto my newly acquired John Deere for the trip to Lister. I was excited. I had never driven a tractor before and, now that I found myself perched in this yellow seat way off the ground, I felt nervous.

"Give me a crash course on flying this thing, Fred."

"That's your two gear shifts down there." He pointed to the two sticks that were between my legs. "You'll want to have it in high range for the drive home but, for most things like swathin' and balin' around the farm, I ran it in second and second…That's the starter button right there. Won't do anything unless you have the clutch in. Your light switch is over here, the emergency over there."

I stepped on the clutch and pressed the starter. The engine roared to life. Slipping the gearshift into second and second, I let my foot off the clutch and rumbled forward. A smile creased my face. I felt like a kid on a go-cart. I had always wanted to try an open-air toy like this when I was younger; now, I was sitting up here for everyone to see. I headed down Fred's drive past his shiny new tractor and out onto the road. I slipped the stick into third gear and pulled back on the throttle.

I couldn't stop smiling; it didn't get much better than this. I felt so free sitting high above the road with the wind blowing through my hair. By the time I had wended my way off the West Creston hills, I was feeling comfortable behind the wheel. I slipped the transmission into high and high, pulled back on the throttle, and headed across the flats. The engine emitted a steady roar; the fluid in the weighted wheels whirled in an irregular fashion, giving the tractor a strange rocking sensation.

A great blue heron rose lazily from the slough adjacent to the roadway. Its long legs dangling and dragging along the water, it flapped slowly towards the Kootenay River. I looked up at it as if seeing one for the first time. I had never realized how gangly and awkward they appeared in the air. Bob and Hazel Rogers rounded the corner on their way home. I smiled and waved.

I rumbled by the pasture land belonging to the Lower Kootenay Band and out onto Highway 3. Spring planting was in full swing. Big dual-wheel tractors idled across the fields, dragging their discs behind them and kicking up long parallel lines of rich, dark silt in their wake.

I passed the Indian Reserve and shifted down for the climb onto the Lister plateau. The golf course was swarming with patrons, some dragging their bag of clubs, some scooting along on their carts. I watched a hefty, middle-aged woman waddle to the tee. Kneeling down, she placed her ball and grabbed a club. She made a few random arcs with her arms before she attacked the ball, wielding the club as if it were a broom she was swinging after an errant dog that had just done its business on her lawn. I could see her look of horror as the ball sliced to the right, hit a tree alongside the road, and ricocheted across the pavement in front of me. I chuckled and gave her a cheerful wave. I wondered if I could ever get into a sport like that. How did people develop the patience to chase a little ball hither and yon for hours on end?

A few days later, I looked at the cows Fred was about to cull and had a talk with Gordon. Cattle had been high for the past couple of years, and I thought they were a good buy. I picked a dozen of the better cows, and we were in the cattle business. Fred delivered them by the end of the week.

"A little to the left! Keep coming. Cut it hard!" The old three-ton lumbered towards the chute and bumped solidly against it. "That's good, Fred. They shouldn't have any trouble getting out there." The truck rocked back and forth as cows shifted from side to side to check out their new surroundings.

I pulled on the rope at the back of the box and a plywood panel rose slowly. Fred poked an old Hereford through the rails; she grudgingly stepped ahead. The end gate flew up as I put my entire weight on the rope. Tying it to the side, I stood back; cows shuffled gingerly down the chute and milled around in the corral.

"Did you buy the whole farm, Dave?" Fred asked. "Sikora had a pretty nice place here."

"Just the eighty acres to the south. Patriquin's dealing with someone else on the home place. He's already moved on...told me I could use the facilities till the end of the month. Doesn't sound like his other deal is finalized yet."

"Who's buying this?" Fred waved his hand at the house and barns that were on the other side of the corral.

"Hasn't said, but he hasn't been around much either. He's pretty busy getting things set up over in Grand Forks."

"I see...dangerous thing, when you have no idea who your neighbour'll be. Well, not to worry...That's the last of the critters. Were you goin' to run 'em out on pasture right away?"

"Thought we'd put the cows through and process them first. Wanted to get the horns knocked off those two old Herefords."

"Good luck with 'em. I'll be headin' home."

As Fred was leaving the yard, Gordon drove in. "Perfect timing, cowboy," I chimed, as he hauled himself out of the car. "Come check out your beasties."

Gordon draped himself eagerly over the corral fence. Clad in a red flannel shirt and new blue jeans, he looked like he was ready for work. "So this is the D and G herd? Do you think we'll make out all right with them?"

"Can't see why not. A few of them have a bit of age but, for the most part, they're good-looking cattle."

"What are you planning on doing today?"

"Just wanted to run them through and get 'em all vaccinated. We need to protect them against the Clostridial complex and for I.B.R., P.I.3."

"What's that? Never heard of any of those things." Gordon was not one to just accept something as the way it had to be done. One of the most knowledgeable men I had ever met, he always had to know the details.

"The seven-way Clostridial vaccine controls tetanus, black leg, malignant edema; I.B.R.'s the disease I've been telling you has been causing all the abortions. P.I.3 is another virus that some people claim can do the same thing."

"So what do we have to do?"

"Just get them in the squeeze so they can't move around. The seven-way goes under the skin of the neck; the I.B.R has to be squirted up their nose."

"Up their nose…how do you do that?"

"Just grab their heads and squirt it in with a syringe. It's really not a big deal."

Gord looked skeptical. "What good could it possibly do to squirt it up their nose?"

"The vaccine's made from a live virus. It's been altered so it can't cause disease anymore, but it's similar enough to the wild virus to stimulate antibodies and protect the cows from aborting. When we squirt it up their nose, we actually cause a mild infection and an immune challenge."

"What do you want me to do?"

"Let's separate the calves first. Don't want any of the babies to get hurt when we're crowding the cows."

"How many calves do we have already?"

"Seven. But I checked the others, and they're all close enough to induce. I'll give them an injection to make them calve early so they can breed back at the same time as the others."

I hopped over the fence and opened the gate at the far end. Several of the calves darted out the moment it was open. Two remained jammed next to their mothers at the other end of the corral. "See if you can cut out that little black white-face, Gord. Don't want her getting crowded any more than she is."

Gord tested the corral rails warily, then hoisted his bulky frame one rail after the other until he reached the top. Looking around hesitantly, he waved his leg at the big black cow below him. She backed up, cramming her calf even more tightly between herself and the old Hereford that stood next to her.

"Yah, back up there, girl! Haaaa!"

Gordon lowered himself one rail and kicked the cow on the forehead. She snorted, backed up a half step, and aggressively shook her head at him. He froze, then hoisted himself back up onto the top rail.

"She doesn't look too friendly."

"Just a sec." The calf was in a press and looking for a way out. Grabbing a pole, I prodded her gently. She pushed for all she was worth and freed herself from confinement. A few seconds later, she scooted out the corral gate followed by the other calf.

"That was good management. You should think of becoming a cowboy, Gord. You're wasting your talents as a realtor."

Ignoring me completely, he scurried down off the fence and quickly took a step back. The black cow whirled and circled the corral in search of a way out. Frustrated by her lack of options, she tried unsuccessfully to squeeze her head between the rails, then gave the Hereford next to her a few quick shots in the ribs.

"Looks like she has a bit of attitude."

"Sure does," Gordon muttered, warily eyeing her through the rails.

"Open the gate to the squeeze there, Gord, and we'll see if we can get this over with."

Gordon fumbled with the bolt on the antiquated gate and heaved upwards. It gave way with a start, and he dragged it open. A red white-face cow lumbered down the chute. I yanked the head gate closed and quickly stuck a pole behind her. She stopped her forward rush, backed up, and struggled briefly. I lifted a tent of skin on her neck and injected the Clostridial vaccine. Drawing up a couple of millilitres of intranasal vaccine, I grabbed her under the chin and sprayed a millilitre into each nostril. As I released her, the cow shook her head and backed up to the pole. When I opened the gate, she trotted off. We put through six more cows without difficulty.

An old Hereford with a gnarled horn that grew back towards her head sauntered up the alleyway. She stood stock-still while I stuck the needle under the skin, vaccinated her, and squirted the other vaccine up her nose.

"See how this horn is growing into her head, Gord?" I pointed to the indentation where the tip of the horn was digging into the skin. "If we don't remove it, it'll end up as an infected mess and have maggots crawling out of it in the heat of the summer."

Gordon wrinkled his nose. "Wouldn't that be a pretty picture." I slipped a piece of embryotomy wire around the base of the horn, then started pulling rapidly back and forth on it. The wire buried itself in the horn. Smoke caused by the friction filtered out from the horn margins, filling the air with the smell of burning flesh. In less than a minute, the horn lay on the ground.

"Boy, that stuff's sure slick. Just looking at it, you wouldn't think it would cut anything." Gordon stared in amazement at the now-coiled wire that he held in his hand. "Would have sworn that was just picture-hanging wire."

I opened the head gate. The Hereford took two steps forward, then turned to look for her calf. Mooing softly, she lifted her tail and ejected a stream of green-soup manure.

"Yah! Get out of here with your crapping." Gordon recoiled in disgust as the watery jet hit the ground and splattered over his shoes and blue jeans. "I'd forgotten just how disgusting these critters are to work around." Tiptoeing around the oozing mass, he whacked the cow on the hip. "Yah! Get going." She shuffled along the fence line as unconcerned as could be and began grazing.

We had processed the mellow cows first; the three remaining beasts were of a more belligerent nature. I grabbed a pole and entered the corral. The black cow that Gordon had had a go-round with earlier ran for the chute. "Get ready on that rope, Gord! This girl looks like she's going to be feisty."

She hit the catch gate with a full head of steam. Gordon yanked for all he was worth, and the metal bar clanked over and locked into place. The cow bellowed angrily then pushed against the cradle. Her hind foot slid out from under her; manure flew in all directions. I climbed over the rails of the corral, determined to get her processed as quickly as possible. She charged back and forth, lifting and banging her head relentlessly.

Gord retreated a couple of steps. The cow snorted and swung her head in his direction. "You sure we want to keep this one? She's crazier than hell."

I quickly grabbed the dose syringe and injected her in the neck. The cow bawled and lurched forward. Her head firing up and down like a trip-hammer, she pushed mightily. I stared in horror as the head gate suddenly lifted from its hinges. "Look out, Gord! Get out of the way!"

The cow lunged in his direction, carrying the entire gate with her. Still fettered by the chain on the corner, she bellowed and twisted her head. Gordon's eyes were wide in disbelief. He pedalled backwards, slipped on the fresh manure, and sprawled out flat on the ground. The cow was still struggling to free the chain of the head gate when Gord started rolling. One more roar and a jerk and she was free. With the metal apparatus still clinging to her neck, she charged across the yard.

Gord rolled like a huge walrus in front of her as she bucked, bellowed, and carried on. Reaching the fence, he squeezed under, then gingerly picked himself up on his hands and knees. "What in hell happened?"

As if in answer to his question, the head gate flew through the air and came to rest with a loud crash at the other end of the yard. The black cow shook her head, snorting angrily at the two of us. I was momentarily in shock. Both hinges of the gate had been pointing in the same direction—one toss of the head was all it took for her to dislodge it.

After a few moments of reflection, we dragged the gate back and finished the two remaining cows. The black cow never did get vaccinated for I.B.R. Gord looked like he had been thrown into a cement mixer containing a bucket of fresh manure. Strangely, he lost interest in expanding the D and G herd.

Hoping Against Hope

"Dave!" The voice was choked with emotion. "It's Michael Carpenter. Hope's been hit by a car...She's really in a bad way."

"Did you see her get hit?"

There was a long pause.

"No...It may have even happened last night..." He was struggling to go on. "She usually sleeps inside, but when I called her, she never came. I thought it was strange—she's so good at sticking around the house. I got up a couple times to check for her, but I was tired and finally drifted off. I thought maybe she'd gone back in the bush behind our place."

Another long silence. I knew Michael was consumed with guilt. "I went to bed...She was out there all night suffering."

"What can you see just looking at her?"

"She...she looks hideous!" The man was obviously on the verge of tears. "Her mouth's hanging open. Her jaw and teeth are all dangling down. She can hardly breathe. Her head's so swollen that I can't see her eyes."

"Has she tried to stand? Can she move her hind legs?"

"I'm not sure, but she got home somehow. The highway's at least two hundred feet away. When I didn't see her this morning, I let the other dogs out for a run—they found her. She was under the picnic table, and Tezron ran right to her. I took one look and rushed in to make sure you were at the office."

"Bring her in. I'll have things set up by the time you get here."

107

"David...the way she looks, I think we may have to put her to sleep. If you think her situation's hopeless, she's been a fantastic dog. I don't want her to suffer."

"I understand, Michael. Let's just see how she looks when you get here. Try not to move her any more than necessary. If Beth can help you, slide her onto a blanket or a board and carry her to your car with support under her."

When they arrived at the clinic, it was still before seven. Doris wouldn't be coming for another hour. I'd hung a bag of fluids from the drip stand and laid out a heavy woollen blanket on the exam table.

Hope was indeed a terrible sight to behold. She was sitting in an unnatural posture with her abdomen and hind end flat to the seat of the car. The usually delicate, well-rounded features of the black Lab's face were obliterated by swelling and a horrible distortion of her lower jaw. Both eyes were so puffy they could no longer open. Her nose was crusted with dried blood and formed clots closed up both nostrils. The front half of her jaw hung down in a grotesque manner, and a combination of blood and saliva dripped from it constantly. Gravel and dirt, which covered every exposed surface, were ground into the depths of the wounds.

Hope gurgled and wheezed as she dragged in air one breath after the other. She bore some weight on her front legs and stretched her head forward in an attempt to breathe easier. Her right hind leg was pulled up beneath her; from the angle she held it, I knew it had to be broken.

"Oh, Hope, you sure got yourself into a mess." At the sound of my voice, her tail wagged as if she were greeting an old friend. Mutilated and tortured with pain, she was still trying hard to please. Michael closed his eyes and turned away.

"Okay sweetie...okay, I know it hurts." I ran my hands gently over her body. Lifting her upper lip, I made a quick evaluation of her mucous membranes. Her gums were pale but, even in the poor light of the car, I was able to see they had a pinkish hue. As I pressed down, the colour blanched, then returned slowly after I removed my finger. Her feet were cool to the touch, but she struggled to pull them away when I pinched them. I ran my hands over her spine in search of abnormalities and checked for signs of pain on deep palpation. Her spine seemed intact, but she was uncomfortable when I prodded her pelvis.

"I think it's safe enough to move her, Michael."

I lifted Hope as carefully as possible into my arms. She squirmed for a moment, her tail flagging as her only means of communication, then lay quietly. When I deposited her onto the exam table and positioned her broken leg, she fidgeted, but settled down with her head extended and her tongue hanging in a hideous fashion.

"I just can't stand to look at her like this," moaned Michael. "Do you think I should just have you put her down?"

"She's eight now, Michael?" I looked from her record card to his tormented face.

"Right, she was eight years old in May."

I explored Hope's fractured hind leg. Manipulating it back and forth, I was unable to find a problem elsewhere. I rolled her over and checked the opposite hind leg. Although it seemed fine, my efforts appeared to cause pain in the pelvis. Slipping on a latex glove, I applied lubricant to my finger and introduced it into her rectum. The pelvic canal was normal in size; no bone fragments were palpable. Applying even a bit of pressure to the left side, though, made her tense and squirm to get away from me.

I returned my focus to Hope's head and began systematically poking and prodding. Gingerly elevating the end of the partially severed jaw, I manipulated it up and down. The joints were still intact and moved without a hint of clunking or grinding. The upper portion of her head and jaw was badly abraded, but I was certain it was intact. A couple of her top incisors were broken at the gum line, but the rest of the teeth looked solid.

No amount of prying at the eyelids allowed me to get a look at the globes. All I could see was tremendous swelling and bruising of the surrounding tissue. It felt as if the inside pressure was normal, and I was hoping that her eyes weren't permanently damaged.

"I tell you, Michael, this is one case where I'd love to have a crystal ball to predict the outcome. She's badly beat up but, if there'd been a major hemorrhage, she'd have died overnight. Her leg is broken, but I'm sure I can handle that with a bone pin. I suspect we have a fracture on the left side of her hip, and we'll sure have to look into that. As bad as her jaw looks, there's still blood supply to all the parts, and I think it can be repaired."

"What do you suggest? Should we try and save her or put her to sleep?"

I shrugged indecisively. "That's a question only you can answer, Michael. There's no one thing I can find that's beyond repair. We won't know about the eyes until the swelling goes down, and we should certainly get some X-rays to make sure I haven't overlooked something. If the pelvic fracture is severe or she's blind, then I would lean towards euthanasia."

Michael gave his dog the most forlorn look and rested his hand at the back of her head. Tears pooled in his eyes as he tenderly stroked her; he cringed when she forced a tortured breath through her mutilated airway.

"She's such a sweet dog, David." He stared down at her almost unrecognizable face. "Beth and I love this dog so much—she's like a child to us."

"I can see you've spent a lot of time with her. Dogs don't just suddenly become as attentive and well trained as she is without someone working awfully hard training them."

"I have spent a lot of time with her, but she had so much natural instinct. She came from the Belmont bloodline; that was real field-trial breeding. She was always so calm and laid back at competitions. Other dogs would be like bundles of dynamite ready to explode—not Hope. She seemed half asleep when it was her turn to retrieve, but when I released her, it was obvious that she'd been watching; she knew exactly what I wanted."

"Why don't we take things in stages until you and Beth can make up your minds? If we're going to treat her, we need to get the swelling down and have a look at her eyes…we obviously have to keep those open wounds from getting infected."

"Go ahead…do some X-rays…See what we've got. Beth and I'll decide what to do after you know more."

With Michael holding Hope, I started an intravenous drip and administered steroids, antibiotics, and Demerol. By the time Doris arrived, the X-ray machine was ready to go, and I had cleaned a lot of the gross contamination from the wounds.

The Demerol helped considerably in easing Hope's pain and allowing her to breathe more easily. She was mellow as we manipulated her and worked our way through one X-ray field after the other. Before long, Doris emerged from the darkroom, her hands laden with various-sized films all fresh from the tanks and still dripping water.

The wing of the ileum on Hope's left side was fractured and her pubis separated, but I had seen a lot of similar cases heal nicely with cage rest. There was no evidence of spinal injury, and X-rays of the jaw showed me nothing I didn't already know. The hind leg was broken in the middle of the tibia and the fibula, as I'd suspected.

Michael had run home and returned with Beth. The pair of them stood beside me, staring at the view box as if it were the crystal ball that would tell them the future of their beloved friend. I held up the last of the X-rays. "So far, there are no surprises."

"How can you ever put her jaw back together so she'll be able to use it again?" Beth's eyes were locked on the X-ray on the view box. "It just looks so hopeless the way it's hanging there now."

"And how's she going to eat and drink while her jaw's healing?" Michael asked. "I can't see how we'd be able to get her to take in enough to stay alive. You can't keep feeding her with the intravenous until her jaw's healed."

"Feeding her is going to be a problem for a while, but there's a new procedure for getting nutrients into critters with severe trauma like this. We install a tube through the back of their mouth so it goes behind the teeth and down the throat. It stays in for the whole time the jaw's not functional. I've never used one, but I can certainly phone the surgeons at the veterinary college for advice."

"That's fine for water, but how would we get food down it?" Michael asked.

"We'd have to whip all her food in a blender...get it fluid enough to be flushed down with water. It's going to need a big commitment of time and effort on your part, though. You should obviously factor that into your decision."

The Carpenters finally looked away from the view box to stare at one another; the answer to their dilemma wasn't coming easily. "Why don't I leave you two to discuss the situation? I'll go check on Hope. Give me a holler if you have any questions."

Hope seemed to be resting comfortably. Although her breathing was laboured, the urgency had somehow lessened and much of the tension had left her body. I had just finished slowing the drip on a new intravenous bag when Michael joined me.

"David, Beth and I have decided we'd like you to make that call to Pullman. We love this dog...owe her a lot for what she's given us over the years. We want to give her a chance."

Seeking advice from the staff of the teaching hospitals at both Saskatoon and Pullman had become one of my most valuable forms of continuing education. It was amazing how much I had learned from difficult cases by following them through to the best of my ability and having someone to challenge my thinking along the way.

I discussed Hope's case with a surgical resident, expressing my concerns with how dirty the wounds were. He was confident that with proper fixation of the fractures and the use of a feeding tube, the jaw would eventually heal. He quoted me an approximate cost for the repair if it were done at the veterinary hospital in Pullman and gave me a rundown for installation of the tube should I decide to go on my own.

After a long talk, the Carpenters and I decided to attempt a repair of Hope's jaw in my clinic with pins and wires. Having the surgery done at Pullman would have been too costly, and the travel back and forth nearly impossible.

It was ten o'clock before we got Hope under anesthesia and began the final cleanup of the fracture sites. The ends of the bones were impregnated with dirt and gravel. We'd do well to get the surgery site halfway clean, and have to rely heavily on antibiotics.

Scrubbing her mouth was a tedious job. As I watched Doris at work, I thought back to the first time we had met—the first time she had helped with a surgery. The bedraggled kitten we had operated on that night had as grungy a wound as I'd ever seen. I'd had my doubts then, too, about Albert's chances and about Doris herself.

Here we were today, again struggling with uncertainty and wishing for just one little look in that crystal ball. To listen to Werner talk about Albert now—how he tears around and rules the farm—I had to have faith. And look at Doris...How could I even imagine getting along without her?

Hope's jaw was in four separate pieces—the portions that articulated with the joints, and the ends with the canine teeth which were almost completely pulled apart. My plan was to first join the two end fragments to try and preserve the soft tissue in that region.

I selected a small pin and locked it into the drill chuck. With a clockwise rotation, I pressed the tip firmly against Hope's jawbone and began the slow procedure of implanting it. Hope was older than most of the animals I had worked on, and her bone was far more dense and compact. It wasn't long before I broke into a sweat.

Placing that first pin took much longer than I had anticipated, but when it was in and I had a figure-eight circlage wire in place, I was happy with its stability. Things looked infinitely more hopeful with both canine teeth perched at the same angle.

The jaw is not easy to work with. Most bones had a better-defined cavity to host a pin than did the mandible of a dog Hope's age. I chose a quarter-inch pin and began driving it into the front portion of the jaw on the right side.

The toughness and mobility of the bone made for difficult drilling indeed. The angle I was working from didn't help either. My hands were tender; sweat was pouring off me by the time the pin emerged from the cortex of the mandible and I could feel it sticking through the skin. Driving it all the way through, I attached the chuck to the opposite pole of the pin and pulled until it was flush with the end of the fracture.

I took a breather to rest my tormented hands. "You have no idea how hard that bone is, Doris. Every twist seems to be that much tougher."

To say that I jinxed myself with those words would leave the false impression that I'm a superstitious man. Whether I hexed myself or was just being prophetic probably matters little. That next hour was far from pleasant for me, let alone Doris. I cranked on that chuck until my hands looked like hamburger; when I first saw blood inside my glove, I was sure I had poked a hole in it and the dog's blood was seeping in. It was little consolation to discover that it was actually my own!

Pressing ever harder on the pin, I struggled to drive it through the bone. Doris diligently maneuvered the hoses of the anesthetic machine back and forth, trying to keep the tube from pulling out of Hope's throat. I was struggling not to blow my cool. Several times, I reached for something to throw; each time I averted the temptation at the last second.

I felt helpless and incompetent. Should I pull the damned pin back and start over, or should I just keep driving and hope that it would eventually worry its way through? I closed my eyes and stood motionless, tears threatening.

"Just a second, Dave," Doris interrupted. "I have to retie the tube. I'm afraid it's working its way out."

I lifted the drapes up and out of the way for her as she untied the gauze that held the tube in place and retied it in its proper position.

"Would it help if I held her head at a different angle...like this? It may make it easier." Doris's hands slipped when she went to lift Hope's head. She tried again. "Dave, I can't move her head!"

"What do you mean, you can't move her head?"

Grabbing onto Hope's jaw, I proceeded to demonstrate for Doris the angle I was looking for. I couldn't believe it; Hope's head was secured firmly to the table! Rather than exiting from the side of the mandible where I had been watching for it, the pin had come out through the bottom of the bone. All the grunting and cursing and cranking I had done for the last half hour had served only to drive the pin through the Arborite on the top of the surgery table and into the plywood beneath it.

This was a watershed moment—one of those split-second flashes that decides the outcome of a day. I could either look for the humour in the situation, or I could explode and fall apart. It was touch and go for a moment: I could sense that Doris was truly afraid to look at me. She started giggling first. Not that I could see it under her mask, but I could detect it in her eyes. Before the moment was up, it was all I could do to breathe, I was laughing that hard.

After ten minutes of steady cranking, I finally backed the chuck out of the plywood. Hope was free. Frankly, things could have been far worse. After all, I had a pin that had a good purchase on the distal bone fragment, and I had access to the end of the pin so I could reverse it and drive it into the main portion of the jaw. In reality, what more could I ask? I felt almost giddy as I looked at how well it was all going to line up. Barring a catastrophe, I was home free.

Doris opened my drill pack. I selected a quarter-inch bit and secured the chuck. Pressing firmly against the bone, I drilled holes parallel to the plane of the fracture on both sides of it. I threaded heavy stainless steel wire through the holes and cinched the fracture together; I was amazed at how well the circlage wires alone held it in place.

I repeated the procedure on the opposite side, tightened the wires, and cut off the ends. Hooking the driver onto the pin that had been buried in the table, I drilled it into the cortex of the end of the jaw. It disappeared steadily until at least three inches was buried deep in the bone.

By the time the second pin was advanced, the jaw felt amazingly firm and my confidence soared. Hope was going to make it. I just knew it! The fracture felt so stable that I questioned even needing the feeding tube; after all, it was uncharted water for me, and we had already been at this longer than I had expected. I moved Hope's jaw up and down to check for any abnormality in movement. I was amazed how freely the jaw moved and ecstatic at how well her teeth lined up. If not for the fractured incisors, her bite would be perfect.

As the resident had suggested, installation of the tube was a very simple procedure, and I kicked myself for even questioning its use. The skin had already been clipped and scrubbed, so it was a simple matter of driving a pair of forceps through the cheek high in the back of her mouth, incising the skin over the surface of the forceps, passing the tube over her tongue and down her throat. A gush of acrid air told me I was where I wanted the tube to be—in Hope's stomach.

I was wishing that I had gone for broke and pinned the tibia before working on the jaw. My logic had told me to repair the jaw first; if that were unsuccessful, we wouldn't go on. Now, it would take Doris at least an hour to clean up the contaminated instruments and resterilize them. The leg would have to wait.

While Doris scrubbed at the open wounds on Hope's head, I turned my attention to stabilizing her fractured leg. I constructed a Thomas splint that would encompass her leg from the outside and keep the ends of the bone from jamming on one another and causing further injury. I had almost finished taping the pieces of the splint together when I couldn't wait any longer. I just had to call.

"Michael, get down here to have a look!"

"She's all right?"

"Come have a look—you tell me. I'm about finished splinting her leg."

By the time the Carpenters arrived, I had finished and Hope was waking up from the anesthetic. The endotracheal tube was still in; there was no hint of the distressing sounds that had been so prevalent earlier.

Beth approached Hope's kennel as if it were a shrine. "Oh, she's breathing so much better!"

"We're just about ready to pull the tube. I hope she'll breathe as easily once it's out. There's still a lot of swelling, but getting that jaw straightened out has to make a big difference."

"David!" Michael had the most gleeful look on his face. "Her mouth looks great! I wouldn't have believed it possible."

They sat with Hope until she was completely recovered from anesthetic. She began to move her legs and finally was able to support herself on her tummy. She swallowed; her breathing became more forceful.

"It's time for her to fly on her own." I untied the length of gauze that held the tube in place. As soon as I removed it, Hope coughed, gagged, and released a mortifying wail. Beth recoiled at the sound of her anguish.

"She'll be vocal for the next hour or so," I warned. "They always are when recovering from anesthetic."

Hope lolled her tongue and flexed her jaw as if trying it out. Her breaths came in rasps.

"Oh, I can't tell you how much better it makes me feel, to see her jaw like this." Michael held Hope's head in his hands and peered at her swollen face. "Now, if only she can see."

"I'm almost sure the right eye's intact. I pried it open just enough to get a look…Sure couldn't get at the left one, though."

For the rest of the afternoon and into the evening, Michael and Beth rotated through the kennel room. They sat with Hope, talked to her, applied ice packs to her forehead and eyes. It was almost ten that evening before I ushered them out the door and went upstairs to bed. I drifted off to sleep immediately.

At half past five, my eyes snapped open. Light shone through the bedroom window. A truck rattled its way over the pothole on Canyon Street. Lug rushed over and stuck his cold nose in my face; I don't know how he always knew the moment I was awake. Pulling on my trousers, I rushed downstairs. Hope was sitting up facing in my direction. Her tail banged wildly on the bottom of the kennel, and she extended her head towards the bars.

"Well, don't you look better this morning!" She dragged herself to me. Her muzzle was wet and slimy; long ropes of mucous hung from the side of her mouth and the hood that surrounded her head. I cleaned away the muck that had accumulated overnight. The smell from her mouth was putrid, but the wounds themselves looked healthy.

Her breathing was much improved from the night before, and she accepted the feeding tube with only the occasional swallow. From the very beginning, it worked well, and Hope got frequent feedings. Within three days, her strength rebounded; I put her under anesthesia to repair her broken leg. I managed to get good fixation of the tibia without drilling more holes in my surgery table.

A week after Hope's initial surgery, she was discharged to the Carpenters. Michael and Beth nursed her diligently, carrying her out several times a day to urinate and defecate, feeding her every couple of hours with a slurry of food and water. Her hip healed nicely and, within a few weeks, she was bearing weight on her broken leg.

The mouth was slow to heal and smelled little better than a cesspool. Only by flushing constantly with mouthwash and water was it possible to stay in the same room with her. By the end of a month, however, the rank smell diminished. She began to lap water and showed more and more interest in eating on her own.

Michael was a happy man when he brought her back to the clinic for removal of the feeding tube. Hope sat on the tabletop as unconcerned as could be as I removed the bandage, cut the sutures, and pulled out the apparatus. After five weeks of tasting tidbits, she paid strict attention to me as I opened a can of cat food and set it on the end of the table. Digging around in it with a spoon, I relished watching the dog's eyes grow bigger by the second. The spoonful of Fancy Feast I held in front of her nose disappeared in a single bite.

"Come now, Hope. There's no way you even tasted that."

Michael smiled as he watched the entire can of food disappear one bite at a time. It had been a long haul, and he and Beth had persevered. The hole from the tube was allowed to granulate closed; soon there was no evidence of its ever having been there. The remaining hardware was gradually removed. Hope's recovery was complete. At the end of six months all her hair had grown back, and she looked as plump and handsome as ever.

I thought better of telling the Carpenters their dear dog had been screwed to the surgery table. At that time of crisis, they may not have seen the humour in it.

Spicing Up the Neighbourhood

"That's just great, Doris. It's debatable that there's enough work for Keith and I in this valley as it is...All we need is a third vet."

Doris gave me her stern, motherly look. "But Bob said that Dr. Dudley was going to be farming. How can he look after three hundred acres and have enough time to work as a vet?"

"He's got his son with him. Maybe he plans on having his boy run the farm, and he'll just cream what he can from a practice."

Doris shook her head at me and returned to making entries in the ledger book. "You worry too much, Dave. Just wait and see."

Wait and see. Wait and see. Doris's solution for everything was "wait and see." I stomped up the stairs, put on a Neil Diamond album, and threw myself on the cushion in the middle of the living room floor. Life was full of surprises. Why couldn't things go smoothly for a while? I had just stuck my neck out to purchase the farm; the last thing I needed was a dramatic cutback in income from my practice. From what Dr. Dudley had been telling his neighbours, money was the least of his worries. They told me his dad had left him eleven million. I thought of Doris massaging the books for enough money to get cheques to everyone at the end of the month. I couldn't imagine having several million in the bank.

I was struggling to keep from being pessimistic, but it was tough when, at two o'clock on a Wednesday afternoon, I was lounging around listening to Neil Diamond sing about love on the

rocks. Maybe Dr. Dudley was already moonlighting. Maybe some of the farmers were already using his services. After all, he had bought land right next door to the Rogers, just down the road from the Hurfords and the Hansons. He was within spitting distance of one of my best beef clients and two of my best dairy clients.

I kept going over and over the same scenario. What if some of my clients really did defect to this new veterinarian? Could I survive? My mind whirled around the problem. The more I thought about it, the more I was convinced I was in trouble—that some of my clients may indeed bail for someone who was closer or cheaper. I squirmed; this pillow was definitely not comfortable enough. I dragged myself from my repose and shut off the turntable. I had to do something. It was dangerous for me to lie around collecting negative thoughts. Darn it anyway, why couldn't I have had just a bit more time to get established? I started the water running in the sink, waited until it was nice and cold, then thrust a cup into the flow. It filled and spilled over the edge; I watched the water rush towards the drain. The problem was that all these farmers were my friends. Losing them as clients was one thing; the thought of losing them as friends was too much. Having them toss me aside for someone else—that would hurt. I took a long, slow drink. Lug longingly watched me, then rooted at my hand.

"So you're thirsty too, are you?" I filled his bowl and he lapped the water enthusiastically.

All the way to the farm I mused about what I could do to keep my clients. How I could improve on my services so no one would want to try another vet. I slowed as I passed the Patriquin place. There was a three-ton truck by the barn and a pickup by the house. A sale must have finally gone through. Who had bought it? I sure hoped it was someone I'd get on well with.

I parked the car at the house site in the trees and wandered across the gully. Several cows were grazing in the creek bottom; they raised their heads as Lug thundered past. He was already playing his favourite game. Holding a stick in his mouth, he howled like a hyena. Running between the cows and their calves, he hesitated just long enough for a cow to give chase, then ran like the wind away from her. How he loved to torment those poor critters, to see how far he could push the game before I bellowed at him.

Having livestock around the farm was becoming routine. I had made a deal with John Bodder, a beef client of mine, for handling the hay crop. He had swathed and baled the first cutting on fifty percent shares, and the old pole barn was brimming. It had been dry for the last couple of weeks, so the pasture was starting to look mowed down. I threw out hay a couple of times a day to keep the cows from depleting the grass. The feed brought them to the shed where I could have a look at them all and make sure they were doing well.

"Come boss! Come boss!" The girls slowly moved in my direction, as if they were performing a duty. They were not really hungry, but none of them wanted the others to get something they missed out on. Number 211 brought up the rear. The last cow to calve, she was finally starting to make a bit of an udder. I had administered Dexamethasone not once, but twice, to induce her.

I had injected the other two late calvers as well, and they had delivered right on schedule; their babies were already bounding around. The white-faced 211 was one of the youngest cows Gordon and I had purchased. She was carrying her second calf, and Fred had parted with her only because she was so much later than the rest of the herd.

In order to ensure a vigorous calf, I would need to induce within three or four weeks of delivery. I was almost positive that the other two had only been a couple of weeks away, and they had both calved nicely within forty hours of their injection. But 211 was different. I knew I was pushing her farther. I had palpated her rectally and felt for the cotyledons again and again to convince myself that she was far enough along to induce. She hadn't responded to the first injection, perhaps because it was too early. For better or for worse, she was responding to this one; I just hoped the calf was mature enough to survive.

I climbed the plank fence next to the hay shed, scaled the stack, and dropped a couple of bales to the ground. From my vantage point, I hoped to catch sight of my new neighbours. There was activity in the house; several times I saw someone through a window. I wondered who it would be.

I broke the twine on the bales and spread them around so there was lots of room for the cattle. The cows milled about, jostling one another to be first to get a mouthful. As usual, 211 stood back from the others, seemingly content to be near the herd. A few of the older calves took a bite of hay while their fellows bucked and chased after one another. The youngest two seemed content to stay beside their mothers.

In an attempt to see who was next door, I approached the fence separating me from the neighbour's property. A boy hustled to the pickup and carried a box into the house, but I didn't get a clear look at his face.

I was distracted by a pair of robins prospecting diligently in the bottom of the draw. Hopping about in ever expanding circles, they pulled up a worm here and there.

"What the hell do you think you're doing, Perrin—buying my farm out from under me?"

I whirled. The familiar voice had come from around the corner of the garage. A shiver ran up my spine as I recognized it. There, with her hands planted on her hips and a look of absolute contempt on her face, stood Verna Levett.

"Oh hello, Verna." My face flushed as I realized that she had been watching me watching them.

"Hello, my ass! *Hello* is for friends…You ain't no friend of ours. You stole that piece of ground right out from under us."

"How do you figure that?"

"If you'd of minded your own damned business, I'd own it right now."

"Patriquin listed it with Veitches. I had no idea you were try-ing to buy it."

Verna strutted towards me, her hands still on her hips. Her face was fixed in a scowl that left little room for interpretation. "Bullshit to that! If that son of a bitch woulda just waited a couple more weeks, I'd have had the money for the whole damned thing. Wanted to get a place big enough for the family to do some farmin', 'n you come along and screw the whole damned thing up."

I could feel my ears flush under her barrage. "Well, I'm sorry, Verna, I had no idea…"

"You all right, Ma?" Verna's son, Len, trotted over from the house. One of her other sons and her daughter hung back at the porch watching the encounter with interest.

"Yeah, I can look after myself!" Verna's green eyes were smoul-dering, her voice dripping with sarcasm. This was the type of response I had expected from Verna a few months before when I had to tell her I'd fried her piglet under the lightbulb. I felt like a flower that had been ripped from its vine and left to wilt in the desert sun.

Len stopped just short of the fence. His ruggedly handsome face was the picture of contempt. His stocky, well-muscled body was bare from the waist up, the veins on the side of his neck engorged. "This is our farm." He sneered belligerently and waved his arm over the woodlot behind me. "You'll figure it out sooner or later."

I could feel the vessels pounding at the base of my temples. "Is that a threat?" Our eyes locked for what seemed several minutes. "Come on, Len." Verna turned her back on me and strode pur-posefully to the house. "We got lots of work to do."

I drifted back to the hay shed. As though in a fog, I turned on the tap to fill the old concrete trough. Water spurted from the decaying rubber hose. This unexpected turn of events had left me perturbed. The last thing I needed was a battle with Verna Levett.

If even one of the dozens of stories that I had been told about her were true, I'd be in for the ride of a lifetime. In this neck of the woods, no name made grown men tremble more readily than *Verna Levett*.

It was after one before I finally went to bed that night. What had I gotten myself into? Everything that I had gained over the past eighteen months seemed to be in jeopardy. First, a new vet, and now Verna. Would there be anything left to salvage?

As I drifted off, I became embroiled in the most difficult case I had ever encountered. Bob Rogers had phoned about a valuable purebred heifer that was having trouble calving. I had started to deliver the calf hours ago and just wasn't able to get anything to go my way. The animal was huge and there should have been lots of room to straighten out the baby.

What started as a simple procedure with just Bob and I suddenly turned into a spectator sport. Sitting on the corral rail was an ever expanding cast of clients. Dan, David, Eve, and Herb Hurford sat next to Morris and Ken Hanson. To my left were John and Jean Partington. Beside them, Hilda and Al Weins watched the action thoughtfully. Everyone was judging my performance. Sweat poured off my face; my coveralls were plastered with manure. I looked down at my arms—they were covered with blood.

I wanted to explain to everyone that this was a difficult case, that for some reason I couldn't get this calf straightened out, that I wasn't usually such a klutz. But, no words would come out. I just stood there looking from one person to the other in search of support.

That was when Verna appeared. On her left was Len smiling a sinister smile; still shirtless, his well-oiled skin reflected rippling muscles. On her right was a handsome, well-groomed young man. The name *Dr. Charles Dudley* was brazenly embroidered across the breast pocket of his spotless green coveralls. Verna grabbed the debonair fellow by the elbow and led him forward. "Let a real vet have a go at her."

Every eye was focused on Dr. Dudley as he carefully rolled up his sleeves and scrubbed himself. He brushed past me as if I weren't even there and, within seconds, delivered the most glorious-looking calf. I could see the admiration in Bob's eyes as he ran his hands over the already dried and half-grown heifer. The flashy vet reached into the cow a second time and pulled out a graceful, long-legged foal.

"That's nothing," Verna pronounced with a sneer. "Look at this." Dr. Dudley explored the heifer's vagina like a magician searching under his cape. He produced piglets and puppies and all manner of critters. I looked from one client to the next. Their eyes were focused with absolute adoration on the fabulous Dr. Dudley. I had lost them. I had lost them all.

I sat bolt upright in bed. My body was covered with sweat; the covers lay on the floor. I had the most horrible feeling of dejection. I glanced at my watch—two-thirty. I rolled over, closed my eyes again, and finally fell asleep.

The following day was thankfully busy, and I had little time to think of either Verna or Dr. Dudley. Herd health at the Weins' dairy went smoothly, and I stayed for lunch with Hilda and Al. It was just after noon, so I had plenty of time to throw out a bale for my cows and make it back to the office for my one o'clock appointment. I parked on the road alongside the woodlot. The cows were nowhere to be seen, so I headed through the trees in the direction of the corral. When I arrived, I could see them milling around the shed. And then I realized why: the boards were missing from the side. Bales were strewn everywhere. I looked in dismay at the mess—at all the wasted hay.

"Damn it, anyway! Yah! Get out of here." I chased the cows back from the carnage. They were as fat as ticks and no longer interested in eating. Three lay stretched out on their sides with big piles of manure behind them. How could this have happened? They had never bothered anything before. I dug at the boards that lay scattered beneath the broken bales. Three-inch spikes had been yanked out.

I stacked the intact bales the best I could inside the shed and tied the boards back in place with twine. I'd bring a hammer and repair it properly later. I got to the office well after one. The afternoon flew by with several small animal appointments. It was almost five and the last vaccination was leaving when Doris came back with the daybook in her hand.

She smiled. "You'll never guess who called this afternoon."

She was making me nervous. "Verna Levett?" I hadn't told Doris about my new neighbours at the farm. As a matter of fact, I still hadn't come to grips with the recent confrontation myself.

"Verna? Why would you say Verna?" Doris looked intrigued. "As a matter of fact, it's Dr. Dudley who wants to meet with you. He asked if you'd stop by his house in Alice Siding...and, by the way, he wants you to bring a sleeping sickness–tetanus vaccine for his horse."

So, this was it. I was finally going to meet the fabulous Dr. Dudley. He must want a showdown, an opportunity to lay out his plans for conquering the Creston Valley. I sorted through the stack of coveralls in the kennel room in search of the new pair—the ones that hadn't shrunk and could still be hidden inside my boots. I had to be decisive about this; had to maintain my dignity and not approach him with cap in hand.

I drove to the address that Doris had scratched onto the notepad. It was a nice home, but certainly not ostentatious. I pushed the doorbell; chimes sounded in some distant room but nobody answered. I rang a second and third time before returning to the car.

A horse whinnied. I wandered towards the back yard, where an attractive-looking bay mare stood at the gate. I checked Doris's note again. This had to be the right place. I glanced at my watch—I was right on time. I settled onto the hood of the car to soak up a few morsels of sunshine. I was beginning to wonder if Doris had made some sort of mistake when a blue Ford pickup with a seat belt dangling from the driver's side roared into the yard and screeched to a halt.

The door flew open and the man behind the wheel quickly got out and made his way towards me. In his forties, he was stocky, dark-haired, and dressed in cowboy boots and pink overalls.

"Dr. Perrin, I presume?" He grabbed my hand and gave it an aggressive shake. "I'm Charles Dudley."

"Glad to meet you, Charles...Call me Dave." An awkward silence followed as we each searched for a means to carry on the conversation. "...So you're a graduate of Colorado?"

"That's right...class of '63. Took me ten years to finally get my degree, but I managed."

"Where did you practise?"

"Never did—veterinary medicine was sort of my dad's idea. I wasn't very fussy about it."

I could feel a smile coming on. "So you're just going to farm then?"

"For as long as I can afford to...Did you bring the vaccine? I just bought a beautiful little quarter horse mare and sure don't want anything to happen to her."

"Have it right here." I grabbed the four-way vaccine from the icebox and was about to hand it to him when he turned towards the back yard. I caught up to him as he was opening the corral gate. Again, I tried to pass him the syringe, but he grabbed the mare's halter and pulled her to him.

"Where do you want to give her the shot?" he asked.

"I'll use the hip." I tapped the horse with the back of my hand a couple of times, then drove the needle to the hub. Attaching the syringe, I injected the thick pinkish liquid. I pulled out the needle and turned to face "the new vet," who was looking in the opposite direction. "All done."

He smiled meekly. "Never could stand the sight of needles."

Full Moon

"Dave, I think you better have a look at this kitten."

I'd heard a commotion in the waiting room just before Doris poked her head around the curtain. She was looking haggard—this was the week of the full moon. Today was one of those days that just couldn't be explained. The office had been filled to capacity all morning, and Doris was still on the phone rearranging appointments.

Mrs. Popovich gave me an exasperated smile. For the past half hour, she had been waiting patiently for me to check on her much loved companion. The Spaniel-cross dog had spent a good part of the night coughing, and Margaret was concerned that Pekoe's heart condition had taken a turn for the worse.

"What's up, Doris?"

"It's Mrs. Dremler. Her kitten dragged itself home a few minutes ago—she thinks it's been hit by a car."

I looked at Mrs. Popovich and shrugged. She smiled meekly. "You go ahead. We can wait."

Bill, the taxi driver, clutched a cardboard box to his chest, dwarfing the tiny, white-haired woman who stood behind him. The frail creature leaned heavily on her walking stick and appeared desperate to perch somewhere. I was sure a good wind could have picked her up and deposited her at the end of Canyon Street.

"Come in here, Bill." I retreated to the surgery room with the

pair on my heels. I indicated the bar chair that I often used while performing operations. "Have a seat, Mrs. Dremler, while I see what's going on with your kitten."

Doris took the old girl's arm and steadied her as she struggled valiantly to hoist herself to seat level. "Oooh…" She closed her eyes and took a half dozen deep breaths as if enduring some indescribable pain. I was as concerned about her condition as I was about the kitten. I watched from the corner of my eye as Doris helped her settle her bony rear end onto the hard wooden chair.

"Are you all right, Mrs. Dremler?"

"See to the kitten, Doctor. See to the kitten." She had her eyes closed and continued to lean on Doris's arm for support. Bill and I exchanged concerned looks.

I agreed with Doris's assessment of the situation: it certainly looked as if the half-grown cat had been rolled by a car. Her hair coat was filthy; chunks of gravel fell to the tabletop as I ran my hand over her. Her right hind leg hung at a grotesque angle, and the white fur over the thigh was red with blood. I gingerly explored the fracture site; a sharp, shiny white fragment of bone jabbed the end of my finger.

The cat's gums were pale, her eyes half-closed, her pupils fixed. Her breathing was forced and raspy; blood bubbled from the left nostril. I probed her abdomen, feeling for distention.

"Mrs. Dremler." She roused herself from her meditative state and turned to me, her face a mask, her steel-grey eyes impassive. "Your cat has a broken leg…She's in shock and may have a concussion. We should start an intravenous and take some X-rays to see how bad the fracture is. The fact that the bone is sticking through the skin isn't good news; we'll get her on antibiotics right away."

"Do you think she'll be all right?" The woman's face was wrinkled like a dried apple, her brow further furrowed with concern. For the first time, I could detect expression in her eyes.

"It's pretty early to tell."

"I don't know what I'd do without her...she's such a good friend. She spent most of the morning on my lap. She wasn't outside for even a half hour this morning."

"I understand how a pet can become such a big part of your life, Mrs. Dremler. I know how you must feel."

"Audrey's my constant companion, Doctor. You do what you can for her." Tears trickled down the old lady's cheeks. She turned to Bill. "Can you take me home, Mr. Miller?"

Bill nodded and helped Doris get the woman off the chair and out to his taxi. As soon as Doris returned, I started an intravenous, added crystalline penicillin to the drip, and got Audrey settled in the surgery kennel.

The rest of the afternoon disappeared in a flurry, as one patient after the other occupied the examination table. By the time I had finished the appointments of the day, it was after seven o'clock. Doris vented the pressure cooker and waited impatiently as the machine gurgled and hissed. She carefully worked off the metal ring; a cloud of steam gushed forth. Pulling on a scorched oven mitt, she quickly removed the sterilized instruments and rushed off towards the surgery. In a hurry to get to the bowling alley, she was in a complete flap.

"Dora's going to kill me...I promised her I'd be there on time tonight."

"Go. There's nothing so important that it can't wait until tomorrow."

As Doris was reaching for the knob, the door opened. In the entryway was Marsh. Teetering dangerously, he stepped into the office. "Is my cousin in?"

"Dave." Doris stepped around him and out the door. "You have company."

Sporting a quarter-inch growth of scruffy grey beard, the man was obviously at the end of a long episode on the town. I guessed that his unemployment check had been depleted. "A bit down on your luck again, Marsh?"

He looked at his feet for a moment. "Yeah, Dave, I'm broke...Can you help me out with a few bucks?" His words were slurred. I caught the strong smell of beer as he exhaled.

"Not if you want it for booze—just if it's for a taxi."

"It is. It is. I promish."

"You borrowed money to get home last time and promised to pay me back. I'm still waiting."

As the realization sunk home, he slumped against the counter. He turned for the door. "Sorry."

"Sit down for a bit. I'll call you a taxi."

He plunked his body down. His whole demeanour was an apology—his face, his posture. Marsh was definitely on the way down from his bender. I called June Miller to order the taxi.

"Here's five bucks, Marsh. Bill will be right over."

"This is it, Dave." Marshall's head lay against the wall; his eyes were closed. "I'm gonna quit...get back in the camp."

"I hope so, Marsh."

"I'm gonna quit." He let out a long breath. When the taxi arrived, I ushered him out.

"Thanksh, Dave...Be in to pay you next week."

The door slammed. Was I helping or hindering Marsh's situation? I didn't want to think about it; I needed to set my mind to something I could control.

I retreated to the darkroom and grabbed Audrey's X-rays. Her condition had improved considerably throughout the afternoon, and I was willing to bet the farm on her survival. Her leg was a different story, however; I had yet to come across another femur that was so badly shattered. Only an inch at the top of the leg and just over an inch at the bottom were intact. The remainder was in splinters.

I stared at the X-ray, trying to convince myself that I could repair the damage. The trick would be to glue all those fragments together and keep them from compressing and dramatically shortening the leg as it healed.

I thumbed through *Canine Orthopedics* and dug out the index for *Veterinary Clinics of North America*. One technique sounded tailor-made for Audrey's leg. I had never used it before, but it made sense, and I was excited about giving it a try. I enthusiastically dialled Mrs. Dremler's number.

Her phone rang and rang. I was about to hang up when a trembling voice answered. "Hello?"

"Mrs. Dremler, this is Dr. Perrin calling."

"Who?"

"Dr. Perrin from the veterinary hospital…I'm calling about Audrey."

"Oh, Audrey. How is she doing, Doctor?"

"Very well, Mrs. Dremler. She looks like she's going to make it, but her leg will be a real challenge. It's badly shattered." There was a long silence. "Mrs. Dremler? Are you there?"

"I'm here." She sounded strangely distant. "Will it be expensive?"

"I'll try to keep the cost down, but it will probably be around a hundred dollars." There was an uneasy silence, then a loud scraping as the phone was set down. I heard a muffled sound in the background. It sounded like sobbing. "Mrs. Dremler…Mrs. Dremler, are you there?"

It was several minutes before she picked up the phone. "Doctor, I…I want you to put Audrey to sleep."

"To sleep? Are you certain?"

There was another long pause. "I can't afford that kind of money, Doctor…put her out of her pain." I waited for her to say more but, instead, heard the click of the receiver and then the annoying drone of the dial tone.

I retreated to the surgery room to check on the kitten. Her eyes were squinting from the pain, but her throat was vibrating and a faint purr was audible. At the drug cabinet, I drew up a syringe full of euthanasia solution. Man, what a terrible job this could be at times. I couldn't have asked the Lord for more as far as Audrey's recovery was concerned and, yet, here I was, admitting defeat before I even gave it a try.

I rested my hand on her head. There was a steady vibration as she droned on—she was going to purr herself to death. Damn! I closed the kennel door and threw the syringe on the counter. This was more than I was prepared to do right now. I knew the kitten was in pain, but she was young and certainly had her regenerative capacity going for her. It just didn't seem fair to end it this way.

I opened the door to the apartment and hollered up the stairwell. "Come on, mutt!" Lug pounded down the stairs and turned the corner with such vigour that he crashed into the wall. His pink tongue dangling, his ear flopping, his eyes flashing with excitement, he bolted exuberantly past me, tore across the clinic floor, and skidded to a stop. Man, how this dog could buoy my spirits. I envied him his energy.

On the way to the farm, all I could think about was getting to the woodlot to stroll through the trees. It had become my communion—my moment of silence in my own forest chapel. I parked at the roadway and followed Lug down the path through the massive pine trees. What a day this had been. I kept thinking about poor Audrey, about poor Mrs. Dremler. I could just see that lonely, wizened-up old lady sitting at home with tears trickling down her face. How she must be wondering why she had let her dear friend outside, why God would leave her alone with no kitten to fill her lap and her heart.

I plunked on a rock on the knoll, looking south towards the border. The alfalfa swayed back and forth; the pine needles whispered as the wind passed through them. We'd had a good rain in the morning, and everything smelled fresh and clean. I imagined that the grass was already starting to sprout. Lug stuck his nose in my palm and flipped his head until my hand rested between his ears. I stroked him, then held his face next to mine. No one knew better than I how much a pet could worm its way into your heart. The cows were nowhere in sight as I headed through the pines. I knew I was in trouble the moment I came out of the coulee and could see the shed. It was a sight that was becoming all too familiar: cows knee-deep in broken bales, cows stretched out on their sides with great mounds of fresh manure behind them.

Tears threatening, I sat on a stump at the brim of the knoll. "Why, Lord? Why are you tormenting me so?" This was the third time in as many days that I had come to look upon this same sad scene. Hay had been pulled out several bales deep, bringing down the entire upper level. Fifty bundles lay in a higgledy-piggledy fashion, one on top of the other; some were broken, some still intact, most were plastered with manure, all were soaked with the runoff from the rain. I chased the cows in the direction of the lower pasture. They waddled laboriously ahead of me, while the calves bucked and played out the familiar game.

I threw the soggy bales aside and pulled the rails from beneath the debris. So many nails poked through them that they reminded me of a dog's nose pierced with porcupine quills. The cows must be using a wrecking bar! I glanced across the fence towards Verna's; I had the feeling that someone was watching me.

It wasn't until I had the rails replaced that I thought about 211. I hadn't recalled seeing her when I chased the others from the carnage. I had an empty feeling in the pit of my stomach; it would just be my luck that she was off somewhere having trouble calving. After watching her like a hawk for so long, I had been lulled into thinking she was never going to give birth.

The other cattle had bedded down a few yards from where I'd quit chasing them. I was right—211 was nowhere to be seen. With Lug romping ahead of me, I crisscrossed the woodlot. I kept searching for the cow's characteristic red colour in the distance. When I got to the farthest reaches of the pasture, I spotted her a couple of hundred yards away against the fence. I quickened my pace, eager to know but fearing the worst.

Turning in Lug's direction, 211 lowered her head and snorted aggressively. The big mutt loved the attention; I could tell that he was ready to play. "Enough! Get back!" Giving me a downcast look, he slunk away to lie in the grass at the brow of the hill.

Long strings of membranes hung from 211's vagina; her udder was full. She circled to keep Lug in her focus. A tiny blob of brown and white stained the green grass behind her. "Oh man…" What had I done? I looked in horror at her calf. He was little bigger than a poodle. A miniature replica of his mother, he lay curled up with his eyes closed, his head held barely off the ground. The hair was half the length it would be ordinarily, soft, yet almost bristly.

He was alive. What a miracle. I rubbed him aggressively and lifted him up. He opened his eyes to give me a vacant stare, then hung there helplessly, making no effort to bear weight on his legs. The cow mooed pathetically and stepped forward to take a gentle lick at her baby's buttock and miniature testicles.

"I'm sorry, girl. What have I done to you?" I allowed the calf to settle to the ground. It was obvious that the baby wouldn't be able to fend for himself. I had pushed this induction way too far; I bet it was six weeks early. I couldn't recall seeing a calf this small that was anywhere near as vigorous. Maybe there was a hope of nursing him along until he could get around on his own. I allowed the calf to sink to the grass. He struggled briefly as his mother licked him, then lay prone.

By the time I had retrieved the lariat, lassoed and milked 211, and carried the calf to the car, I was beside myself. The last few trips to the farm had been far from restful. Something had to give! Maybe I should just sell the place to Verna and concentrate on being a vet—the practice alone was a full-time job.

Back in town, Lug bounded over me to get out of the car. He was excited about having the calf on board, knew that something out of the ordinary was going on. I opened the hatch. The calf lay curled up with his tiny white head tucked into his flank. The way he lay was encouraging; at least, he was able to sit up on his own. There was a glimmer of hope.

I packed the calf upstairs, lay a blanket on the verandah, and corralled him with a few boxes. After warming 211's milk, I syringed some into his mouth and was delighted to see him swallow; as tiny as this critter was, he appeared to have the will to live. I was ecstatic at how much colostrum I got into the baby. If he kept up like that, I may just redeem my blunder.

The whole time I was feeding the calf, I kept thinking of Audrey. It wasn't fair that she was lying downstairs in pain. If I was going to put her to sleep, I had no right to drag it out. It was time to get it over with.

I reluctantly headed downstairs. Everything was exactly as I had left it. Audrey had hardly moved; the syringe of death still sat on the countertop. I picked it up, flipped it end for end. How I hated being an executioner; moreover, I hated to quit when I knew I could win.

I opened the kennel door and checked the IV. It was still running; the kitten looked fine. The mechanics of what I had to do were simple: just hook the syringe to the catheter, depress the plunger, and stuff Audrey into a black bag. My training said: Don't think about it—it's your job. I was sure a lot of Nazi guards weren't callous when they first started either. I wondered if I could have been trained to turn on a gas valve to kill children and old women because it was my job.

I stroked Audrey's head. Her eyes opened and she extended a front paw to knead my arm gently. I could hear the steady rumble of her purr. I closed my eyes and sighed. The only thing that was stopping me from repairing this cat's leg was money—money an old lady happened not to have. Why didn't I just repair it for nothing? I could consider it a payment on my karmic debt.

Verna Digs In

Gordon was at the farm with his tractor and posthole auger by seven-thirty on Sunday morning. Within the hour, he had drilled a dozen holes, and Brian and John were busily tamping dirt around newly planted posts.

"Put some muscle into it, Brian," I hollered. "Make sure the soil is real tight around the bottom of the post—otherwise they'll be wiggly." John threw another shovelful into the hole and smiled. The boys had been taking turns flailing away at the loose dirt with a long pole, and he loved watching his brother sweat.

By the end of the morning, we had erected a fence to keep the cattle twenty-five feet from the hay shed. As long as I could keep the cows from starting the tractor and running the bucket through the rails, this should put an end to wasted hay.

There was a commotion on the neighbouring property, and I couldn't keep myself from looking. Hollering directions to the driver of her old yellow pickup, Verna met my gaze across the fence, turned, and strode purposefully towards the house. I watched after her as she disappeared around the corner of the garage. She was one tough cookie to deal with. I could understand her frustration with wanting this property, but damn it, it was mine!

"Yah! Get off there!" Len was banging at the sideboards of the truck. He was answered by a loud squeal and a few deep-throated grunts. A huge boar with enormous tusks lunged from the vehicle,

regarding his handler with defiance. Len lowered the sliding gate on the truck box, glaring contemptuously in my direction. Our eyes met briefly before I looked away to pound on another rail.

The last week had seen a flurry of activity on Verna's property. She and her family had dug in posts and pounded together a series of connecting rails. Today, the younger kids were busily nailing on the slabs of rough-cut lumber for the upright fence. Before the day was out, fifty sows would be rooting for treasures in their new surroundings. The neighbourhood was becoming more interesting by the moment.

A backhoe had dug a series of trenches parallel to the fence line. I assumed I'd soon see a barn; by the look of things, Verna was going at this venture in a big way.

The last few days had been a blur. What with the work at the office and the daily torment at the farm, I was beginning to question the wisdom of my new hobby. I was still milking 211 twice a day, and her calf, which I affectionately named Dudley, was making remarkable progress. This morning, he had tackled the lamb's nipple with such vigour that he sucked it right off the Coke bottle. After I teased him with it, he got excited enough that he struggled to his feet. A few more days like this and I'd take him back to his mother. I was praying she still wanted him.

The situation with Audrey, the kitten, remained unresolved. I had sutured the wound over her thigh, but had still not tackled the surgery on her mangled leg. I wanted to make sure she was completely stable before putting her under anesthetic.

I needed a good sleep. Doris was coming in early in the morning for the procedure. When I was certain Audrey's surgery was successful, I'd call Mrs. Dremler and tell her what I had done. If the situation didn't look promising, I'd just put the cat to sleep and the poor woman would be none the wiser.

Maaaa. Maaaaaaaa.

I rolled over and reluctantly opened my eyes. Lug felt me stir and crawled forward to stick his nose on my face. "You bum—the next thing, you'll want under the covers." This was the second morning in a row that I had awakened to find my faithful companion sharing my pillow. "Get down on the floor, you big boob. What do you think you are, a poodle?" He rooted at my hand, absently stretched, and stepped down off the bed.

Maaaaaa, maaaaaaaaaaa.

"It sounds like Dudley's ready for breakfast." I swung my feet to the floor; another day had begun.

I filled a pop bottle with milk and set it in a pot in the sink with hot water running over it. Lug pushed past me as I opened the door to the balcony. He trotted out and sniffed with interest at the small creature that teetered on the other side of a cardboard corral. "Aren't you a sight this morning?" The calf stood bravely on all fours pushing at the rickety enclosure in an attempt to get at me.

"You're starting to think I'm your momma." I rubbed his tiny head as he stretched his neck and nuzzled at my hand. His delicate pink tongue curled out to corral my finger and, before I knew it, he was sucking away. "I think it's time you met your real mom, little boy...sure hope she remembers you."

The milk was still cool, so I wandered downstairs to premed Audrey. The moment I opened the kennel door, she reached out her front paws, gently kneaded my hand and licked at my finger. What a delightful critter. I could see why Mrs. Dremler was so attached to her. Her motor ran constantly, with only the barest of hesitations in her purr as the needle pierced her skin. I dearly wanted this kitten to return to being functional and happy. Scratching under her chin, I closed my eyes and pictured her well. I could see her tearing around Mrs. Dremler's apartment doing somersaults and tackling the curtains. This was going to be a slam-dunk!

I had fed Dudley and was boning up on the new pinning technique in *Vet Clinics of North America* when Doris arrived. I wanted to get on with the show. I had never tried this technique before; to be able to use it without pressure from a worried owner was a treat. This just had to work, for Audrey's sake.

"What will you be needing?" Doris was in her efficient, get-your-ducks-in-a-row mode. What would I do without this woman? She had the pin pack, the small animal surgery kit, and several packages of stainless steel wire assembled on the counter. Her smock pocket brimmed with packs of suture material.

"Looks like you have me outguessed, as usual. You go ahead with Audrey if you like." I studied the X-rays on the view box as Doris tucked our now placid patient into the cat bag. The flow volumes on the anesthetic machine looked perfect, and Audrey's breaths through the mask were deep and regular. The X-rays were something else: the middle portion of the long bone of the cat's right leg had been shattered. I carefully studied the ends near the articulations at the hip and the knee. It was important that they be intact and able to hold a pin without splitting the bone.

"She's ready, Dave." Doris had Audrey out of the bag and her mouth open, set for me to squirt lidocaine down her throat. Cats were like humans. If their windpipe wasn't frozen before a tube was inserted, the larynx would go into spasm and the airway would completely close up.

I stripped the hair from the cat's abdomen, hip, and hind leg before I began my own scrub. Doris tied one end of a string to Audrey's toes and the other end to the surgery light in order to have easy access to the leg. She began washing. "It's hideous, Dave. It's as if the whole bone were mush." Doris frowned as the leg squished beneath her fingertips.

My mind was whirling with anticipation as I clamped on the drapes and proceeded with the skin incision. I located the separation in muscle groups, cut through the fascia, and thrust my finger towards the bone. Dozens of sharp little spicules poked at me. A massive clot peeled out and a pool of dark, stagnant blood soaked the drape margins. I mopped at the mess with a sponge, salvaging all the larger shards of bone. Surveying the mass of splinters, I was beginning to wonder how I could possibly fashion it into a functional leg.

Probing the remnants of the femur, I located the round hollow ends. Both portions of the bone were intact. As near as I could tell, neither portion was cracked.

"Not much left to work with, is there?" Doris was peering intently over my shoulder. "You were talking about doing this one differently from the others. What are you going to do?"

"With the other legs you've seen me repair, I entered with the pin through the broken end, drove it up through the middle of the bone to come out the top of the femur in the hip region. Once the pin was through, I pulled it all the way up, then threaded it into the bottom end to hold them together. But, the whole middle of Audrey's bone is shattered; if I did that this time, the bone would compress and shorten. I'm hoping to cut a pin to length first, then lever the broken ends of the bone onto it."

Doris nodded, but the look on her face suggested the procedure was still shrouded in mystery. I chose a pin that slid snugly into the shaft of the femur, then held it up to the X-ray to guesstimate the length of the medullary cavity of the healthy bone. I slid the pin into the cutter and leaned on the handles. There was a decisive crack as the stainless steel severed. Sliding the short portion of the pin into the upper fragment, I pulled steadily downward on the knee to stretch the muscles as gently as possible. Slowly tipping the lower fragment onto the pin, I straightened it and impaled the bone like a wiener on a skewer.

"So that's what you meant." Doris stared skeptically at the repair. The middle half of the pin still glistened under the surgery light. "How in the world will the bone ever fill in that huge gap?"

"That's where the wire comes into play. We'll place all these fragments around the pin and wire them in place. A callus should eventually form around them and use all the materials to restructure the bone."

By the time I had girded the pin with the bone chips and wired them into place, Doris's look of skepticism had diminished. I closed the muscle fascia and sutured the skin. A wire splint around the limb to keep it from rotating, and Audrey's ordeal was over. I could hardly wait to call Mrs. Dremler! The old girl was going to be so happy to hear that her dear comrade was coming home after all.

I pulled out Audrey's tube and sat with her as her breathing became more rapid. Her ear flicked. Her front legs moved in and out as if she were kneading bread; she growled and opened her eyes. I put her back in the kennel. She sat there on her tummy, her leg stuck out beside her. Her throat was vibrating, her eyes were closed; she had resumed her raspy purr.

Within ten minutes, I had Dudley loaded in the back seat of my car and was heading for the farm. It was hard to believe he was a calf—he still couldn't see over the edge of the seat. I steamed through Lister. The cows would be wondering where I was. Bouncing down my rutted back lane, I peered anxiously towards the hay shed. I had become so used to finding a huge mess that I dreaded each arrival.

The cows were lying in a cluster close to the fence. Ah, everything was still intact, and 211 was near the entrance to the corral so it would be easy to chase her in. I was hoping she was still interested in her baby.

It wasn't till I was almost to the shed that I noticed a big mound of dirt in the middle of my lane. I was squinting in wonder when Verna trotted out from behind her garage. In her hand, she carried an axe.

I stopped the car and hurried to the hole that Verna now occupied. Digging like a badger, she was firing dirt in all directions.

"What's going on?" I asked warily. The woman didn't look rational, and I wasn't at all sure how to approach her.

She continued her shovelling. "You think you can steal my farm, you son of a bitch!"

"You know I bought this farm, Verna. I never stole a thing from you."

"You may have bought the land, Perrin, but you didn't buy the water." Verna stopped digging, leaned on her shovel, and gave me a venomous glare. Her forehead was sweaty; hair dangled in her eyes. "I checked with Leonard Huscroft, and you aren't on Lister water. He told me to cut you off." Her green eyes sparkled as she smiled at me wickedly.

"What do you mean, I'm not on Lister water? Why wouldn't I be?"

"Sikora only had water rights to one block of his farm...He just ran the water across the road to his cattle. Huscroft says he had no right to do that!" Verna stomped with both feet on her shovel, driving the blade into the hard clay soil. Lifting it high over her head, she drove it into the clay a number of times in rapid succession before beginning to shovel with a passion. Dirt hit my legs and settled on my boots.

I was tempted to drag the woman out of the hole and tell her to go home, to mind her own damned business. Somehow, I thought better of it. Instead, I climbed over my corral fence and turned on the tap that fed the water trough. Verna stopped shovelling as the water spurted from the end of the hose. She glared at me. "That's my fricking water, you son of a bitch!"

She shovelled madly, as if possessed by a water-seeking demon. The trough was two-thirds full when I heard the sound of metal striking metal. Verna had found the pipe. She threw down her shovel, picked up the axe, and began flailing away. She beat on the rusted conduit until water sprayed from the bottom of the hole. I looked at my water trough. The tap was no longer running.

"Drink that, you big dink!" She stood there puffing, her chest heaving from the exertion. Leaning on the axe at the edge of the crater she had created, she sighed with satisfaction as it rapidly filled with muddy water. Exulting, she retreated to her own side of the fence, the axe in one hand and the shovel in the other. I stood

148

dumbly staring into the whirling pit. What in the world would I do now?

I got back into the car in a state of total confusion and turned the key in the ignition. Lug pressed his nose into my hand, begging for attention. "Not now, boy. Sit down and let me get going." I'd head over to Huscroft's and sort this mess out right now.

Maaaaaaaaaa!

"Damn, Dudley, I'd forgotten completely about you." My adopted bovine son stretched his head towards me from the back seat and stuck out his tiny tongue in search of my finger. I sighed and shut off the car. The lack of water on my property was certainly not a concern to Dudley.

Number 211 headed reluctantly for the corral; she loved her grain but was still not convinced that she wanted to be a milk cow. I threw the lariat on her, tied her to the corner post, and went back to retrieve Dudley. I carried the fawnlike creature to his mother's side and released him. The cow strained against the rope and turned to look at her offspring. As I maneuvered him towards her head, she mooed softly and gave him a few swipes with her raspy tongue. Dudley closed his eyes, braced himself, and leaned towards her. Hallelujah! My blessing for the day.

I released the lariat from the pole and allowed the cow to reach her baby without hindrance. I couldn't help but smile as the little critter bucked tentatively and scampered around the corral. These days, I had to take my moments of victory how and when they were presented, because they were certainly not unfolding as they should.

I tromped back to the vehicle to let Lug out. Verna was a different cat, but even so, it seemed strange that she'd just whack a hole in the pipe and wander off. After all, her water was now flowing freely in the middle of the road. What had she been thinking? On the way past the hole, I realized something was amiss. The flood was in fact receding; the water level was now an inch below the lip.

I inspected the hole for evidence of the water that had been swirling into it only moments before. It was completely still—not a trace of movement. I froze; I had the strangest feeling that I was being watched. As casually as possible, I turned my head and glanced across the fence. Verna leaned against her little red barn, her arms folded and a smile on her face. She was studying me intently. This whole thing had been nothing more than a show, a few moments of theatrics to test my resolve. She had known from the outset that all she had to do was turn off the tap in her barn. I guess that was just too benign—just not Verna's way.

Witches

I pulled up in front of the tiny building at the far end of the dairy. A manure-caked Ford tractor was parked beside it. I rapped on the door. A wiry young man, still munching his toast and jam, stepped onto the makeshift stairs. His cotton shirt was tattered, his blue jeans worn through at the knees. Pulling on a pair of mucky gumboots, he stepped down onto the freshly gravelled driveway.

Wayne looked worried. Every time I'd seen him this month, he had been trudging around as if the weight of the world were on his shoulders. "One of the cows you told me was pregnant six months ago was showing signs of heat this morning. Just barely moved her to the dry lot...and 61 is limping something awful, hardly had a drop of milk this morning. We're struggling to meet quota—I don't need to lose her."

Wayne amazed me. Barely in his twenties, he was the youngest dairyman in the Creston Valley. To date, he and his wife Eileen, who was several years his junior, had poured every slab of concrete and either erected or supervised the erection of every stick of wood on the place. They had been building for months now, and the makings of a dairy were definitely taking shape. The one-room shack they were living in was still propped on four-by-fours several feet from the ground and skirted with weathered straw bales. Their energy was focused on what was paying the bills—the cows.

Wayne grimaced, clutched at his stomach, and leaned forward. He'd been worried about an ulcer for months now but was too

stubborn to actually go to the doctor. I flinched in sympathy as he slowly straightened. He wasn't one to whimper about his infirmities.

Harvest time was tough on a dairyman to begin with; add the stress of building on top of it, and it was beyond my comprehension how he could possibly cope. He had been heading for the field with his baler when I checked the cows the night before, and I was sure he was up before five this morning for milking.

"How's the haying going?"

"Pretty good," he grunted, composing himself and managing a half-hearted smile. "Pounded out six hundred bales last night."

I followed him through the milk house and out into the free-stall barn. Four cows lounged in the sick pen. Three of them stood up and turned to face us as we entered. The fourth remained recumbent, her feet tucked under her abdomen. She didn't look happy.

"I don't know what's going on with 61." He gave her a boot in the hind end; the cow stuck out her tongue and extended her head in protest, but made no effort to get up. "She won't even touch her foot to the ground." Wayne shook his head in disgust. "She was milking over nine gallons a day this time last week."

We caught the cows one at a time in a head squeeze. There was the faintest trace of a smile on Wayne's face after I pronounced the first two pregnant. It disappeared as I grabbed the tail of the big black cow in the corner and pushed my gloved hand into her rectum.

"This is a cow I bought as a heifer from Douma. She milked good last lactation, and you told me she was pregnant way back in April. She comes due right when I have a big hole in my breedings...I was sure counting on her."

He watched in anticipation as I shoved my arm forward up to the shoulder in search of the cow's uterus. I hated this sort of situation. Although there were lots of reasons for a cow to abort her fetus, farmers never wanted to overlook the possibility that I might have been wrong about the pregnancy in the first place. I was delighted by the presence of huge cotyledons floating in a uterus full of fluid. I maintained a straight face and pushed forward—there were the calf's front feet and there, his head. I withdrew my hand and folded the glove inside out. Wayne stared at me expectantly. I grinned. "She's still pregnant."

Wayne struggled to keep from smiling. "That'll keep my banker off my back for a few more days; I still need to buy some more, but that one would be hard to replace."

He opened the gate and released the critters into the herd. Only 61 remained, struggling to get up. Holding her right front leg out from her body, she touched the inside claw to the ground and hopped towards the exit. Wayne jumped in front of her, then quickly slammed the gate. The cow's entire body quivered as she stood waving her foot in the air.

"She's in a lot of pain," I observed.

I caught just the faintest flash of blonde hair in a sea of black and white. Weaving her way quietly through the herd was Eileen. "Have you found out what's wrong with her?" she asked.

"Not yet," Wayne replied. "But the three cows were pregnant."

"Oh, good." The tiny woman squeezed between two cows that dwarfed her. One looked back casually, the other stood stock-still, chewing her cud lazily. Eileen put her foot on the bottom rail of the pen and rested her hands on her ponderous belly. She was pregnant herself, and by the look of her, rapidly approaching her due date. Raised on a dairy where pregnancy was looked on as a condition rather than an infirmity, she was constantly at her husband's side.

"See if you can get a halter on her while I grab a few things from the car." I climbed over the railing and worked my way through the curious throng of bovine onlookers. By the time I returned with a rope and my farrier tools, 61 was secured to the corner post in the stall. I formed a loop around her neck, tied a bowline so it couldn't tighten, then made a half hitch behind her front legs and in front of her hind legs. Standing behind her, I pulled on the rope. The cow took a half step backwards, leaned against the halter shank, and collapsed with her legs to the side. This trick never ceased to amaze me, but it always worked; for some reason, a cow just couldn't resist those pressure points.

I washed aggressively at the cow's foot with my boot brush, certain that I'd find some sign of injury. With tractors driving back and forth over freshly gravelled roadways and, with all of the construction going on, I expected to find a stone or, at least, an abscess caused by stepping on one.

"See anything?" Wayne was at my elbow, staring intently at the newly cleaned foot. I poked and prodded the soft tissue around and between the claws looking for evidence of tenderness.

"Not yet…looks clean as a whistle." I grabbed my hoof testers and began checking the inside claw. The way the cow had been waving her foot around and winging it out, I anticipated problems with the other one.

"That's a wicked-looking thing." Eileen frowned in disgust. I moved the huge pincers from one area to the other on the bottom of the foot and got no reaction. I shifted to the outside claw; the moment I put pressure on the underside, the cow ripped her foot away from me. Flailing her leg back and forth, she struggled to get up. Wayne jumped to his feet to pull on the rope. She lay still. I probed the sole of the foot with the testers until I had a gut feeling for the most sensitive area, then carefully began peeling away horn. Focusing on a small area of discoloration in the centre of the pad, I rotated the hoof knife in a circular direction, cutting out a core of the sole.

The cow flung her foot madly about, jerking away every time I touched it; I braced myself, grabbed hold, and continued deeper. I pressed harder, made another swipe.

"You sure you're diggin' in the right spot?" Wayne looked skeptical.

As if in answer to his question, a jet of pus shot from the cow's foot. I closed my eyes a split second before I felt the sensation of warmth on my forehead. The watery, foul-smelling liquid dripped from the end of my nose.

"Oh, gross!" Eileen turned away as I wiped my face on the sleeve of my coveralls. Sixty-one lay still for me to pack and bandage her foot. It was as if a tremendous burden had been lifted from her. I was wishing that I could as easily relieve my own.

The previous day had been one that I would certainly not choose to relive. I drove to Leonard Huscroft's the moment I left Verna and her tantrum about my water. He confirmed that I was, in fact, not in the water district, and that Verna, as owner of the deeded water rights, was legally required to sever the connection.

I was left with no alternative other than to dig a well—one more expense that I hadn't budgeted for. My watch said eight-thirty. I had half an hour before the backhoe would be arriving at the farm. Where to dig? We'd start in the draw by my proposed building site; surely, we'd find something there.

I parked my car at the clearing and headed through the trees. The battleground was quiet this morning. Not one of Verna's clan could be seen. I threw out a couple of bales for the cows and carried a big flake to Dudley's mother. I approached the pen apprehensively, hoping that nothing untoward had befallen my little buddy. The cow was lying in the centre of the corral; Dudley was nowhere to be seen. I was about to panic when I caught sight of him. There he lay, curled up between his mother's legs. He had sucked well before I left him yesterday, and his belly still looked nicely rounded. His mother stood up as I approached; Dudley lazily followed suit. Stretching out one little leg after the other, he meandered complacently under 211's belly. I closed my eyes, hoping that she'd sense he was there and not tromp him underfoot. Rooting with his nose as he went, he latched onto the very tip of his mother's teat and began to slurp. I shook my head and smiled at the pair. They were going to do just fine.

The night before, I had phoned everyone I could think of with a backhoe in hopes of getting my well dug quickly; everyone was busy for at least a week. As happened so often, Gordon came to the rescue. A few minutes on the phone with Ed Veale, and we were in business. He'd be out first thing in the morning.

Now that he was due to arrive, I felt like a groom waiting for the much anticipated event—full of hopes for what was possible, full of dread for what could happen. Wells in the Lister area were unpredictable. Not only was volume of water a problem, but also quality. My neighbour, Johnny Ivany, had taken great pains to tell me of the hardships the pioneers of the area had endured in order to get enough water to drink and care for their livestock.

Ed arrived right on time. We started digging in the draw next to where the creek had recently been running—surely, there'd be an underground stream somewhere near. By eleven o'clock, we had filled in one dry hole. While Ed was working on the second, I heard Gordon's familiar voice over the noise of the backhoe. "How's it going, Doctauri?"

The glum look on my face told the story. "Not worth a damn."

Ed was cleaning off the face of the hole; the bucket was reaching as far as his machine was capable. The surface was wet and water oozed from the muddy-looking clay, but nowhere was there evidence of a stream. Gord looked grim. "That'll never give you enough to bother with."

He returned to his truck and came back with a pair of copper wires about three feet in length. Bending them at right angles four inches from the end to form a handle, he followed the bottom of the draw, holding the wires out in front of him. He traversed the area several times; each time the wires crossed at a place ten feet from the fence, about twenty feet from the hole we had just filled in.

"Pappie!" he yelled at Ed. "Try here."

I looked at him skeptically. "I suppose you're going to tell me you're a witch on top of all your other talents."

Gordon took his wires and fired them in the back of his truck. He looked hurt and avoided me as I attempted to pacify him. Ed finished filling in the second hole and moved to the new location. Gord looked apprehensive as the hole grew deeper and deeper. We were at ten feet when Ed hollered and pointed to the material in the bucket. It was a different colour and loaded with gravel. I stared in amazement at the water that spurted from the edge of the face.

"Take a few more scoops over here, Pappie!" Gordon pointed to an area on the right where water squirted four to five inches from the clay wall. He was working hard at concealing a grin. Scoop after scoop of sloppy soil came up laden with gravel. Soon Ed was having difficulty flailing the muck out fast enough to keep up with the inflow of water.

"We better head to town for a culvert." Gord was in complete control of the operation now. "Pappie!" he hollered over the noise of the backhoe. "We'll be back in a bit…Go as deep as you can."

We returned within the hour with a fifteen-foot culvert loaded in the back of Gord's truck. We had stopped at Bill Irvine's shop to get a section burned out for the passage of pipes and wires. Gord had it all figured. He called for a couple of loads of pit run gravel from the builder's supply, and the first load arrived as we lowered the culvert into the hole.

I left the farm shortly after two o'clock with a well full of water and a plumber working diligently at installing a pump. Doris had managed to put off all the appointments until the next day—things were beginning to look up!

"Your cousin Marsh has been in half a dozen times. What are you going to do with him?"

"Did he give you any trouble?"

"No, he never does. But he won't take no for an answer either. Are you going to just keep on doling out money to him? You know you aren't really helping him out."

"But he came in the other day and paid me back for everything he's borrowed. He was so appreciative. When he's sober, you couldn't ask for a nicer guy."

"Well, he sure wasn't sober this morning. I swear he gets a bit worse each time he comes back."

"What do you suggest, Doris? You know I'm a soft touch. I always try to make sure he spends that money on a ride home."

"I don't know…I'm glad he's not my cousin."

"Take five bucks and put it in an envelope in the top drawer— we'll call it his float. If he comes in for money and it's there, then give it to him. If it's already gone, then he's out of luck until he brings it back."

I couldn't dwell on the Marsh situation. It was time to give Mrs. Dremler a call. I was certain her kitten was out of the woods, and I was ready to step forward and take a bow. I grabbed the patient record, dialled her number, and waited as it rang. I could picture the poor old girl struggling up from her seat and making the trek to the phone. It had rung a dozen times, and I was beginning to think she must be out when she finally answered.

"Hello." She sounded tired and frail.

"Mrs. Dremler, it's Dr. Perrin."

"Who?"

"Dr. Perrin, the veterinarian…Audrey's doctor."

"Audrey's here."

The poor girl was confused. I hadn't realized that the woman was that disoriented. "Do you remember when Audrey got hit by a car, Mrs. Dremler? I'm the doctor you brought her to."

"That Audrey's dead," she replied gloomily.

"That's what I'm calling about. Audrey's still alive. I did surgery on her for you, and she's coming along just fine." There was silence as I waited for the message to sink in. "I know how much she meant to you, Mrs. Dremler, so we did the surgery free of charge. She's doing really well; all you'll have to do is keep a close eye on her at home and bring her back so I can check her from time to time."

I waited in anticipation of the joyful response I knew was coming. This may have come as a bit of a shock. It would take her a moment to adjust to the news that her dear friend and companion was still with her. I wish I could have been standing there to see the look of delight on her wizened face.

"Who do you think you are, young man?" Mrs. Dremler's tone was terse. "I gave you instructions on how to handle my cat— what didn't you understand?"

"Pardon me, Mrs. Dremler, I thought you'd be happy to know that Audrey is going to be sound again. I could see how much you cared for her."

"I told you what I wanted, Doctor! What I didn't want was charity from you; you had absolutely no reason to assume otherwise."

My mouth was hanging open. I stood staring at the receiver, not knowing what to say. The woman was correct. I had no right to take the decision of Audrey's surgery upon myself, no right to assume that I knew what was best for Mrs. Dremler.

"What do you expect me to do, young man?"

"I don't understand. Audrey's surgery's done; she's recovering nicely. If you'd like me to keep her until she's completely well before you pick her up, that's fine. We can look after her for you."

Mrs. Dremler's voice was shrill now. Anger dripped from every word. "You're missing the point, you little pup…What am I going to do with two Audreys?"

"Two Audreys…I don't understand."

"I got another kitten the day after you were supposed to put my dear Audrey to sleep. I liked her so much, I named the new one after her."

I was trying to digest the sequence of events. "Oh my. What do you propose we do, Mrs. Dremler? Would you like me to find a home for this Audrey?"

She paused again, and I could almost hear the wheels grinding. "No…she's my cat…I don't want anyone else to have her."

"Please…tell me what you want me to do, Mrs. Dremler."

"You've placed a tremendous burden on me, young man. You realize I'm a pensioner—I have enough trouble feeding myself and one cat."

"Would you like to think about it?"

"No…I'll have my homemaker stop by and pick her up. You have her ready…and write a note for Dr. Marling about what you've done to her. You won't be seeing her again."

There was a click of the receiver and, once more, the sound of the dial tone. I took a deep breath and hung up the phone. What a turn of events. I drifted into the kennel room and opened the cage to check on Audrey. Stretched out on her blanket, the cat was the picture of contentment. The swelling in her leg was almost gone. I squeezed her toes and smiled as she pulled her foot away and licked at my fingers. Drawing herself over to me with her front legs, she rubbed her head back and forth on my hand. Each time, she paused for effect and waited for an ear rub. She looked up at me with her bright green eyes and broke into an appreciative, raucous purr. What more could I ask?

Too Little, Too Late

"Could I please talk to the doctor?"

"He'll be busy for a few minutes longer," said Shirley. "Can I tell him what it's about?"

The young fellow shuffled his feet, pushed his rumpled cowboy hat back on his forehead, and looked wistfully towards where I was working on June Miller's poodle. He scratched at a week's growth of sparse red beard, then looked at the floor. "I'd…I'd rather wait, ma'am."

I finished clipping Mooch's nails and rose from my knees at the end of the exam table. "Was there anything else, June?"

"That should keep him out of trouble for a few months, Dave. If I don't get you to do his glands now and then, he gets to scooting on my carpets. I hate being after him all the time to quit it."

"I can appreciate that. Let's just keep on top of them."

While Shirley finished with Mrs. Miller, I approached the young man, who was wistfully watching the fish in the large aquarium. "Hello, Dan."

He turned with a start. "Hello, Doctor."

"How have you been? It's been a while since I last saw you."

"Bin over a year. Surprised you remember me." He shifted his feet again. His blue eyes made contact with mine for a second, then focused on the toes of his well-worn cowboy boots. "I'm afraid we got trouble again. We don't seem to be havin' very good luck with our bulls."

163

"Oh no, what's up this time?"

"Don't exactly know, but he's all swoll up."

"Swoll up? Whereabouts is he swollen?"

Dan squirmed uncomfortably. "Down below."

"Under his belly or inside his sheath?"

He flushed. "Looks like his dick," he whispered.

"Have you seen him try to mount a cow lately? Can he still get his penis out?"

Dan shook his head slowly from side to side. "He mostly just stands around feelin' sorry for hisself. Had an old cow jumpin' all over 'im this mornin', 'n' he just stood there for a bit, then tried to get away from 'er."

"That doesn't sound good. Are you pretty much done with the breeding season for the year?"

"Not hardly. You remember how we lost that other one right at the start last year…took us quite a piece to buy him a replacement. The cows 're spread out pretty bad with calvin'."

"Well, we better have a look at him then. Do you want me to see if I can make it out yet this morning?"

"I'm sure Dad'd like that. I took 'im down to the barn to see the bull and he was 'bout fit to be tied."

I had a look at the day page. "I can try and change a few appointments around. Could you go home and get him in for me right away?"

"He's at the corral already. Dad 'n' I tried to have a look, but we couldn't see much, other than him bein' swoll up bad."

Shirley managed to shift a few appointments to later in the afternoon; within twenty minutes, I was on my way towards West Creston. It seemed strange to be pointing my vehicle across the flats instead of towards the ferry landing. Once the bypass road made the old relic obsolete, the ferry had been towed up the river to Kootenay Lake. By now, it was probably already being chopped up and hauled away to some scrapyard.

I thought back to the first trip I had made to the Rockwell ranch. It was hard to believe that it was only last year. I had recently moved into Grampa's old house, and I still wasn't comfortable in my surroundings. Two bantering roosters woke me up before six o'clock each morning, and I could never get back to sleep.

On that particular day, I had finished washing up and was smearing some peanut butter on a crust of bread, when my neighbour, Fred MacKay, arrived. Even though he was a distant relative, I didn't know him well at the time. Now, I was the proud owner of his old John Deere and several of his cows.

Fred had inspected me from stem to stern. "Good mornin'. Didn't expect to see a city fella like you up and around already."

"Got to get a good start on the day." I was lying through my teeth. "By the way, are those your roosters?"

"Nah, never had much use for banties. They've been running wild here since last fall when them other folks left."

"Ahhh." Visions of banties roasting over an open fire danced through my head.

"I just got a call from Wilson Rockwell over to the other side of us." Fred had pointed vaguely in a southerly direction. "He wants some help with his bull; his son found 'im down in the bush and they can't get 'im up by themselves. I mentioned that you'd moved in here, and Wilson wondered if you'd come along and have a look at 'im. Marling's in Nelson today—won't be back 'til tomorrow."

I recalled rushing eagerly into the kitchen to grab the black wooden kit that I had bought secondhand from a resident at the veterinary college. Picking my way down the rickety stairs to the root cellar, I pulled a couple of bottles of penicillin from a storage case, dropped them into the box, and scurried to the back door where Fred was waiting.

"Hadn't you better put on some shoes?"

"Wouldn't hurt." I felt more than a little foolish as Fred stared in disdain at my bare feet.

A few minutes later, I was ready to leave, equipped with both shoes and coveralls. I threw my rubber boots into my Volkswagen sedan and turned to Fred. "Do you want to ride with me?"

"How 'bout we take my truck?" Fred looked dubious about crawling into my vehicle.

"Fine with me."

It was just as well that Fred drove because, within a few minutes of leaving the house, I was confused. We were the last properties on our road and, in order to get to Fred's neighbour to the south and west, we had to drive northeast several miles to get off the hill, turn east to the ferry landing, and then south again across the flats. When we were at the end of that road, Fred turned west, drove by a few houses and onto a narrow lane through the bush that again ascended to the West Creston bench.

"This here Rockwell's an American fella. Came up from Colorado a couple of years ago. Rumour is he was a senator and came up here so his son Danny could stay out of Vietnam."

"What kind of cattle has he got, Fred?"

" 'Bout what he's picked up here and there at auction sales. He's bought some lately that I haven't ever seen."

We climbed steadily up the drive until the road levelled off. Coming around a corner, Fred stopped in front of a galvanized metal gate.

"I'll get it." I hopped out, unhooked a chain from a nail on the post, and swung it forward. After Fred had driven through, I swung it closed. The road led into an opening that had been cleared only recently. Most of the area was covered with stumps and boulders, but a few acres around the house and barns had the furry green appearance of newly seeded pasture.

We stopped in front of a white, two-storey stuccoed home that was perched over a carport. A hefty German shepherd–cross announced our arrival. Woofing and muttering, she loped towards us, followed closely by a larger-than-life pig that lumbered up to the truck and peered in Fred's window. She grunted softly, chewed playfully with the door handle, then rubbed her way along the side of the box.

"Arnold! Arnold! Go lay down! There's a good girl."

"That's Wilson." Fred stepped out to meet the slight, sandy-haired man who had materialized from the basement door.

"And that's one hell of a pig!"

"She's a sweetie, really," Wilson responded with a smile, "the best watch pig you'd ever want to have. But, she sure is hard on Enid's garden. She's rooting constantly, and anything she hasn't dug out she's laid on."

"Where does she sleep?" I was in awe of the massive animal.

"She's totally taken over that part of the garage." Wilson pointed in the direction that I'd seen her disappear. "Spends a good part of her day gathering stuff from all over the ranch to build up her bed. If we ever need a piece of twine or an extension cord, that's where we'll find it—tucked away in Arnold's bed.

"Damned shame about the bull," he went on. "Don't know what could've happened. We hadn't seen him for the last few days and, when Dan went to check on him last night, there he was mired down in the water hole. We tried to get him on his feet, but he didn't seem to want to work at it...just looked like he'd given up completely. Enid gave Bob Rogers a call, and he helped us drag him out. Good man, that one—really knows how to handle critters. I'm sure we didn't hurt him much when we dragged him out. He slid on out pretty easy."

"What breed of bull is he, Wilson?" I slipped my shoes off and pulled on my gumboots.

"He's a Charolais. Just bought ourselves a good bull to breed up our Hereford cows, and here he's out of commission before the breeding season even gets started. Good Charolais bulls are hard to come by."

"Well, let's have a look at him." I picked up my black box. "Maybe you'd better grab a rope if you have one handy, Wilson; we may need it before we're done."

"I'll bring mine," Fred interjected. From behind the seat in his pickup, he drew out a neatly coiled lariat.

Following Wilson's lead, we climbed up a set of stone stairs by the side of the house, through a "well-rooted" garden, and over a rail fence. Wilson set out on a cow trail that angled across newly seeded pasture and disappeared in the bush above it. The trail meandered along what must have been an old logging road. Pine and poplar seedlings struggled to obliterate the path and, in some places, spring runoff water had gouged deep ditches.

"We're coming up to the first dam." Wilson paused to catch his breath. "We get the water for our house from this one and have another one above that we use for sprinkling."

The sound of water tumbling in the distance and the rich, aromatic smell of moss, cedar, and decaying vegetation were welcome reminders of my mountain heritage. God, how I had missed it all! The sights, the sounds, the smells of the forest—an addict's fix.

"Only a couple hundred yards more," said Wilson.

As the path wound its way into larger timber along the edge of the creek, cedar trees became abundant; grass and small evergreen seedlings competed more vigorously.

"Dan's with him just up ahead," motioned Wilson, as we came around the next corner.

"He's eatin' some feed, Dad!" the young man hollered as soon as we came into sight. Not taking his eyes off his father's face, the slender, unshaven redhead picked up a handful of hay and stuck it in front of the bull's face.

The bull was much smaller than I had expected. The ton of muscle and bone that I had pictured in my mind shrank to the nine hundred pounds of dejected and muddy flesh that lay in the middle of the roadway. His ears drooped and his right eye was swollen totally shut. His coat, covered with a film of mud, cracked in sections as if composed of scales. Flies crawled over his back and around his eyes. One of the insects landed on the surface of his partially open left eye and wandered around the centre of it. The bull didn't flinch.

"He certainly looks about done in," I remarked quietly.

I removed a penlight from my kit box and shone it in first one eye, then the other; his pupillary responses were normal. "He bashed his right eye in the struggle but, as far as I can see, there's no evidence of permanent damage…See if you can hold him up a bit, would you, Dan?"

I pushed the animal into a more upright position. Dan shifted his battered cowboy hat to the back of his head, then obediently thrust his shoulder against the bull's chest. I flipped out my stethoscope and jammed the head into the muddy crevice between the bull's front leg and his chest.

"You're gettin' yer thing all dirty," the young man pointed out. He watched my face attentively. "He soundin' all right?"

"His heart's slow but strong, and I can't pick up any abnormal lung sounds." Wiping my muddy hands on my coveralls, I fished a thermometer from my kit and lifted the bull's cold, manure-plastered tail to insert it.

"When you tried getting him up, Wilson, did he put any weight on either end, or did he just lie there?"

"He pretty much let us do all the work."

I grabbed the bull's front leg and levered him onto his side. "Give me a hand here. Just hold his head down while I check out his legs."

"Don't think you need much help," quipped Fred.

Palpating and flexing, I began a systematic examination, moving from foot to fetlock, to elbow, to shoulder.

"No problem here."

Checking the hind leg, I moved methodically upward from his foot to his stifle. Prodding, lifting, and rotating back and forth caused no discomfort, no reaction whatsoever; all the joints moved freely with no signs of a problem.

"Okay guys, let's flip him over on his other side." We held the front and hind legs together and easily rolled him over. Starting my examination on the back leg, I picked up the foot.

CLUNK!

The noise was unmistakable. I lifted the leg at right angles to the body to find that it bent abnormally above the stifle. There it was again—that same clunk and the grinding that followed—the sound that results when the ends of two bones grate against each other, then suddenly slip past.

"I'm afraid it's broken, Wilson…high in the upper part of the leg. I suspect it's mid-shaft in the femur."

Wilson received the news with a look of resignation.

"Just stick your hand here while I rotate it. There, feel that?"

"Umph, damn. Guess that means doing away with him, does it?" Wilson sighed.

"I'm afraid so. With an animal his size, repair would be both difficult and costly."

We left the bull lying in his dejected state and completed the return walk in silence. It seemed that even the birds had quit singing. The creek was mumbling rather than babbling, and the view from our perch on the mountain seemed brash and gaudy.

My first bovine case had gone the way of many that were to follow. I correctly diagnosed the problem. I prescribed the right treatment, taking into account the quality and size of the animal. I informed the owner of the condition and advised him as to the best means of handling the patient. Everything had been done by the book. I knew the forces of nature were at work in ways I couldn't control. Why had this case left me feeling so inadequate?

Now, here I was again, following the road to the Rockwell ranch. It was like reliving a dream from the night before. As I pulled the galvanized gate closed behind me, I found myself wondering how big Arnold had grown since last year. I had never come across a more impressive pet.

I craned my neck as I approached the house, certain that she'd come lumbering into sight at any moment. There was movement at the barn; it was Dan waving. I stepped out of the car, to be greeted by the fat old shepherd dog. Dan was close on her heels.

"Where's Arnold?"

Dan frowned and pushed his battered hat way back on his forehead. "She's in the deep freezer. Mom decided she wanted a garden again, an' Arnold came out second best."

"Sorry to hear that."

"Yeah, she was quite the critter…Made her into sausages, but none of us kin get 'em down."

Across the yard, beside an old wooden chute, Wilson stood looking woefully at his bull. This one was long-legged and much larger than the last. He looked to be some sort of Simmental cross.

"Hope you can do something with this one. We have some fantastic calves on the ground from last year's crop."

"Let's have a look at him." I inserted a thermometer and knelt for a closer look at the problem. The bull's penis was dramatically swollen; a large mass of pink tissue protruded from the prepuce, the fold of skin at the end. The long wavy hairs that dangled from his underbelly were coated with pus. I cautiously dabbed my finger on the material and held it to my nose. It reeked.

Wilson watched the procedure with the same look of resignation that I recalled with his last bull. "Am I going to have to send him down the road, too?"

I checked my thermometer. The temperature was way up—just under forty-one Celsius. I moved to the far end of the chute and threw the bull's massive tail over his back. Grasping it a foot from the base, I indicated for Dan to take over my purchase.

"Hold it like this; keep a slow steady pressure on it."

"What does that do?" he asked, leaning into his task.

"It's called a tail-jack. It keeps him from kicking my head off. For some reason, when you push forward on his tail like this, it keeps him from moving his back legs."

Dan raised his eyebrows. He had learned a new trick.

"Keep a steady pressure." I crouched beside the chute and manipulated the bull's penis. The huge animal leaned against the front of the cradle and shuffled his feet back and forth. Shaking his body from side to side, he bellowed in anger.

"Boy, he sure doesn't like that." Dan was straining to hold on.

"I can see why." As I pushed forcefully back on the bull's prepuce, the very tip of his penis protruded. A cut ran as far back as I could see; underlying flesh bulged like meat through the casing of a European wiener. "Looks like he tried to do some breeding through a barbed-wire fence."

"Oh no," moaned Wilson.

I straightened. "You can let go of his tail for now, Dan."

"So he's history, then?" Wilson face was downcast.

"He's probably finished breeding for the rest of this season, but I think he's salvageable for the long term."

Before redirecting his attention to the bull, Wilson gave me a long, sad look. I had the feeling that, once more, I had fallen in league with a hapless critter to bring hardship on the Rockwell ranch. How great it would be to be presented with a case where I could produce immediate, dramatic results. Why couldn't I tell Wilson something he wanted to hear for a change? I smiled ruefully and hiked to the car for supplies to begin treatment. Some days, even when things were going one hundred percent in my favour, the results didn't satisfy anyone.

Dog Under Pressure

"I don't know how Doris does it, Dave. She looks after the books, helps you in surgery, has all your equipment ready to go..."

Shirley was running around like a chicken with her head cut off. Doris had taken the morning to visit with her daughter, and our fledgling trainee was getting the first taste of flying the office on her own.

The telephone rang; Shirley feigned a look of terror as she ran to pick it up. "Creston Veterinary Clinic, can I help you?...That's okay—ask away...No...No." She laughed out loud and looked at me with a grin that spread from ear to ear. "I've never heard of anything like that! What does he do about it?...Really!" Shirley broke into laughter. "Just a second, I better let you talk to Dr. Perrin."

Shirley's behaviour had certainly piqued my interest. I gave her a quizzical look as she passed me the phone. "Dr. Perrin speaking."

"Dr. Perrin, this is Veronica Hadikin. I've had our dog, Voyou, in to see you for vaccinations."

"Yes, Veronica."

"I know this sounds odd, but can a dog become gay?"

"Become gay?"

Shirley was watching me with a big smile on her face, waiting for my reply.

"Some dogs, especially when they're younger and flowing with

173

testosterone, will mount other male dogs—and even people—when they get excited."

"I've seen that…" Veronica answered hesitantly, "but this is different. Voyou isn't after other males—they're after him. This is more like when you have a female dog in heat. I've had them camping on my doorstep for the last week. I have to go outside with a broom to keep them away from him. The poor dog looks so embarrassed when they jump on him, but now he just stands there."

"Well, that certainly doesn't sound normal. Voyou may well have a problem." Shirley waited intently for me to go on.

"Has he been peeing more than normal?"

"Not that I've noticed but, when he pees now, he squats and he always used to lift his leg."

"Could you get a urine sample for me?"

"I could try. What would that tell you?"

"I'd like to rule out a urinary infection that may just be attracting the attention of other dogs…Could you bring him in for me to have a look?"

"I hope it's nothing serious, Doctor. John and I just got married and things are pretty tight for us financially."

"Would you be able to bring him in this afternoon?"

"I'll talk to John and see what he says…I should be able to get some urine."

"What do you think?" Shirley asked the moment I hung up the phone. "Have you ever heard of such a thing?"

"I haven't…Almost sounds like something hormonal though. Male dogs can pick up on a female in heat from quite a distance. They're obviously hanging around for a reason."

Shirley answered another call as I was leaving for a herd health at the Riehls. Lines of worry had etched her forehead while I slipped into my coveralls and gumboots. I'm sure she'd have been eminently more comfortable coming along with me to work with the cows. I touched her arm to get her attention and whispered, "You'll do just fine." She rolled her eyes, then continued negotiating an appointment time for a dog to be vaccinated and neutered.

It's impossible to stick your arm up the rear ends of twenty or thirty cows without getting some of their contents on you, and this morning was no exception. Although I pulled my boots and coveralls off before leaving the dairy, I could see in the office mirror that I had brought plenty of manure home with me. My shirt collar was decorated with brown flecks. A couple of blobs clung to my cheek.

"What's that stink?" I asked. A wretched odour permeated the clinic. It smelled like a smouldering garbage heap—the stench that hangs around the metal burn barrel in a farmer's back yard.

"You come in here reeking like a dung wagon," Doris chided, "and you're asking us what smells. You better go change your shirt." She was back from the morning visit with her daughter. By the looks of her, they had spent a good part of that time with Norm and Tom at the House of Manell Beauty Salon.

I headed up the stairs. "Don't forget to wash behind your ears," she hollered. There were times I felt Doris was my other mother.

"Man, what reeks?" The smell was worse in my apartment. I wrinkled my nose and surveyed the neighbouring buildings along Canyon Street to see if someone might be tarring a roof.

I whipped off my shirt and headed for the bathroom. Doris was right, as usual. There was manure behind my left ear. I had a quick sponge bath, then flung open the door of the refrigerator. Something was different—my assistants had cleaned the thing. There was nothing but bare racks. They'd even thrown out my mouldy cheese! I turned and surveyed the room. The dishes had been washed and, for the first time in a long time, I could see the bottom of the sink. I spotted a large red throw rug under the kitchen table. I shook my head. Sometimes I was embarrassed about being such a slob. Doris and Shirley must have decided that my pit had gone past the humiliation level and laid the carpet down to make the next cleanup easier.

They were insinuating I was a regular pig. The next thing, they'd be replacing my table with a big trough. I thrashed through the cupboards and plucked out a box of corn flakes. It was empty except for the few crumbles trapped in the wax paper lining. No matter, seeing there was no milk or sugar to be found.

We had vaccinated a cat for Mrs. Walker, and I was putting the final stitch into the forearm of an old black Lab when Veronica Hadikin showed up. She sat chatting and joking animatedly with Shirley as I gave my patient an injection of penicillin. I noticed a lilt to Veronica's English; I guessed the slight accent to be French. I heard her ask about the "ghastly" odour but didn't hear the response because Shirley lowered her voice considerably. They both laughed, but stopped as soon as I appeared.

At Veronica's feet lay a large woolly dog that was spread out full length on the floor. "This is Voyou…and here's your sample." She offered me a mayonnaise jar a quarter-filled with sparkling yellow urine.

"That looks clear enough."

"I thought so, too."

"Have you noticed any changes in his activities lately?"

"He's like this most of the time at home these days." She pointed to the recumbent creature. "This is not like him. Usually, he'd be up here begging to be petted. And his hair—he used to have such a beautiful coat. Look at it now. It's terrible and he leaves clumps all over the house."

I bent down to stroke the dog; his hair was dry and brittle, his coat sparse. Portions of the hair on his flank and tummy were totally missing, leaving a dark, leathery appearance to his skin. Voyou opened an eye and heaved a big sigh.

"I'm not sure whether this has any bearing on his present condition," Veronica began, "but Voyou has never been normal. If there's such a thing as a mentally challenged dog, he's it. My mom's dog, Tara, had seven puppies. Mom sat with her as she delivered the first six—dried them off and made sure that they sucked. Hours after we thought she was finished, we found this blob under the corner of the basket. Mom tore the sac open and breathed into his mouth. He finally came to, but he never was the same as the others. We held him on the tit for weeks before he could find one on his own. It was always obvious he was different. People told us to put him to sleep, but he was the kindest, most loyal fellow—always at your side looking to be petted."

I took the sample to the back and dipped in a urine stick. Except for its being dilute, the urine was normal. "Can you bring him in?"

"Voyou…Come Voyou." Veronica walked past him and slapped her hands on her knees to coax him to follow. The dog lay motionless except for the slightest twitch at the end of his tail.

"Come on now, boy." She grabbed the dog by the collar, half lifting him to his feet. "He hardly lives up to his name," she said. "It means *hooligan* in French." Once up, Voyou plodded resolutely behind her into the exam room.

"There's a boy." I cradled him in my arms and lifted him to the tabletop. His feet slipped on the stainless surface; he sank rapidly to his tummy. I stroked the dog's head, checked his eyes, and raised his eyelid. His conjunctiva was pale. "You're pretty tired, aren't you, you old hooligan?"

"Do you see something?" Veronica stood behind me peering over my arm.

I exposed Voyou's gums. "Do you see how white they are—that's why he has no energy."

"Ahhh." Veronica's big brown eyes were filled with compassion. "Poor Voyou. You are sick, my boy."

I slid my stethoscope down the dog's chest. Whoosh. Whoosh. Whoosh. Each stroke of his heart produced rumbling turbulence as watery blood regurgitated through the valves. I watched the telltale pulsation of blood back into the jugular.

"Voyou is still intact, Veronica?"

"Pardon me? Intact?"

"He's never been neutered?"

"Oh no, he's such a placid creature…We never thought it was necessary."

"How old is he now?"

"Almost seven."

I reached between his legs in search of his testicles. "Over we go, Voyou." I lay the dog on his side and carefully palpated his groin. I traced the one testicle I found to the right side. Pressing deeply into the left inguinal ring, I felt for any lump of tissue that didn't belong.

Veronica was puzzled. "What are you looking for?"

"A testicle."

"A testicle?"

"That's right—there's only one down."

"You think there's a problem with the other one?"

"I'm willing to bet there is."

My hands migrated to the dog's abdomen. He had looked plump and rather pendulous from a distance. Now, I realized that was only an illusion—the dog was devoid of fat. My face flushed. Was this possible? His entire abdomen was occupied by a singular mass! Running my fingers around it, I could follow its knobby contour through Voyou's thin abdominal wall. It was huge. I removed my hands from the dog, stood back, and leaned resignedly against the wall.

"What's wrong?" Veronica's face was flushed.

"Voyou has a very large tumour."

"He has cancer?"

"I'm afraid so."

"Can you operate?" Veronica shot a worried look at the dog that lay prone on the table before her. "Is there any hope?"

"He's weak—very anemic—but I think there's a good chance that the cancer will be localized to just the testicle."

"But what about everything else—his blood, the other dogs?"

"They're all related. Unless I miss my guess, Voyou has an exaggerated case of male-feminizing syndrome. It happens when cells in

179

the testes start producing estrogen instead of testosterone. The loss of hair and the changes in his skin go along with that condition, and lots of estrogen in his system would certainly explain why all the neighbourhood dogs are thinking he's a female in heat."

"And the anemia?"

"That's probably because of the high estrogen content as well, but huge tumours can have strange effects on the body all on their own."

"Oh, Doctor." Tears flooded Veronica's eyes and rolled down her cheeks. "I don't know what to do." Shirley passed her a box of Kleenex. We all stood staring down at poor Voyou.

We were a sombre crew as we sat around in the back room that night. It was amazing how individual cases could have such an effect on morale.

"Do you think they'll do surgery?" Shirley asked.

I shook my head slowly. "It's a hard decision for them, I'm sure. When you've only been married a month, you have a lot of things to be spending money on."

"Speaking of money, Dave…" Doris gave me the *Mother Superior* look that never failed to get my attention. "You've been promising for months to order an autoclave. That poor old pressure cooker of your mom's is on its last legs."

I cringed. The last thing I needed was another bill from Haver Lockhart. We had picked the machine out of the catalogue months ago, but farms and cows and wells always seemed to divert my attention from purchasing it.

"Okay, call it in—you already have all the information."

Doris winked at Shirley, who blushed clear to her scalp. I peered at Doris again; there was something about the look in her eye. "What am I missing here? You already ordered it, didn't you?"

She gave me a wicked little smile, slipped into her jacket, and left without a word.

It wasn't until a week later that we heard from Veronica again. Voyou's situation had changed little—if anything, he was weaker.

Veronica's Uncle Abel had stopped for a visit, and one look at Voyou was all it took. They were bringing him right in. Abel would pay for the surgery.

"He's just so tired all the time." Veronica held Voyou's head in her hands. "He hardly moves around now except to pee."

"I can believe it." I rolled back the dog's lip to expose parchment-coloured tissue. "He's going to need a transfusion before we consider surgery."

"A transfusion?" Veronica spoke to her uncle in French. He nodded and replied with a torrent of language that left my French 201 in the dust.

"My uncle wants to know how you do matching in dogs. Where will you get the blood?"

"Lug! Come, Lug!" My faithful comrade trotted out from the back room and made the rounds from one extended hand to the other. "There are a lot of canine blood types, and we can usually transfuse even from unmatched dogs the first time around. We just happen to be lucky that Lug is a universal donor."

Abel squatted on the floor, took Lug's head in his hands, and chattered away to him in his native tongue. "Eh bien, mon petit chien," he cooed.

"My little dog" glanced up at me as if with a smile. How he loved being the centre of attention.

The tables turned all too quickly. Lug frowned as the clippers removed a blob of hair from his front leg. From the moment I picked him up and plunked him on the table, he knew what was coming. Sometimes he was just too smart for his own britches. I placed the tourniquets above his elbow, wiped him down with alcohol, and drove the huge needle into his forearm. Lug licked his lips and appealed to Doris. How he hated this part of the exercise. "It's okay, boy," she reassured him.

Blood snaked its way through the long plastic tubing into the bag at my feet. Doris squatted and massaged the receptacle to mix the blood with the anticoagulant. Both of Lug's ears were pressed close to his head; right then it was hard to pick out the floppy one.

"What a good boy you are, Lug," Doris chimed. "You get to be the hero again."

Within twenty minutes, the bag had assumed the shape of an overfilled water balloon. Lug was getting antsy. Doris remained by his side, giving him encouragement. "Don't let Dad forget about the Dairy Queen," she chirped. Lug's ears perked up—he knew exactly what she was saying.

"There we go, Bud." I pulled out the needle, drained the blood as far down as possible and tied off the plastic tubing. Doris kept pressure on the gauze over his puncture for a couple of minutes. When I returned him to the floor, he gave my hand a lick of forgiveness. "Are you ready?" His tail wagged furiously; he whined and jumped up on me. "Just give me a second, boy."

Voyou was stretched out in the kennel with a blanket over him. He lay motionless with an IV dripping away. If not for the occasional movement of his chest, the dog may well have been dead.

"Voyou. Voyou." His eye opened. Nothing else moved. I hung the blood bag on the same hook as the intravenous fluid and connected the drip. It felt good to watch Lug's blood disappear one drop at a time into the poor creature. I ran my hand over his side—he felt so cold.

Lug dug eagerly at my hand with his nose. "Okay. Okay. Let's go." He yelped with joy and bounded to the door.

"Be back in a bit, Doris. Dairy Queen time."

"Okay, boys. Have fun."

As I drove up the block, Lug became increasingly animated, anticipating the familiar red and white sign. The moment I turned into the parking lot, he howled in excitement and spun around twice on the seat. I parked in the lot and left him staring out the window.

"One plain burger with mayo…no mustard."

"Is that all you want on it?" The girl looked at me skeptically. "Would you like fries?"

"No."

"Will that be all, sir?"

"No. I'd like two regular soft ice creams."

"Two?"

"Yes, two."

Lug was still craning his neck when I got back to the car. His nose was pressed against the glass, his tail wagging madly. I opened the door and passed him the hamburger; it disappeared within seconds. He looked longingly at the ice cream cone. I extended one and he licked enthusiastically. He settled down after we finished our dessert. The only evidence of his indulgence was a dab of mayonnaise on the tip of his nose.

By the end of the afternoon, the addition of German shepherd blood had done wonders for Voyou. His ears perked up and he missed no opportunity to garner attention from any passerby. His surgery was slated for the morning; I was praying it would go smoothly. That tumour was massive; I wondered what it would be like for a body to have twenty to thirty percent of its cells suddenly removed.

Would his bone marrow respond and start cranking out red cells? Would the tumour be completely encapsulated within that one mass? Would his heart recover from months of abuse and deprivation? We were about to find out.

Lug sat pensively watching as I cooked supper that evening. Although I kept him on a dog food diet, he never quit hoping that I was cooking for him. I fried the hamburger, chopped in an onion and a pepper, and tossed in a can of mushrooms that I had hastily picked up from the Daylight Grocery.

I hadn't spent a lot of time in my kitchen lately, but I was annoyed at Doris and Shirley. Putting that red carpet under my table as a slop-guard was an insult. It wasn't as if I ate at the table anyway. I shook some salt, pepper, and a pinch of garlic powder into my concoction, then threw a lid on the pan. The insult had to go!

Dragging the table to the side, I pulled up the new carpet and took a step towards the exit. My hand was almost on the doorknob when I stopped short and looked back towards the table. There in the centre of the floor was a huge black charred circle. I ran my hand over the blemish. The existing carpet was burned through clear to the floorboards.

I contemplated this discovery for a few moments. Was there a connection between this and Doris's insistence last week on a new autoclave? I hadn't seen the pressure cooker for some time. She usually left the thing on my stove or in the back room of the clinic on the hot plate. I looked everywhere I could think of, upstairs and down. There wasn't a trace of my mother's old pot. I was on my way back upstairs when I noticed the pressure cooker box in a corner—way up under the workbench. Someone had taken great pains to hide it. I got down on my hands and knees to dig it out. Sure enough, there it was.

I lifted it out and set it on the counter. With it came a faint acrid odour. The scorched remains of the pressure cooker teetered back and forth on a bottom that was warped to the shape of an egg. So that was the vile smell that had lingered for days! I shook my head knowingly and chuckled. Shirley really must have had a whale of a day by herself.

Voyou was tipped upside down on the surgery cradle. The hair on his underbelly was sparse, the skin darkened and oily.

"Clip him way up on the chest, Doris. I'll have to open him up from stem to stern."

"Will he get a normal coat back when we get rid of the tumour? His skin feels like leather."

"I sure hope things get back to normal. Most male-feminizing cases respond to castration, but Voyou's situation is one in a million. It's not too often you have to be a weightlifter in order to remove a testicle."

"You think it's that large?"

"The way this one feels, it's big enough to do a rhino proud."

"Amazing it could grow so big." Doris poured surgical scrub down the middle of the abdomen and worked it into a lather. "Are you ready to shave him?"

I was still in the teaching mode. "The incidence of testicular cancer is way higher when it's inside the abdomen or the inguinal canal. That's why I'm always harping at people not to leave the testicles when they're retained."

"Why do you think that would be?"

"Probably the higher temperature. The testicle needs to be cooler than the rest of the body—even sperm production drops terribly when it isn't."

"So, if you just left Voyou, it would keep growing until it took up the whole body cavity?"

"It's close to doing that now. Feeling it, I can't see how there's much room for anything else in that tummy."

I shaved a strip down the centre of Voyou's abdomen. The poor dog looked like a plucked turkey ready for the oven by the time we were done. A catheter protruded from the end of his penis to a collecting pouch; cloth girded the surgical site, leaving a narrow rectangle of exposed skin toward the centre and right side of his body. Doris carefully unwrapped the disposable paper drape that she had prepared in her brand-new autoclave especially for this procedure. I carved a fair-sized hole in the material, then clamped it to Voyou's skin.

Doris's eyes widened as I sliced the skin from the end of the rib cage to a point just in front of the pubis. "My Lord, you weren't kidding about splitting him open."

"Unless I'm mistaken, it'll be a tight fit getting the tumour out even with this opening."

I made a tiny stab at the umbilicus and extended the incision in both directions with the scissors. The muscle layers separated to expose the huge, irregular mass within.

"Oh, my God!" Doris's eyes bugged behind her horn-rimmed glasses. "It does take up his whole tummy."

I slipped my hand inside Voyou's abdomen and worked my way entirely around the outside of the tumour. "What an ugly-looking thing." Pinkish-tan in colour, the mass was covered with dark brown and black blotches. Huge lobules of tissue struggled to expand in all directions. I located a peduncle at the bottom and traced a pulsating vessel to the base of the kidney. "Now you know what an estrogen factory looks like."

Doris craned her neck to get a closer look as I slowly elevated the bulky structure through the incision. When it wouldn't squeak through, I extended my cut further towards the rib cage. Pushing the mass in that direction as much as possible, I spread the muscles apart and eased the far end through.

"Oh, my God," Doris repeated. The huge structure emerged from Voyou's abdomen, surfacing like a bulky marine creature from the depths of the ocean. I balanced it on the draped surface and felt for the artery and vein that supplied it.

"You better put on some gloves, Doris. I'll need your help while I tie off these vessels." As she prepared herself, I explored the remains of the abdomen. Both kidneys looked normal; the liver was smooth, its edges sharp. The bowel looked normal. There was no evidence that the cancer had spread.

Doris helped balance the mass as I ligated the vessels and severed the connection to Voyou's body. That amorphous blob of tissue weighed in at twelve pounds and represented close to a fourth of the dog's body weight. It was the largest testicle I would see in twenty-five years of practice.

With the removal of the tumour, Voyou's coat regenerated, and his red cell production returned to normal. His heart had been permanently damaged, which slowed him down in his later years. But, much to the delight of the Hadikins and Uncle Abel, the hooligan's career as a doggie poster boy came to an abrupt end.

The following morning, I placed the corpse of the pressure cooker on the counter before Doris and Shirley arrived for work. Doris

186

snickered when she saw the remains, but Shirley was upset. "Oh Dave, I'm so sorry…It was that day you left me alone in the office. Things got out of hand…"

"I'm all ears," I said, enjoying every minute.

"Well…I was preparing the instruments on the hot plate and I blew the breaker. So I had to use your stove upstairs. Then Herb Hurford came in for medication and Joan Watt brought in her sick cat…Her daughter was crying and…"

"Yes…and then?"

"…And I forgot about the pressure cooker. By the time I could smell it, it was too late. I panicked because smoke was pouring from the vent…It was so hot I couldn't even touch the handles. I grabbed a towel and moved it onto the floor…and, of course, it scorched the carpet and then I didn't know what to do."

"So you consulted Doris," I said sternly.

"Well, of course she consulted me," snipped Doris. "And what do you expect with the primitive state of this…"

"All right, all right—I agree with you. We'll just forget it," I said.

Shirley was completely remorseful. "I wouldn't blame you if you fired me."

"Oh come on, let's look at the bright side. We've taken the plunge into new technology, and you can see that Doris is as happy as a pig in you-know-what with her spiffy autoclave."

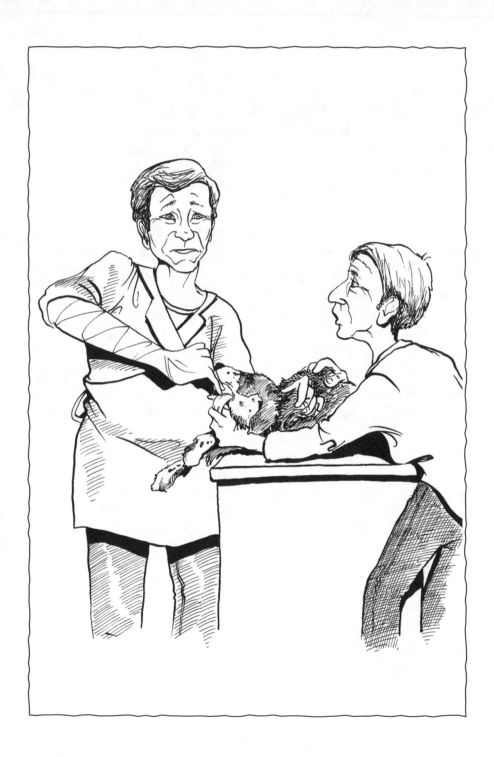

Poison

It was quarter past two in the morning. I don't know how long I managed to ignore the ringing before I finally succumbed and fumbled for the phone.

"Dr. Perrin, this is Bob Milne. Terribly sorry to bother you at this time of night, but my dog, Missy, has had a stroke or something. She was out on the lawn with the children and started acting strangely. The girls are having a sleepout tonight—she was with them."

"Could she have gotten into something?"

"Yeah, she could have, but she sticks pretty close to home."

"Have you noticed anything unusual about her behaviour over the past few weeks?" I was fighting to clear the fog that still drifted through my mind.

"Now that you mention it, a half hour ago she nipped at one of the girls. That's when we brought her into the house—it's not like her to do something like that. She's never bitten anyone before."

"Is she getting worse?"

"Worse by the second. She's under our bed—there's drool and watery poop all over. She's shaking something awful, even looks like she's having trouble breathing."

"When did you first notice problems with her breathing?"

"About twenty minutes ago. What should I do?"

"It sounds like you better get her down here right now. How far away are you?"

"Five minutes. I live right next to the brewery grounds."

"Great," I moaned, hanging up the phone. The brewery poisoner was at it again!

Over the past few months, there had been a rash of poisonings in the area adjacent to the brewery. Dozens of dogs and cats had been poisoned with a variety of toxins. It seemed as if some demented fool was trying every concoction from ant killers to herbicides to reduce the dog and cat population in his neighbourhood.

Please don't let it be a repeat performance of the last episode, I prayed. The thought of five dogs on intravenous fluids at the same time, with the terrible rank smell of vomitus and diarrhea hanging heavily in the air, was more than I could contemplate at this hour of the morning.

Bob arrived in front of the clinic in the time it took me to get dressed and go downstairs. The light blue dress shirt that he wore had been hastily tucked into a pair of grey sweats. His sneakers had been pulled over bare feet and had yet to be tied.

"I'm afraid she's gone." His tone was deadpan, his round face drawn. "I'm never going to have another dog—this is it!"

In the back of his station wagon, in a pool of saliva and diarrhea, lay the body of a small black and white Border collie.

"She was only just breathing when I loaded her…didn't expect her to be alive when I got here."

He had no sooner spoken than the dog made a feeble attempt to draw air. It was just the faintest of agonal movements, but she had tried. Scooping her up, I rushed into the clinic. Her body was cold, her coat slimy with excrement and drool.

Virtually a dead dog, her gums and tongue were a sickly blue-grey, her eyes glazed in a fixed, vacant stare. I touched my finger to the surface of her cornea; there was no reaction. I pressed the gums to check her capillary refill time, and a blanched ring remained where my finger had been.

"What do you think? Is there any hope?"

"From the history and the way she looks right now, I think she's been poisoned with an organophosphate insecticide. She's in respiratory failure, probably drowning in her own secretions." I grabbed an endotracheal tube, opened Missy's mouth, and pulled out her tongue.

"Hold this!" I instructed Bob, who gingerly grasped the tip of her tongue while I smeared away long, stringy ropes of mucous. I slipped the tube through her epiglottis and down the trachea. Missy made no attempt to breathe. I pushed on her chest to get the first few puffs of air into her. Grabbing a syringe, I inflated the cuff around the outside of the endotracheal tube and blew into it.

A bubbling sound rattled from the tube as air gurgled through the accumulated secretions in the dog's airway. Hanging her head over the edge of the table, I pounded her rib cage. Gobs of slimy mucous streamed onto the floor.

I turned on the valve to send oxygen flowing into the large rubber bag that acts as a reservoir for the anesthetic machine. Closing the pop-off valve that vents the system, I squeezed the bag and expanded Missy's chest. I felt frantically for a heartbeat; there wasn't the slightest vibration.

"Bob, take over here! Expand her lungs for four or five seconds, let it collapse, then start over again."

I placed a hand on either side of the dog's rib cage and began compressing vigorously. Less than a minute later, I stopped to check. There it was! Faint but present—the vibration of her chest wall as her heart contracted. A couple of minutes of resuscitation did wonders—the dog's heart went from an occasional erratic burst to strong rapid contractions. Her gums and tongue took on a pinkish hue.

While Bob continued the rhythmic expansion of his dog's chest, I adjusted the flow of gas to provide for small amounts of nitrous oxide and halothane. Without them, it would be impossible to control both her voluntary movements and the muscle spasms caused by the poison. Now that Missy was being ventilated, I concentrated on starting an intravenous. Quickly assembling a bag and drip, I shaved her forearm. I rubbed it down with alcohol, held the cephalic vein off with a tourniquet, and drove a catheter into it. The flow of blood was brisk, the colour a bright red.

"Look at that. We're making fantastic headway with our oxygen uptake."

"That's a good sign, isn't it?" Bob's tone was hopeful, almost buoyant.

"Yeah. Oxygen was top on our list of priorities. She was as blue as any dog I've ever seen."

I started the fluids running, then grabbed a stethoscope. Her heart rate was rapid, but strong. I was surprised that the lung field was clear; I had been expecting to hear fluid bubbling in the deepest airway.

Bob took a deep breath, sighed, and tipped his head back. "Man, are the kids going to be upset if Missy doesn't make it."

I nodded. "I bet they will be. I wish the s.o.b. that's doing his dirty work over there would take a dose of this himself."

With the emergency treatment underway, I quickly retreated to the books. I had little trouble remembering dosages of drugs that I used on a daily basis but, for this, I needed help. The reference claimed that, in order to counteract the effects of the organophosphates and reduce the production of secretions, I'd need to use atropine at levels of ten times normal. Bicarbonate would reduce the tremendous carbon dioxide debt that Missy undoubtedly accumulated while unable to breathe.

Protopam, a direct antagonist to the organophosphates, was one of those obscure drugs I cursed when taking inventory—it could sit for years without being needed, then suddenly become a lifesaver. I hoped it would do the trick tonight. Book in hand, I rushed back to the dog and administered the drugs through the intravenous portal.

"Hold it for a bit, Bob." I opened the stop valve on the anesthetic machine. "Let's see if she'll breathe on her own." A minute passed with no effort on Missy's part. "You'd better start again…we'll try her later."

Rummaging through the cupboards, I dragged out the half-inch tube I used to pump the stomachs of poisoned dogs. I lubricated the bevelled end, passed it down the esophagus, and ran a litre of water into Missy's stomach. By maintaining steady pressure on her abdomen, I was able to force the water to flow back through the tube. An assortment of goodies from grass to all the makings of chicken soup dribbled into a five-gallon bucket.

"She certainly never got any of this stuff from home." Bob shook his head in disgust as gobs of chicken fat, meat, and noodles plopped into the bucket. "I don't know who put that stuff out for her, but they must have left it close to our place—I didn't think she lost sight of the kids all night." Bob stared at the floaties in the bucket as if he were a soothsaying gypsy reading tea leaves. "Where would that idiot be able to get hold of poison anyway?"

"Probably from almost any gardening supply store. An orchardist would get it from the packing shed. Organophosphates are commonly used as an insecticide." As I manipulated the tube and ran more water into her stomach, there was the slightest twitching of the abdominal muscles. "Quit bagging for a bit. I think she wants to try it on her own."

I unscrewed the pop-off valve of the anesthetic machine so that the bag wouldn't be distended by excess air. This time, the wait was rewarded by a definite tightening and movement of the abdomen. A feeble first breath was followed by others. Each attempt seemed to move more and more air. Finally, the bag filled and emptied in a rhythmic fashion that was for all intents normal.

"By God, I didn't think I was ever going to see her take another breath." Bob smiled and ran his fingers through his short black hair.

Ecstatic with Missy's progress, I resumed the chore of evacuating the contents of her stomach—running a couple of litres of water in, manipulating a slurry of water, chicken, and noodles out.

Bored with the procedure at hand, Bob's attention fell to the open volume of *Veterinary Clinics of North America*. A look of genuine astonishment swept his face as he read, first to himself, then aloud: "Signs of organophosphate toxicity are excessive salivation, watery diarrhea, constriction of the bronchi with resulting dyspnea, miosis, muscle fasciculations, ataxia, paralysis, and death from respiratory paralysis...I'm not sure what all those words mean, but she sure had what I recognize." I smiled. It was nice to be right.

A couple more flushes were sufficient to complete the cleansing of Missy's stomach; the final water came back almost as clear as it went in. Certain that I had accomplished what I was going to with the lavage, I chased down a mixture of charcoal, Kaopectate, and water and withdrew the tube.

With the busy work of the evening over, all we could do now was wait. Missy was breathing deeply and rhythmically. Her colour was good; for the most part, she looked no different from any other anesthetized dog.

"You may as well go home to bed, Bob. There's not much you can do here anymore. I'll keep her under anesthetic for a while longer to control her muscle tremors and prevent her from going back into convulsions."

"How long will you keep her asleep? Will she be normal when she wakes up?"

"We won't know if there's been brain damage until she recovers from the anesthetic." I didn't want to sound too confident but, deep down, I was sure she was out of danger. "If her brain was starved of oxygen for too long, some damage certainly could have occurred. Right at the moment, all we can do is wait and see."

Bob yawned. "Well, maybe I will head home for some sleep then."

"I'll get in touch if anything goes wrong." I stretched and poked casually at Missy's rosy gums. What a tremendous difference a few hours could make! I was elated to yank the dog back from the jaws of death, but found my thoughts turning more and more to the sleep that was slipping away from me. My eyes were burning; I struggled to suppress a yawn.

Doris and I had a full day booked for tomorrow, and sleep between then and now was looking doubtful. Forcing myself to move, I began cleaning up. By the time an hour had passed, the floor was mopped, the table cleaned, and the garbage buckets emptied. It was time to see if Missy could manage on her own.

I turned off the halothane and nitrous oxide to leave her on straight oxygen. Five minutes passed with slow, regular breathing; I disconnected her from the anesthetic machine and returned her to room air. Missy's recovery was typical of any other dog that had been anesthetized for two and a half hours. Within a few minutes, she began to breathe more rapidly, shivered a few times, then made a feeble effort to swallow. Gradually, she swallowed more aggressively, and I removed the tube that had been her lifeline.

After an initial attempt to gag, Missy fell into a pattern of deep breathing punctuated with a high-pitched whine on expiration. Within a half-hour, she was able to maintain herself on her sternum and was making uncoordinated efforts to stand. Her breathing appeared normal.

I grabbed the cushions from the waiting room and threw them in front of the surgery kennel. I stretched out, confident that if Missy seizured again, I would hear her and be able to respond quickly.

"What on earth are you doing sleeping there?" Doris stood next to the surgery table looking down on me. I sat up and gazed around, slowly coming to grips with my surroundings.

"Rough night." I stiffly picked myself up from the floor. "Another poisoning."

Missy was stretched out on her side, still enjoying a slumber that I envied. I opened the kennel door. My patient bounded to her feet and stood wagging for attention.

The resilient collie survived the ordeal with no damage that either the owner or I could detect. She had become one of scores of dogs to be poisoned over the years within a few-block radius. Never could I predict how many cases I would see in an episode, and never could I presume the same poison had been used. Some were organophosphate poisonings, as with Missy, but far more of them were strychnine, metaldehyde, or paraquat. My success in treatment varied tremendously with the agent used, the dose consumed, the size of the animal, and the amount of time that passed until I could treat the victim. Never did I have a survivor come closer to death than Missy.

The local detachment of the Royal Canadian Mounted Police put forth an extensive effort to find the guilty party. Although several officers had personal reasons to find an answer—their own dogs had been poisoned—nothing concrete was ever determined. There were always suspicions about the culprit. Angry pet owners accused various people who didn't like dogs, or who expressed a hatred of cats, but the allegations were never substantiated.

Were we dealing with some demented individual who enjoyed inducing pain and suffering, or someone who had no idea of the misery he caused? I became convinced that the poisoner felt somehow removed from the events. He never saw the salivation, the vomiting, the convulsions, the agonized gasping for breath. He was never left to deal with the bodies of the victims.

I often thought that if he were forced to witness his heinous handiwork firsthand, or endure the tears of the children as they stroked their friends a final time, the poisonings would come to an end.

Bob was thankful for my help that night. A week following the incident, he sent his two happy daughters to the clinic with Missy to show me how the dog had recuperated. He promised to pay me as soon as payday rolled around. I hope he gets paid soon—I'm still waiting patiently.

Heavy Metal

Freshly spread gravel crunched under my boots as I stepped onto Esther's drive. I couldn't help but look out over the valley. The view from this vantage high in the West Creston hills was always breathtaking, but today it was truly magnificent. The sky was as blue as only a crisp autumn day could produce, and the foliage of the deciduous trees blazed yellow, orange, and red. The Kootenay River was a shimmering strip of silver, fenced from the rich browns of partly harvested fields, complemented by the glowing yellows of the cottonwood and poplar trees that lined her banks.

The town of Creston, sleeping in the foothills beneath Thompson Mountain, spilled out jagged rows of houses, then blended gently with the agricultural land that stretched across the valley. Sheer rock ledges of the Purcell peaks confined the green alfalfa fields of Canyon and Lister to the rolling hills below.

The banging of the screen door diverted my attention to the house. "Hello Dave, Brenda's still on her feet." The tall, willowy woman strode briskly in my direction, brushing back tassels of curly blonde hair. "I don't know for sure that it's milk fever, but if it is, I'd like to catch her before she goes down."

Esther had moved from Calgary with her husband, Ken, and fallen in love with the little farm in the hills. For a city girl, she had adapted well to the life of a small-time farmer. The condition of her gardens, grounds, and outbuildings was a testimony to the energy that she put into her new endeavour.

"Can I get you anything?"

"I'll need some water." I threw a bottle of calcium solution into the bottom of my bucket. "We'll have to warm it before giving it to her."

Esther turned back to the house with bucket in hand.

Calcium, thermometer, stethoscope, syringe case, ketone test tablets, rectal palpation sleeves, soap—that should be it. Only too well, I remembered the long climb to the barn, the fences that would have to be scaled, and the string on the barn door that would have to be untied each time I returned for forgotten items.

I headed up the path past the cedar-sided bungalow. The pole fence, which surrounded the yard, separated a well-manicured lawn and orchard from the pasture which, by this time of year, looked like a poorly trimmed putting green. Fumbling with the chain on the gate, I was still trying to decide which end unhooked when Esther caught up to me.

"The cows haven't figured it out, either." She smiled, then simply lifted the chain over the first picket of the gate. "I don't know why this one has them baffled; they seem to be able to open every other one on the place."

"I'm not sure myself..." I wondered how much longer I would have struggled to open it before stepping over.

We puffed our way to the corral and crawled through the rails. "I left Brenda in the pen behind the barn after milking," Esther gasped between breaths. "I didn't strip her out completely. She had hardly anything there to speak of."

In the far corner of the paddock, on the other side of six sliding rails, stood a Guernsey cow with a green sleeping bag draped over her back. Her calf lay in fresh straw under the lean-to near the other end, its head tucked contentedly into its flank.

I studied the old tan and white cow as Esther struggled with the rails separating us. From what I could see of Brenda under the sleeping bag, she appeared to be in good flesh, not overly fat like she had been in early summer. Her head drooped slightly; a long strand of mucous hung from the margin of her nostril. She was steady on her feet—not what I would have expected with a milk fever cow—and she made no effort to back away as Esther juggled the rails in front of her.

The sleeping bag sat squarely on her back, evenly distributed on either side, as though thrown on only moments before. That was strange; most healthy cows would have taken great joy in flinging it off and tromping it underfoot. Standing over a flake of timothy hay, she fixed her big brown eyes on me.

The eyes bothered me. They were droopy, inattentive; more than that, there was the look that I had come to associate with pain. And the hay—that flake of timothy was beautiful considering the amount of rain we'd had this year. It had been baled soon enough to maintain its gorgeous green colour, but was dry enough to keep it from becoming musty. A healthy cow would have torn into that hay and devoured it in five minutes flat!

As far as cows go, Brenda was an old girl. Her gut was prominent, her udder sagged, and the bones of her skeleton were more pronounced than normal. The broad blaze of white that started at her poll and widened towards her nose was no longer crisply separable from the surrounding tan hair; her muzzle was completely white.

As I stepped through the rails, her eyes widened. She took a hesitant step in retreat and looked desperately towards her benefactor for help.

"I'll get her." Esther slipped a rope halter over Brenda's head, pulled it tight, and snugged her to the post in front of her. "She seems leery of you."

I hung the sleeping bag on the fence, walked behind Brenda, and started a rhythmic massage of the region beneath her vagina. Most cows, when manipulated in such a manner, would promptly hunch and urinate as if on command. Several times Brenda started to pee, released a few dribbles, then stopped as though the hunching of her back caused her pain. I worked a thermometer into the cow's rectum and went on with the examination.

"Has Brenda ever had problems with mastitis?" I massaged the bulky udder back and forth between my fingers, searching for signs of pain, swelling, or unusual scarring.

"Never a bit..." Esther shook her head emphatically. "She has beautiful milk and is such an easy milker."

Grabbing the teats one after the other, I sent jets of milk across the toe of my boot and watched as it flowed to the ground. There was no evidence of clots or the excessively watery consistency that usually occurred with a mammary infection.

"Just as clear as can be." I removed the thermometer. "She's running quite a fever...40.8."

"She looked fine last night." Esther's forehead was suddenly creased with wrinkles. "She calved early yesterday morning and never looked a bit off. I milked some for the calf, but nothing more. She was real slow to get up this morning and shaking badly. When I came back out this afternoon and she was still shivering, I was sure she had milk fever, so I covered her up with that sleeping bag and called you. She hasn't had it since two calves ago, but I guess once they've had it, they're always prone."

"Yes, it is likely to recur once you've seen it, but I think we have something else going on here."

"Something else? It's not hardware and ketosis like before, is it? You remember the trouble we had last year, how sick she got."

Withholding my diagnosis, I plodded ahead with my examination. I listened to both lung fields for the rattle of fluid in the bronchial tree or the squeaky sounds of dry rales that would indicate resistance to flow. There was nothing unusual, except a momentary hesitation on expiration, that slightly audible sound of air being forced past a closed glottis.

Moving down the left side, I centred the stethoscope in the triangle formed by the ribs to the fore, the pin of the hips to the rear, and the vertebrae above. The rumbling of Brenda's normally active rumen was gone. Thumping with my forefinger over the rib cage and rumen area presented a dull thud; I detected no distended bowel, no gas in the rumen.

"Her tummy's as quiet as a church."

I examined the right side in a similar fashion, but found nothing unusual. Returning to the left, I slid my stethoscope forward over Brenda's trachea and prepared myself for the crucial test. A decisive grunt would mean that a swallowed nail or wire had penetrated the first stomach and was causing infection or pain. Putting my right hand on the cow's back, I clenched down hard over the vertebrae. She emitted a tremendous moan and dropped to her knees.

"That hurts her terribly!" Esther seemed to feel the old cow's pain. "Oh Brenda, not hardware again. I don't want to see her suffer any more. Let's just put her to sleep." Falling to her knees and holding Brenda's head in her arms, Esther burst into tears. "I think we should put her to sleep." She repeated her plea, and proceeded to drench the old cow's neck with her tears.

"Take it easy, Esther, we have to give her a chance. She's a tough old girl—she made it last time."

There was just one more possibility I wanted to rule out. I rolled up my coverall and slipped on the rectal palpation sleeve. "Sometimes an infection of the kidneys can look exactly like hardware." I squirted soap on my glove, lifted Brenda's tail, and pushed my hand into her rectum. Her stool was hard and compacted. I struggled to extract it. When the dung hit the ground, the pieces were so solid that they rolled away intact.

Carefully advancing, I proceeded until only the uppermost portion of my arm was exposed. The right kidney, which is the one readily palpable, was of normal size, and the indentations that separated its lobes were easily discernible. Firm manipulation of the organ caused the cow no discomfort, and a quick examination of the rest of her abdominal cavity revealed no abnormalities.

Hardware! It never ceased to amaze me what cows would cram down their gullet. How they could swallow a nail or a five-inch piece of wire was beyond me. Only a month earlier, I had gone into a cow's rumen in search of metal that I could remove. The animal was obviously dying and hadn't eaten in days. Conservative therapy seemed to be getting us nowhere. I pulled out a magnet that was literally covered with trash—pieces of wire, staples, nails. I had hoped to pull out the one that had penetrated her stomach wall and was causing the infection, but no such luck. I could feel nothing but the small indentation in the reticular lining where a wire had disappeared. Her heart beat under my fingertips only a fraction of an inch from the wound.

I performed a postmortem several days after the unsuccessful surgery. The cow's stomach was almost empty. I chopped through the ribs and folded back the chest wall to reveal a massive sac of fluid around the heart. The pericardium was filled with gallons of pus; a two-inch piece of well-worn wire was protruding from her heart wall.

Esther brought me back to Brenda's predicament. "How could she have more metal?" She dried her tears with her shirt sleeve. "I'm so careful with what I feed her. We watch how we handle nails and staples when we're working around the buildings or fixing fence. You put in a magnet last time...Why didn't that help?"

"You remember how we put Brenda on antibiotics to treat the infection? How we kept her quiet till it was walled off? Often we get an abscess that forms where the metal pokes through the gut. The cow produces a thick fibrous wall to separate it from the rest of her body, and there is sort of a standoff between the cow and this sac filled with pus. All the pushing and heaving associated with calving can break down that wall and allow bacteria to creep out and start a new infection."

Esther sniffled. "I'm sorry to carry on like this, but this old cow means so much to me—that's why I never breed her to a Guernsey bull. I don't want another milk cow. I get so attached. I can let the beef steers go to the butcher, but not Brenda. She's just so special."

"I can understand the way you feel, but let's be patient."

"What do I have to do?" The look on Esther's face suggested that she wasn't convinced she was doing the right thing.

"We'll have to watch her for ketosis. If she starts burning off too much fat without eating, the ketone bodies will skyrocket and she'll be in the same shape as she was before. I'm going to get some medication from the car." I climbed over the rails and headed towards the gate.

I thought back to my previous visits to Esther's paddock as I struggled through the second fence. Surely there had been one visit when I had carted everything I'd needed the first trip up the hill. Maybe the time I'd been out to pregnancy-check Brenda this spring…No, that was the day Esther decided to castrate Brenda's bull calf while I was there—I had to return to the car for the emasculators.

Brenda's treatment regime fell into place as I sorted through the vehicle. Chloramphenicol would get her started on broad-spectrum antibiotic therapy, and dextrose would help supply the energy that she wasn't getting as a result of not eating. B vitamin complex might just stimulate her appetite. As an afterthought, I grabbed the compass. I'd check to make sure she still had the magnet.

By the time I had hiked back up the hill, Esther was regaining her composure. "I faint at the sight of blood, remember." Esther glared in horror at the two-inch needle that was poised ready to strike over Brenda's vein.

"Just hold her tight, then, and turn your head." I bent the old cow's neck in an arch and drove the needle to the hub. My thrust was rewarded by a gushing flow of blood that ran freely over her neck and onto the ground.

"The tube, please."

Esther passed me the intravenous apparatus, swinging her arm in an exaggerated arc in an effort to avoid looking in my direction.

"Okay, tip the bottle over and let it run."

She stared at the bottle as the level of dextrose declined and air glugged in. Alcohol and air spurted from the metal end of the IV tubing. I waited until the syrupy solution started trickling out, then connected it to the needle hub. I took the bottle from Esther and held it high over the cow's head. There was a steady blurp, blurp, blurping as the sugar water running into the vein was replaced by air bubbling in through the flutter valve.

When the bottle was almost empty, I crimped the tube to shut off the flow. Grabbing the second bottle of dextrose, I squirted in the B vitamins and reattached the administration set. Brenda stood quietly, paying little attention to me as Esther stroked her forehead and whispered in her ear. When the last of the dextrose ran into her vein, I injected the chloramphenicol and pulled out the needle. Finally, I dragged the compass back and forth under the cow's abdomen.

"She still has that magnet," I pronounced, as the needle twirled madly in circles.

"So what am I going to have to do with her now? I despise giving those needles. Last time she hated the sight of me coming. You have no idea how much that bothers me."

"I'm sorry, but you'll have to be tough. She'll need a shot twice a day for the better part of a week. I want you to give her the propylene glycol twice a day just like last time until she starts eating on her own."

"Oh no!" Esther screwed up her face in obvious disgust. "I don't know what I hated most, sticking that needle in or wrestling with her to give her the drench. It just tears me apart when she runs away from me. She's such a pet; she usually follows me around like a puss."

To her credit, the woman persisted with both the injections and the drenches over the ensuing week and, little by little, Brenda recovered. It was a month later that I was called to castrate a colt for a neighbour at the end of Esther's road. As I drove by her farm, I slowed down to see if I could catch sight of either her or her old cow. Sure enough, Esther was out in her garden harvesting carrots; as I pulled into her yard, she ran over to the car.

She was all smiles. "Brenda's doing great! You just have to see her."

Before I could reply, she was off at a jog. I had just reached the gate to the field when I saw her returning. Close on her heels was Brenda. Trotting as though nothing had ever been wrong with her, she followed behind Esther like a kitten.

Cold Delivery

It had been getting progressively colder throughout the week, and tonight the thermometer was forecast to drop to forty below zero. For those of us who weren't born and raised to think metric, minus forty degrees had the dubious distinction of being the point at which the Celsius and Fahrenheit no longer need conversion—forty below was forty below.

"I had all I wanted to see of this weather when I was at the vet college," I whined to Doris. "I expected it in Saskatoon, but I can do without it here."

The back room of the clinic was a maze of extension cords as we battled to keep the water in the bathroom from turning to ice. Space heaters whirred constantly to keep the temperature a few degrees above freezing. Furry parallel lines of white frost decorated the walls as moisture condensed and froze at the junction of all the boards.

"This is ridiculous." I was fuming as I stomped back through the darkroom. "Call the landlord again and tell him we need some insulation in that bathroom. We should just let it freeze up, and then he can deal with the mess. It's too bloody cold for us to use anyway. Be damned if I want my ass frozen to a toilet seat!"

I dreaded going outside to plug in the block heater. My car had started only with great difficulty earlier in the afternoon, and I was determined not to be stranded in case of an emergency. I dragged a cord through the back door of the clinic and rushed it to the

parking lot. As soon as I pulled my hands from my pockets to plug in the cord, my fingers turned numb. Quickly stuffing them inside my coat, I ran to the clinic. It wasn't until I slammed the door behind me that I noticed an ominous silence. The draw of that one additional heater was more than the breaker could handle.

I retrieved the end of the cord from outside and plugged it into an inside receptacle, then tried the microscope in the adjacent plug-in. Its light came on; the breaker was still intact. Without bothering to remove my coat, I plunked myself on the gas heater and basked in the warmth that gushed forth.

Very few of our clients were willing to brave the elements, and only a couple of appointments showed up throughout the afternoon. I wandered about the clinic with bats of insulation, trying to block as many drafts as possible around the perimeter of the building. All heating units were running constantly to try and keep the place warm, but even then, we soon felt the chill if we didn't keep moving.

"I didn't realize it ever got this cold in Creston," I complained anew, as Doris was bundling up to leave for the evening. She prickled and was immediately on the defensive; she hated anyone making even the slightest derogatory comment about her home town. "It doesn't happen often, but we do seem to get a cold snap from time to time."

"The shorter the snap, the better I'll like it."

"It's been awful quiet the last few days." Doris fluffed up her scarf and carefully buttoned her coat. "For weeks you were getting a calving a day, and you haven't had one for ages now. What's happened?"

"Who knows, maybe the cows have pulled a pucker string until the weather warms up."

"One of these nights, you're going to pay for the time off." Doris pulled up the collar of her coat and dashed out into the Arctic air.

She was right. It was just a few minutes to one when the telephone woke me. I had to convince myself to throw back the covers and leave the sanctity of my warm cocoon.

It was a very apologetic Glenda Davis. "I hate to call you out on a night like this, Dave, but we have a heifer that's been pushing for the last two hours without making any progress at all. Murray stuck on a plastic sleeve and put his arm in her. He doesn't think she has enough room for him to deliver it on his own. Can you come out?"

"Okay, I'll be there as soon as possible."

As I grudgingly stuffed my legs into my long underwear, a shiver ran up my spine. The thought of going outside again was daunting. I pulled on my jeans and looked longingly at the wool sweater hanging on the door, but knew I would only have to strip down to my bare arms before doing the calving. What a job. It was tough to decide what to wear on a night like this when, no matter how cold it was, I would be shedding my clothes to perform the procedure.

Lug enthusiastically thrust his wet nose into my hand. Rhythmically wagging his tail, he was absolutely delighted by this rude awakening. I roughed up his ears, then took a few moments to stroke his head.

I trudged downstairs with Lug hot on my heels and paused for a moment in front of the gas burner as it cranked out the heat. I was determined to store every last morsel of warmth before plunging out into the night. Lug whined in anticipation and danced back and forth between me and the exit. I stood with my hand on the doorknob, mentally preparing for the wall of frigid air that would envelop me the moment I stepped outside. When I did, it seemed noticeably colder than earlier in the day. My face tingled as the wind whipped against it, my sinuses burned, and frost immediately built up on my nasal hairs.

The crusty layer of frozen snow on the sidewalk crunched loudly under my boots. Shards of ice splintered in front of my feet and scattered across the roadway. Lug bounded ahead of me full of his usual zest, his left ear flopping up and down with each step.

The car started easily. The stick shift moved resentfully into reverse and we backed out into the alley. Frost accumulated immediately on the inside of the windows, and I scratched at it in a futile attempt to keep the glass clear. The entire vehicle vibrated and thumped on flat-bottomed, frozen tires. Not until we were at the edge of town did they begin to limber up. Sensing something different about the car, Lug sat with his nose pressed firmly to the glass, leaving trails of slobber that froze into a mosaic.

It wasn't more than three or four miles to the Davis farm, and the car never really had an opportunity to warm up. I maneuvered past the house. Peering through a tiny portal that I scratched at fervently with the back of my glove, I aimed at a beacon of light that bobbed towards me from the corrals. Lug emitted a low, deep-throated grumble as a swaddled figure approached. I knew it was Murray Davis but, completely buried beneath layers of clothing, he was unrecognizable.

"Hi Dave." His voice was muffled by a frost-tinged ski mask. "I hope you're able to work some magic with that heifer and get that calf delivered—sure feels tight to me." Clouds of steam ejected as he spoke; he rubbed impatiently at the mask with the tip of a leather mitt.

"Is she a pretty good size, Murray?" Lug struggled to follow me out of the car, but I pushed him back.

"I'm afraid not." There was a note of disgust in his voice. "This is one of the heifers I'm looking after on shares. She seemed to start out about the same size as the rest, but somehow got left behind. She was out of one of the better cows too; I'm really disappointed in her."

"Isn't that the way of it? And what a night for her to decide to calve!"

"I've never had a critter that had to have a Caesarian before, but I think that's about to change."

Murray was right; the heifer was small. As I looked at her, half buried in the straw of the lean-to, the prospects of producing a calf without surgery didn't look good. Lying on her brisket with her feet tucked beneath her, her white face turned into her flank, she pushed sporadically on the feet that protruded from her vagina. Jets of steam burst like geysers from her nostrils; a layer of frost and tiny icicles had formed on the hair of her hind leg and flank.

"Do you have some water out here that hasn't frozen yet? I'll scrub up and see how she feels."

"You bet. Just brought some hot water out here a few minutes before you arrived. It should still be plenty warm."

Murray produced a steaming bucket. I peeled off my coat, stripped down to my shirtsleeves, and quickly rolled them up. Adjusting the scarf around my neck, I zipped my vest to the top and did up the snaps around the collar. The exposed skin of my forearms tingled with the bite of the frosty air. Kneeling in the deep straw behind my patient, I wasted no time getting my arms into the bucket of water and slopping it over the lips of her vagina. I squeezed the soap container firmly to cover her back end, but nothing happened. The normally slippery soap was frozen into an amorphous glob of sludge.

"Here, try mine." Murray tossed me an Ivory soap container. "Forgot it out here the other night, and it did the same thing."

I squirted on the thick, brown soap, then scrubbed aggressively at some manure that had dried along the margins of the heifer's rectum.

"Would she survive having her gut opened up when it's this cold?" Murray lifted his ski mask and scratched at his face. He looked tired. "I know I sure wouldn't last long without all these clothes on, and I sure as heck wouldn't want my guts dragged out on a night like this."

"I'm always impressed with what a cow can handle. I've never done a Caesarian at this temperature before, but they're tough and, if we can give her half a chance, she'll make it through."

I rinsed in the bucket of warm water, then quickly slipped my right hand over the calf's feet and into the cow. She bellowed plaintively, rolled onto her side, and strained against my intrusion. The calf's huge feet occupied most of the pelvic canal. I pushed forward, feeling for the head, but ran out of space immediately. There was no room for my hand to go in, never mind the calf's head and shoulders to come out.

"Not good, is it?" Murray pulled off his mask and scratched aggressively at the back of his head.

"Not good at all. There's just no way that calf's going to be delivered through the vagina—not in one piece anyway." Withdrawing my hand, I grasped the calf's foot and spread his toes apart enough to cause discomfort. The foot jerked back and forth. "The calf's still alive, so there's no way we're going to take it out in pieces. Somehow we're going to have to do a Caesarian."

"Would it help if we could get her into that little shack over there?" Murray pointed to a squat shed that looked as if it had provided many years of service as a chicken coop.

"Sure would. Even if it did nothing more than cut the wind, it's bound to give us a bit of an edge."

"Well, I've got one of those propane space heaters; it won't exactly warm the place up, but it'll cut the cold a bit."

After a few minutes of coaxing, we got the heifer to her feet. By pulling on the halter and cranking on her tail, we coerced her to take a few faltering steps in the right direction. We stuck her head through the door of the shack, locked our hands behind her, and pushed her forward one hesitant step after the other. By the time we cleared the door and were finally able to swing it shut behind her, my hands were numb and my arms were a mass of goosebumps.

I pulled down my shirtsleeves and rushed back outside to grab my coat. I slipped it on; my body was shivering convulsively and the very thought of stripping for surgery kept the waves coming, one after another. Trying to focus on something other than the raw weather, I fetched the surgery box from the car and ducked back into the shed. I had to maneuver to avoid the rafter cross-ties that traversed the structure at two-foot intervals, conveniently at forehead level. At times like this, my height was a definite disadvantage.

"You have power right there." Murray pointed to the plug-in on the opposite wall. "I'll run over to the shop and get that propane burner if you're all right by yourself for a few minutes."

"I'll be just fine." I fished my hair clippers from the surgery box and plugged them in. "We better get on with this before we all freeze up."

I flicked on the switch, but there was no movement from the clipper head—only a low hum from within the body. Flipping off the blade, I watched in fascination as the plastic finger wagged slowly back and forth. After a couple of minutes, the motor warmed up enough to produce a slow whine. I clicked the blade back into position. The motor ran at quarter-speed, but at least the blades were moving.

The heifer stood expectantly on the other side of the shack, her head half turned in my direction. Her back was arched against the feet that protruded from her rear end, and every now and then she gave a halfhearted push in an attempt to expel them.

"Easy, girl. Easy, girl." I approached her with caution. Straining against the halter that held her fast to the building, she looked back and twisted her body sideways until her right side was in contact with the wall. I touched her gently on the hip and scratched along the base of her tailhead. She lifted her left hind leg and lashed out in my general direction. It wasn't the vicious, well-aimed kick of a cow intent on doing damage—more a protest, a warning.

With the clippers droning at an agonizingly slow pace, I took a swipe over her tailhead, lifting away a clump of dry, fluffy hair. I worked my way forward along her spinal column and stripped her to the skin. I felt guilty as the insulation that fell from the heifer accumulated in a pile around my feet. By the time Murray returned with the propane heater, I was laying waste to a large triangle of hair on her left side.

"My God! Do you have to shave her bare? She'll freeze to death even if she does survive the surgery."

"She can cope with it. I can't possibly do surgery without clipping her."

I was making a few final passes with the clippers when the heifer simply crumpled in protest. It happened without warning and, even after loosening the halter shank, she wasn't interested in getting back up.

"Is that good or bad?" Murray asked.

"To be honest with you, I'd rather have her standing; but if she's going to go down, it's better now than after I start cutting."

Glenda arrived with another bucket of warm water just as I finished blocking the nerves in preparation for surgery.

"Oh, you poor dear," she crooned. "You're going to freeze to death."

"I am kinda cold," I quipped, "but I think there's a pretty good chance I'll survive."

Glenda smiled and countered through chattering teeth. "Actually, it was her I was feeling sorry for."

I scrubbed the heifer and sprayed her side with alcohol. Murray brought a bale of straw and I laid out my instruments and surgery gown. Backing away, I began shedding my clothing. Murray and Glenda stared at one another in amazement as I stripped down to my undershirt, then threw my vest back on.

"Oh my God!" Glenda gasped. "You can't be serious! You *are* going to freeze to death."

I began my scrub, though my skin was stinging in the icy air. I repeatedly slopped the warm water over my arms to try and warm them up.

"Why can't you leave more clothes on?" Murray asked. "I can't even stand looking at you like that."

My teeth were chattering uncontrollably. "I have to reach

inside her up to my armpits. I sure don't want her to end up with an infection."

When I was finally satisfied with my scrub, I grabbed a sterile towel to dry off. The material, cold and unyielding, chafed my skin. I slipped my arms into the frigid sleeves of the surgery gown and turned for Glenda to do up the ties. Waves of shivering coursed through me as the cold linen pressed against my flesh.

I opened a package of sterile gloves and wiggled my fingers to force them inside the stiff latex mould. They were as inflexible as cardboard; only by working them constantly so they would warm to my hand temperature could I finally slip them on. I grasped a scalpel blade and tried to insert it into the handle. I fumbled miserably.

I chose my location in the centre of the flank and pressed the scalpel firmly to the heifer's side. The blade sliced easily through the skin, leaving behind a trail of raw flesh that spurted fine jets of blood and emitted a foggy mist into the open air.

"Oh my!" A great gush of steam exploded from Glenda's mouth. "You are making a big cut."

"We want a long enough incision so that the calf slips out easily. Besides, I may need a hole big enough for me to crawl in to warm up."

I opened my hand upside down to drop the scalpel. The heifer's blood had frozen solid, and the instrument clung to my glove as though glued in place. I stuck my hand back inside the incision, held it there until I felt warmth returning to my fingers, then quickly deposited the scalpel on top of the instruments.

Cutting a large hole in the centre of the blue crepe surgery drape, I spread it over the animal's side to protect the site from contamination. I clipped towel clamps one by one through the corners of the drape and into her skin.

Although I had been joking with Glenda about the cold, it was no longer a laughing matter. My hands were numb and, again, I had difficulty holding onto the scalpel. I cut through the muscle to the level of the peritoneum and sliced through the thin mem-branous structure. Biting air rushed into the heifer's abdomen. She coughed. A tremendous cloud of steam gushed from the rent in her side. I extended the incision through the remainder of the muscle tissue, then tried to set the scalpel down. Frozen again!

Once more, I thawed myself on the rumen so I could detach from the instrument. Reaching deeply into the abdomen, I felt for the position of the calf and revelled in the luxurious warmth of the heifer's body cavity. While the fingers of my right hand were bask-ing at thirty-eight degrees Celsius, those of my left were exposed to the cold skin of her bare flank.

"What are you feeling for?" Murray looked puzzled as he watched my arm disappear to the depth of my shoulder.

"I'm looking for the calf's hocks…trying to see which way I have to rotate its body to bring them to the incision."

The heifer was small and the calf lay in a perfect position, with its butt away from me and the hocks within easy reach. I grasped the uterus over the calf's lower leg and slowly elevated until the toes stuck out over the flank and the hocks lodged at the bottom of the incision.

Glenda was excited. "Are those the calf's legs?"

"Yes, those are the hind legs still inside the uterus."

Fixing them in place with my left hand, I reached for the scalpel and lay open the uterus from the calf's toes to its hocks. The feet popped up through the incision, the long filamentous tips soft, flexible, and white. I grasped the calf's legs.

"Okay, here comes your baby!"

Lifting the calf from the womb, I pulled until legs gave way to rump and rump to abdomen and abdomen to chest. A final tug, and the calf lay stretched out on the straw steaming in the chill, dry air like a hot roast fresh from the oven. Shaking his head, he raised himself to his sternum, then rolled back onto his side.

"He's all yours. You better get him dried off as soon as possible."

Turning my attention to the gaping womb of the heifer, I cut away as much of the extraneous membrane as I was able to and stuffed the remainder into the uterus. Murray held the spool of gut suture while I pulled out enough to close the wound. My hands were numb, and I fumbled pathetically with the needle until finally managing to thread the thick gut suture through the eye.

My hands seemed detached from the rest of my body; I struggled to hoist the uterus up and out of the abdomen. Trapping it against the side of the incision, I pierced the needle through the uterine wall, tied off the suture material, and began the methodical procedure of sewing it together. Although the propane heater was keeping my back from growing numb, it was doing little for any other part of my body. It was now all I could do to hold the needle firmly. Paroxysms of shivering ran through my body.

I wasn't alone in my reaction to the bitter conditions. The calf shivered violently; the hair over his ears and tail was crisp and starting to freeze. Glenda rubbed at his slimy body as he struggled to get his feet under him. The ends of the towel had hardened like parchment.

"We better be getting this calf in the house, Murray." Glenda was frustrated by her lack of progress. "He's freezing up already. There's just no way I can get him dried off properly here."

"Just keep on rubbing until we're done here," he replied, "and I'll throw him in the front of the truck and get him to the house."

I finished suturing the uterine wall and daubed it gently with a towel to remove the blood that had congealed along the margins of the incision. I lowered the uterus into the abdominal cavity and checked it for proper positioning. With both arms buried in the heifer's abdomen, I waited expectantly as warmth slowly crept back into my hands. I was almost finished in more ways than one; the surgery was over except for the closing of the abdominal wall, but my ability to perform was now seriously in question. My pants were soaked from kneeling in the wet straw, and I was on the verge of losing the feeling in my feet. Sensation slowly returned to my fingers, but now they were aching.

I fumbled my way through the suturing of the peritoneum and muscle wall using a continuous pattern and tying only once at the top of the first layer and again at the top of the outer layer. By the time I had placed the final sutures to complete the closure of the skin, I was on the verge of tears. My body was aching. My ability to function was all but gone. I removed the skin clamps and threw them in with the rest of the instruments. Pushing myself up with my arms against the heifer's back, I struggled to straighten my legs. Like stumps of wood, I dragged them one after the other under me. My toes burned as though on fire; my calves and hamstrings shook violently.

Fighting for balance, I took a step back. My right leg gave out; I stumbled and my head struck the rafter cross-tie. I crashed to the straw like a windblown tree.

"Are you all right?" Glenda gasped.

I lay for some time without even attempting to answer her. I gingerly probed my skull and my fingers came away tinged with blood. Bright lights danced before my eyes. A decided lump was forming on the back of my head. I struggled to my knees, then pulled myself to my feet by grabbing the wall.

By the time we'd gathered my instruments and rounded up my clothing, I was more or less able to stand erect. I struggled to get my arms into my shirtsleeves but, by the time I got to my coat, I was shivering so violently that I merely draped it over my shoulders. The wet portions of my jeans were frozen stiff. Murray and Glenda carried my things to the car; I could hear Lug's savage bark warning them not to open the door.

I stumbled in their direction to find Murray standing beside the vehicle with his flashlight trained on the window and the surgery box still in his arms. Lug barked aggressively and attacked the window with his teeth. Occasionally, the frosted surface was disrupted when his wet nose melted the thin layer of ice and provided a brief glimpse of the beast within.

"That's enough, Lug!" I hollered without a trace of humour. "Go lie down!"

I struggled with the door latch until I finally depressed the button. Lug stuck his nose out to greet me, his body swaying back and forth to the rhythm of his tail. I shoved him aside brusquely. As I flopped my butt onto the driver's seat, he settled onto the passenger side with a look of dejection. I managed to drag the ring of keys from my pocket, but couldn't close my fingers over the right one. Fumbling repeatedly, I just couldn't get that key to the ignition.

"You'd better come into the house and warm up," Glenda counselled. "You're in no shape to be driving."

She was right, but all I could think of was getting into my own bed and pulling the covers over my head. I could already imagine how that warmth would feel. I focused all my ability on closing my fingers over that key but, no matter how hard I tried, I couldn't grip it well enough to work it to the slot. Murray and Glenda, their arms still laden with supplies, watched in disbelief.

"Murray, will you start this thing for me and get it pointed in the right direction? My hands don't want to do as I tell them anymore…Just stick that stuff in the back." I struggled to pry myself from the seat and get out of his way.

"Do you think it's safe for you to be driving in your condition?" Glenda persisted. "I don't want to find you frozen to death in a ditch tomorrow morning. Come in and warm up first."

"I have to get home to bed, Glenda. Lug…Come on out here for a pee and let Murray get in."

Throwing the instruments on the back seat, Murray hopped in the car and quickly closed the door. The light from his flashlight sent eerie reflections through the frosted windows as he familiarized himself with the vehicle. The engine turned over with difficulty, then fired up in clouds of steam and exhaust. Certain that he was being left behind, Lug came tearing across the yard. A look of terror etched on his face, he ran to the driver's door, raised himself on his haunches, and peered expectantly into the window.

"Over here, Lug!" I hollered. "It's okay. Come over here."

He whirled and ran to my side, still uncertain about what was going on with his car. Murray scraped vigorously at the window to clear a small spot, then ground the gear shift into reverse and slowly backed into the yard. Glenda, her figure at times disappearing completely in a cloud of smog, shone the flashlight to guide him around. Murray revved the vehicle several times before he got out.

"You're going to have one hell of a time seeing where you're going with those windows frozen up," he cautioned. Lug wasted no time in getting himself positioned on the passenger seat, simply content to be back in his vehicle.

"Thanks a lot for your help!" Murray hollered over the roar of the engine.

"You be careful on the way home!" Glenda yelled. "Are you sure you'll be all right?"

"I'll be fine." I pushed the stick shift with the heel of my hand and eased the vehicle down the driveway. Scratching frantically at the small portal that Murray had created in the mural of ice on the window, I managed to crawl along the lane and out onto the roadway, turning towards the haze on the horizon that I knew to be the lights of Creston.

I worked continuously at the window to maintain a small glimpse of the world. It wasn't until I was almost home that half-moon circles appeared above the defrosters. The frost had not actually melted, but had softened enough to allow me to remove it with the scraper. I navigated into the parking lot, shut the car off, and fumbled the keys from the ignition.

I wrestled my feet to the ground and pushed myself erect. Lug shoved past me, then trotted off to check out a few of his favourite scent posts. I grabbed the surgery box from the back seat, slammed the door closed, and took a few faltering steps in the direction of the clinic. Only a matter of minutes and I'd be standing in front of the heat register with hot air blasting around my body.

"Oh no!" I stopped in my tracks. If I didn't plug the car in, I'd be stranded for sure. I located the cord at the back of the clinic. It was frozen stiff, and I couldn't bear to touch it with my naked fingers. Sliding my hands up my coat sleeves, I clutched the wire tightly to my body and dragged it to the car.

I struggled to plug the two cords together with hands that were numbed beyond cooperation. Tears trickled down my cheeks as the simple task suddenly grew in complexity. In desperation, I fell to my knees in order to get closer to the struggle. The plastic of the plug-in was unyielding; I simply couldn't hold onto the ends well enough to join them together.

"AAAAAAhhhhhhhhhhhhh!"

The wail that parted my lips was an entity unto itself. It had lain dormant inside me like a disembodied being, waiting for this very moment to escape. I collapsed to the frozen ground and stuffed my hands inside my coat. I sobbed uncontrollably; tears rolled down my cheeks.

Lug shoved his nose into my face. Whining, he dug forcefully at my back with his paw. I took a deep breath and concentrated on the burn of the icy air as it filled my lungs. Stretched out on the ground eyeing the heater plug that dangled inches from my face, I was possessed with a tremendous resolve to join those cords. At the moment, I could think of no worthier task in the universe.

With the palm of my left hand, I jammed the receptacle of the cord firmly against the bumper and surrounded the block heater plug with the unfeeling fingers of my right hand. I advanced the prongs to the two dark slits of the plug-in and completed the reluctant union. For a few seconds, I lay staring with a certain grim satisfaction at the orange cord, which now dangled from beneath the engine.

I rolled onto my belly, pushed myself upright, and stumbled towards sanctuary. In the alcove of the clinic, I fumbled with my key ring. Kneeling close to the knob, I planted the office key between the fingers of both hands and guided it into the slot. It slid in without resistance, and there was a clunk as the door unlocked.

A blast of deliciously tepid air engulfed me. I lurched through the door and leaned against it to slam it shut. Shuffling to the heater, I unfolded my fingers before the warm currents. My entire body was wracked with wave after wave of shivering, and the muscles of my abdomen and back ached from the incessant contractions. My face burned as the blood rushed to my cheeks and forehead; my fingers ached as the circulation returned. I backed up to the flow of air and sat directly on the register like a chicken on a barbecue spit. I basked in the newfound source of strength.

I was reluctant to leave the heater, but all I could think of was getting some sleep before the return of the sun, settling into my nice, toasty bed and pulling the covers up over my head. I tore myself away from the luscious flow of hot air and picked my way up the stairs. Opening and closing my hands repeatedly, I was frustrated by their lack of dexterity.

I stalled in front of the gas burner in the kitchen and began to peel off my clothing. I unbuckled my belt with difficulty and worked my pants down past mid-thighs. Shackled by jeans and long underwear that refused to release me, once more I felt tears building. I jammed my hands into the crotch of my pants, pushed them to my knees, and stood shivering and fighting for breath. The cumbersome clothing had thawed and clung to my calves. By stepping on my underwear with my left foot and lifting my right leg with all that was left of my strength, the wet cloth finally peeled off inside out. The long limp tube of cotton, stained blood-red and manure brown, lay on the floor. Repeating the struggle with the other leg, I was finally free.

I turned on the tap in the tub and steam rose. I worked off my socks and shirt and stepped into the water, impatient for it to impart its heat to my aching feet. As the warmth penetrated, the shivering persisted. I cooled the water slightly and carefully eased my body beneath the surface.

I'm not sure how long I lay revelling in the flow of hot water, alternately submerging the top half, then the bottom half of my body. My skin was red from head to toe. The waves of shivering became intermittent. I rose wearily from the tub, towelled dry, and made my way to the bedroom. This was the moment I'd been waiting for. I crawled beneath the blankets. Pulling them up over my head, I huddled into a ball and closed my eyes. The covers were cold, and I was careful not to move and disperse even a morsel of body heat. I was floating in a weightless state of pleasure when the telephone rang.

This wasn't possible! I'd had enough for one night. "Hello." I emitted a barely audible croak.

"Dave, this is Lynne Hornslien. We have a problem with a cow calving. Bob's been out several times to check her and nothing's happening."

"Ohhh, no…Lynne…Is this a mature cow?" I was searching for a bit of light in the gloom.

"Oh yes," Lynne chirped. "This is her fourth calf, and she hasn't had problems in the past."

"Has she broken water yet?"

"The membranes have been hanging since twelve last night. That's why Bob's so concerned. He stuck his arm in her quickly a few minutes ago, and all he could feel was a mass of legs. As soon as he felt her, he said, 'Call Dave'."

"What time is it now?"

"Six forty-five."

"Ummph…Okay, I'm on my way, Lynne. Could you try and have the cow tied up? We'll need hot water."

"No problem; she's halter broken and already has one on. I'll have the water ready."

I moved like an automaton as I pulled on clean clothes and prepared to go back into the winter darkness. I refused to allow myself to even think about what lay ahead, concentrating only on the physical process of pulling on one garment after the other. Lug sat at my feet watching my every move, as anxious as ever to go on another adventure. His tail wagged exuberantly.

"Not this time, boy." I crowded close to the door to prevent him from sneaking out. "You've already steamed the car up enough."

I opened the door a crack, pushed the knob in to lock it, and slipped out into the bitter morning air. Lug emitted a mournful howl as the door closed in his face, and he realized that I was going without him. A transport truck rolled along Canyon Street dragging a whirlwind of dry snow in its wake. I turned my face to cut the force of the blast, then trudged down the street to the parking lot.

I pulled the plug from the block heater, giving scant thought to the struggle that had gone on just an hour before. The car started easily and I was soon making headway down Canyon Street, scratching at the windshield as I went. The Hornslien farm was across the flats on the other side of the Kootenay River. Nick's Island, as the area was called by long-time residents, was one of the last pieces of land diked and reclaimed from the flood waters of the mighty Kootenay River.

As I approached the bridge, the car was immersed in a blanket of fog that hung like a canopy over the river. I dimmed my lights and slowed the vehicle to a crawl. Keeping my eye on the yellow line, I inched my way across the bridge. I peered into the fog for the next hundred yards in search of the service station lights that I knew were there. They appeared as a yellow haze on the left, and I turned onto the narrow dirt road that doubled back on itself towards the river.

I passed the murky glow of three other farms along the three-kilometre route. By the time I got to the Hornsliens, the roadway had become a narrow one-lane path between two fence lines. It eventually entered a farmyard where I could see the taillights of several other vehicles reflecting through the fog.

Bob stood in the yard, a flashlight in one hand and a bucket of water in the other. He was a big man. A transplant from Saskatchewan, he seemed perfectly at home peering from the hood of his bulky Ski-Doo suit. Leaving the car running, I grabbed my bucket, soap, and chains.

"Sorry to get you out of bed on a morning like this, Dave." Lynne's voice drifted to me from somewhere out in the mist. "You sounded like you were having such a good sleep."

"I was trying hard."

"Well, if it's any consolation," Bob drawled in his slow, easy voice, "we didn't get much sleep here either. I was sure she'd calve last night; checked her every hour. Cold as it was out here, we couldn't bear the thought of a newborn baby layin' out there freezin' his ears and tail off…wanted to bring the calf in the house to get dried off first."

Bob led the way through the corral gate and across a small paddock, towards a blur of light in the distance. Compacted snow crunched underfoot. "Fog sure is thick," he noted. "Came on about ten last night, been gettin' heavier ever since."

We reached a metal gate, and Bob set down his bucket. Wearing thick leather mitts and still gripping his flashlight, he fumbled with a spring latch, grasped the bolt with both hands, and pulled it towards him. The gate swung open and he waited for Lynne and me to pass through. There was a metallic clang as it slammed shut; cattle stirred at the far end of the paddock.

"Easy, girls." Bob spoke in a reassuring tone. "It's amazing how they pick up on someone different. They don't pay the slightest attention to me comin' and goin'."

The calving shed was partitioned into individual pens. Bob went in before us and turned on overhead lights. There was a rustling as critters stood up and moved into position to get a better look at me. A big Charolais cow whirled in her stall, tossed her head, and snorted. Steam shot from her nostrils into the nippy morning air. Awakened by her performance, a snow-white calf sprang to his feet and retreated behind his mother.

"Easy, Smokie," Lynne crooned. "Dave's not the least bit interested in your baby."

Bob swung open a gate and stepped into the end stall with a brindle-coloured cow. She lay on her brisket, her head stretched comfortably out in front of her.

"Up you get, Tubbs," Lynne urged. "Get up and let Dave see what's going on with that baby of yours."

She snapped a shank onto the cow's halter and gave her a few gentle taps with the flat of her hand. Tubbs turned her head in Lynne's direction and stuck out her tongue as if looking for a handout.

"Up you get now, Tubbs!" Bob slapped her on the side and gave her a knee in the ribs. "Come on, girl."

The cow reluctantly stood on her hind legs, then casually pulled first one, then the other front leg under her. She shuffled to the corner and rustled through the hay in the feed rack. Grabbing a mouthful, she munched on it as though fulfilling an obligation.

Bob tied her to the feed rack. "I'm not sure what's going on in her. All I could feel was feet everywhere. I tried to find the head, but there's just no way."

I peeled off my coat and rolled up my coverall sleeves. The cold was as biting as it had been a few hours before, and goosebumps again proliferated on my exposed flesh. Grabbing the bucket of water, I scrubbed up my arms and the cow's vagina. Not the least bit concerned, Tubbs stood stock-still, chewing contentedly on her hay. I rubbed my arms down with soap, then slipped my hand into her. "I can see why you were confused, Bob. We have more than our share of legs here."

I flexed the joints of the limbs that were sitting in Tubbs's pelvic canal and found that two of them bent upward and two bent downward. Following the leg of the foot that bent upward, I arrived at a hock and finally a tail. "Looks like twins. They both want to be first to get out here and freeze with the rest of us."

Lynne moved through the gate to crowd closer to the action. It

227

was obvious that she was excited about the prospect of twins. Her eyes were glittering, her mouth pursed in anticipation.

"You look like you need a job to keep you occupied." I handed her the end of Tubbs's tail.

I grabbed a calving chain from the bucket, lingering long enough to allow the warmth of the water to soak into my fingers. Reaching past the brim of the pelvis, I slipped a loop over one of the feet and pulled with my other hand until it had tightened above the fetlock. My hands still ached and their movements were sluggish. I fumbled with the chain until I had a half hitch just above the hoof, then reached into the bucket for another chain.

Bob waited expectantly as I placed it. His face was creased with worry; he chewed constantly on his lower lip.

"Just give me a bit of a pull here, Bob." I flexed the fetlocks one more time to make certain that I had snagged the right ones.

Bob hooked the handles on the chains and leaned back to pull. I could feel the hocks slide beneath my hand, and the hind feet of a calf soon protruded into the frosty air.

"Just keep a steady tension. Let me work at getting the other calf out of the way." I manipulated my hand over the hind legs of the first calf and pushed against the chest of the twin. It shifted slightly and I crammed it further back into the uterus. "Slow and steady Bob. We just have to make sure there's room to get this one by."

The thighs of the calf slid easily through the vaginal lips, and I maintained my hand over its tail as it passed through the pelvic canal.

"Easy Bob! Easy!" I cautioned, as the baby rocketed into the raw morning air. I grabbed frantically for the calf's chest as it shot past me and managed to ease its slimy body to the straw. He blinked one eye and made a feeble attempt to draw a breath.

"Doesn't look like he's very strong." I dropped to my hands and knees next to him and raked a strand of mucous from the back of his throat. The calf lay in a lifeless heap, making no effort to draw another breath. I grabbed a straw, stuck it up his nose, and wiggled it back and forth in his nasal passage. There was a passive contraction of his abdomen, and then he lay still. Except for the constant throb of his heart, there was no sign of life, no indication that he wanted to live.

"He doesn't think much of the world we've brought him into." I lifted his shoulder to expand his chest. Picking him up by his hind legs, I swung him back and forth. Long trains of mucous drained from his mouth and nostrils as he dangled in the biting air. I dropped him to the straw and quickly cleared away some remaining slime. I closed his mouth and one nostril and blew into the other; his chest and abdomen expanded as the air forced its way in. I shoved the straw back into his nostril and got a deep breath in response.

"Grab a bucket of cold water from the trough, will you, Lynne? He doesn't want to live, but he doesn't want to die either."

I blew in the calf's nostrils several more times, expanding his chest, but getting air in his stomach as well. Working with the straw, I coaxed another couple of breaths, each one seemingly stronger than the last.

"Here's your water!" Lynne panted as she rushed back from outside. "It's cold as all get-out. Are you sure you want to use it?"

"Just give him a blast along his side."

Lynne slopped the frigid water over the calf. He gasped, fully expanding his chest. I threw some warm water on him from the other bucket, then gave him a few sharp slaps over his chest wall.

"Okay, give him some more!"

Lynne dumped another shot across him and, sure enough, he took a couple of deep gasps. We alternated warm and cold water until we ran out and, each time, we were rewarded with several deep breaths. Lynne hurried away for more water as I knelt beside him, jamming a straw up his nostril and coaxing breaths one after the other.

"Hit him again?" Lynne puffed, as she returned with her bucket brimming.

"I think we've gotten him started."

The calf lay stretched out on the straw drawing deep, regular breaths. His eye flickered as if he might be gaining consciousness.

"Boy, that was close," Lynne huffed. "For a while, I thought he was a goner." Her face beamed in a smile and her eyes twinkled with excitement as she grabbed a towel and rubbed aggressively at the baby's sides and chest. I lifted him towards the corner, then returned to Tubbs. The old cow was quiet, but her tail now stuck straight out and she pushed occasionally as if wanting to deliver.

"Sure hope the other one's in better shape than this one." I passed the tail to Bob and doused my hands in soap. My fingers were numb again and my palms were getting the same aching feeling that they had earlier on. I slipped my right hand into Tubbs's vagina and waited for warmth to penetrate my fingers. Both of the calf's feet were in the pelvic inlet, but its head was nowhere to be found.

A shiver coursed through my torso. I waited until it abated, repeatedly flexing my hand to try and regain some feeling. Tracing the calf's legs to its chest, I followed the neck as it made a lazy curve into the depths of the cow. The calf's head was tiny; under normal circumstances, I could have grasped the forehead to bring it around into the pelvic canal. This morning, my hand was not going to cooperate.

With the first calf gone, there was plenty of room in Tubbs's uterus. All I had to do was straighten the head and she could do the rest. I hooked my fingers behind the calf's ear and dragged it easily towards the pelvic canal.

"I think we're in business, Bob. The calf is small. She'd have popped them out like nothing if they hadn't gotten all balled up."

Lynne threw aside her towel as she realized she was close to acquiring another ward. She picked up her bucket of water and moved to the cow's side. Her face revealed a mix of worry and determination. This calf was going to live if she had anything to say about it.

"Do you think this one's going to be stronger?" she asked, her bucket poised at waist height.

"I hope so, but I never felt movement when I straightened its head, and it's certainly not very big."

Lynne's eyes were riveted on my hand as it disappeared once more into the cow. I was about to ask Bob for the calving chains when the cow started straining. The calf advanced through the pelvic canal, its head and forelegs protruding. I reached for the front feet just as Tubbs gave a mighty heave. I fell over backwards and the calf sailed through the air to land squarely in my lap.

Lynne had been prepared like a trap cocked and ready. The moment she saw the calf, the trigger was sprung. Her arms swung forward and the bucket was launched. The calf and I gasped in unison as the water cascaded over us.

"AAAAAAAAAhhhhhhhhhhhhhhhh!"

"Oh, Dave, I'm sorry!" Lynne screeched. "I just couldn't help it."

The calf's eyes popped wide open and it shook its head in shock. My mouth hung open like a goldfish as I gulped for air. The cold water was quickly soaking through my coveralls; I struggled to get out from under the calf.

"Oh, my God! Oh, Dave, I'm so sorry!" Lynne exclaimed in horror and disbelief.

I picked myself up into a squat position, trying desperately to pull the soggy clothing further from my skin as the cold took hold. Frigid water oozed into my boots. The calf we had just delivered struggled to stand but sprawled backwards onto the straw next to its sibling.

"Well, you sure got him going," I chattered.

Lynne's eyes were still wide with astonishment as she stared at the drenched figures shivering before her. She glanced at Bob and back to me and produced the most impish giggle. "Oh Dave, I don't know what came over me."

Tubbs strained at her rope, stretching her head as far back to the calves as the halter would allow. She uttered a very maternal little moo in their direction.

"Can I let her go now?" Bob asked.

"Can't see why not; she sure couldn't have torn herself with that calf. It hardly touched the walls on its way out!"

Bob fumbled with the rope, then finally slipped one hand from his cumbersome mitt to unbuckle the snap and release the halter. The cow shuffled her back end around until she could see her babies and sniffed each one in turn.

I shoved my hands under my armpits to warm them as Bob gathered up the chains and the calving handles. He remained to fuss over the calves as Lynne and I departed.

"Thanks a lot, Dave," he fired after me as we left the barn.

Waddling along like a toddler with his pants full of poo, I followed Lynne across the paddock. My coveralls had frozen stiff from my chest to the top of my boots, and water squished between my toes with each step. My teeth chattered incessantly. But, the night from hell was over!

Light was filtering through the veil of fog that enveloped the West Creston flats. I pointed the car towards town and my first appointment of the day.

Eleanor and O'Brian

In the dying days of January, the cold weather loosened its grip on the valley. The last week had been rainy and overcast. Doris was promising that winter would be over by the middle of February, and I was going to hold her to it.

On one of those dreary days, Eleanor Blair called just before lunch. She was in a quandary about getting deworming medication for her horses. Although I had long since stopped billing her for my services, she tried diligently to pay for her medicines. Today, she was flat broke and wouldn't have money until she got her social assistance cheque at the end of the month. I assured her that she could stop in and pick up what she needed.

Late in the afternoon, I slipped up to the apartment for a bite to eat. I was polishing off a tomato sandwich when Doris huffed up the stairs. She carried a rather bedraggled-looking plastic sack.

"You'll never believe what I have here." She deposited the Overwaitea Foods bag with a rattle on the kitchen table.

"What in the world?" I grasped the receptacle by the bottom and turned it upside down. A haphazard collection of spoons, knives, and forks clattered onto the tabletop. I picked up a couple of pieces and looked at the handles; each implement bore the lion rampant—it was English silver.

I shook my head. "Eleanor?"

"Yes. She said she really appreciates your help, doesn't want to be a burden."

At six that evening, I retrieved a message from my recorder that Eleanor's horse, O'Brian, was doing poorly. I had just finished supper at Veitches and was struggling with that uncomfortably full feeling that I most often got after pigging out on one of Ruth's home-cooked meals. I hopped in the car and headed for Canyon. Eleanor had sounded distressed; I didn't want to keep her waiting.

All that remained of the winter snowfall was a dirty brown ridge on either side of the roadway. I pulled off in front of Eleanor's gate, running the wheels of the vehicle well onto the compacted snowbank. It was twilight but I could make out the silhouette of my friend and her big grey gelding as they trudged across the yard towards me. I clicked on my flashlight and shone it on O'Brian's frame.

He had probably been a raw-boned horse even in his younger days. Now his hips, spine, and withers protruded in an exaggerated fashion and his back swayed ever so dramatically. It was hard to know if the critter was in poorer shape than the average horse his age, because I honestly had nothing to compare him with. To this day, I haven't examined another horse that has lived to the ripe old age of thirty-four.

"He ate this morning." Eleanor stopped in front of me and took a deep drag on the half-burnt cigarette that dangled from her lower lip. It glowed brightly in the gloom, then faded. I shone the light in Eleanor's direction; she squinted and looked away to avoid the glare. Smoke encircled her face as she spoke. "Tonight, he just stood there and let Honey eat everything."

"Has he been colicky?"

"He's been a bit sweaty...keeps looking at his flank. Hasn't actually tried to get down and roll though."

I ran my hand over his back and rib cage. His hair coat was rough and lifeless; he was moist with sweat. This horse was emaciated. I slipped a thermometer into his rectum, and then felt for his pulse at the angle of his jawbone. His heart rate was only forty-five—about what I'd expect for a fellow of his age. Folding back his upper lip, I shone the light into his mouth and checked the colour of his gums and mucous membranes. They were pale but not blanched. I pulled his tongue to the side of his mouth and ran my finger along the inside of his cheek. The front teeth were extremely angular, the back worn to the level of the gums.

"Have you watched him when he eats? Does he seem to chew more than normal or spit out his food?"

"Well, he sure has been taking longer to eat than he used to. I've fed O'Brian and Honey together for years. Lately, Honey finishes first and comes over to steal the rest of his. In the past, O'Brian was always boss."

"I'm afraid his teeth are all but worn out, Eleanor. He's probably having difficulty chewing long hay and may well be impacted as a result of it."

I listened to his chest. His heartbeat was strong and there was no sign of a murmur. Placing the stethoscope head over the last ribs, I waited for the normal tinkling sounds that I'd expect to hear as gas and fluid moved through the small bowel. His tummy was ominously silent. The thermometer showed his temperature almost a full degree below normal. Moving to the other side, I listened for several minutes before I heard even a faint rumble.

"What's wrong?" Eleanor hadn't taken her eyes from me. She knew I was troubled.

"His gut is terribly quiet." I thumped along his side, dreading the possibility of the high-pitched ringing sound that would indicate a torsion. I was relieved to hear nothing but the dull thud of my finger contacting his emaciated flesh. "Have you seen him pass a stool in the last few days?"

"No." Eleanor stared at the remains of the cigarette butt that rotated in her nicotine-stained fingers. "And he hasn't made water since I've had him out this morning…Do you think his kidneys have quit working?"

"Let's bring him to the shed so I can do a rectal examination." Eleanor led O'Brian around the perimeter of the yard, then headed to a rickety old building that was every bit as decrepit and sway-backed as the horse. I retrieved a rectal sleeve and lubricant from my car. By the time I got back to Eleanor, a new cigarette hung loosely between her lips. She looked tired—very tired. Maneuvering the horse next to the old barn, I wrapped his tail to keep the long hairs from abrading his rectum.

"Hold him steady, Eleanor."

I applied lubricant, gently introduced my fingertips into the anal sphincter, and pressed forward until my hand slid into a rectum filled with rock-hard pellets of feces. As I manipulated them, they plunked to the ground one by one and rolled in all directions.

I checked the other organs I could reach. The remainder of the colon was full. The caecum—the horse's main digestive organ, which is normally pliable and full of fluid—was firm and hard-packed. I pushed steadily against it; deep indentations remained from the impression of my fingers.

I withdrew my arm and pulled off the palpation sleeve. "I'm afraid he's badly impacted. At his age, we could be in for a real battle to get things moving again."

Eleanor gazed pensively into the overcast night before turning towards O'Brian. Tired old eyes stared into tired old eyes as the two friends communicated with silent understanding. Several minutes passed before Eleanor finally looked away from her companion. Grinding out her cigarette on the heel of her boot, she faced me resolutely. "Let's get started!"

She slogged to the house to heat water in her electric kettle. O'Brian was obviously in discomfort. His ears drooped, his nostrils flared. Whenever I released his head, he turned to look plaintively at his flank.

Eleanor returned with a kettle. Steam billowed up as I poured the contents into my bucket. I diluted it with cold water from the trough until I could bear to stick my hand in it and added a laxative called Dioctol. After warming a stomach tube in the bucket, I inserted it into O'Brian's nostril. His eyes grew wide as I slowly advanced it; he stumbled backwards, almost collapsing. I moved with him and slid the tube through his nasal passage and into the pharynx. Puffing on the end of the device, I introduced it into the stomach, and gas erupted.

I handed Eleanor the flared end of the tube. "Hook onto the stomach pump and let's get started."

As she gamely stroked the handle, I held the tube in position in the horse's nose and watched the soapy fluid flow up inside the clear plastic conduit. O'Brian accepted the intrusion with indifference as Eleanor struggled to empty the bucket. By the time the pump finally started sucking air, her face was drawn and her breaths were coming in gulps. With a look of desperation, she threw me the pump, fell back towards the barn wall, and leaned her head against the rough-sawn boards.

"Are you sure you're up to this, Eleanor? We could be in for a long ordeal. These impaction cases take a long time to get to this point, and they can take just as long to correct themselves."

Eleanor coughed violently. Leaning forward until her forehead almost touched her knees, she struggled for composure. "I'm fine!" she finally blurted. Brushing a few locks of grey hair from her sweaty forehead, she fumbled with her jacket pocket in search of her cigarettes.

"How about heating up some more water, Eleanor? I'd like to give him an enema as well." I placed my finger over the end of the tube and pulled it from O'Brian's body with one slow, steady motion. The horse shivered as the hot fluids began warming his body. He took a half step forward, then shook himself so hard he almost lost his footing. Emitting a low-pitched groan, he turned his head into his right flank.

"Oh dear," moaned Eleanor, lighting a cigarette. "He is in pain."

Afraid that he was about to drop down and roll, I flicked the horse with the end of the halter shank and pulled towards me. He straightened his head and hesitantly started plodding at my heel.

Eleanor brought another bucket of water that sent billows of steam into the evening air. Her feet still dragging, she trudged along with the receptacle barely inches from the ground. Her breaths were even, long, premeditated; not even drawing air came easily for the poor woman at this moment. I could tell she was dreading another session with the pump. I directed her to hold the tube and delivered the enema as quickly as I could. The old gelding strained to evacuate his rectum, so I pushed his tail down firmly and motioned for Eleanor to lead him away. We walked the horse off and on for several hours. He was obviously in discomfort, but made no effort to roll or cast himself.

Even though O'Brian had been a perfect gentleman all evening, my experience with colicky horses had taught me to take nothing for granted—things often got ugly very quickly. I hated leaving Eleanor alone with him, but exhaustion and the thought of a full slate the next day finally dictated that I head home.

Although it wasn't particularly cold, the air was damp and I found myself shivering often. I kept looking at Eleanor in her threadbare jacket, almost sure that she had nothing but bare feet inside those holey rubber boots. She looked worn-out already, and I doubted that her head would hit the pillow tonight.

"You'd better try and get some rest, Eleanor. He should be all right if you leave him out here and peek at him from time to time. It's not such a problem if he lies down. It's only when he starts to roll that you need to get him up."

"I'm just fine." Her voice was hoarse, her reply less than convincing. "Don't you worry about me."

I stepped through the gate, thankful for this respite. "I'll come and check him in the morning. We'll have to keep pumping fluids into him to soften that mass."

As I lay shivering beneath the covers that night, all I could think about was Eleanor still out there in the cold, stomping around in those flimsy rubber boots. How frustrated she must be at times like this. She hated to be seen as a charity case by anyone yet, with all those strays and such a limited income, how could she afford to pay a vet for an emergency like this?

The morning saw little change in O'Brian's condition. Although Eleanor was ecstatic about his passing some cow-pie-like stool, he had no desire to eat, and his caecum was as hard-packed as ever. Twice that day, we pumped hot water and Dioctol into him. Each time, he offered less resistance than the time before. Because he had been so long without eating, I administered dextrose and injections of a vitamin B complex. He was sinking fast, and I was concerned that he wasn't going to rally. How I dreaded the moment that I'd have to discuss the topic of euthanasia with Eleanor.

The following morning, O'Brian refused to stand. With his nose pointed towards his flank, he lay subdued and totally uninterested in what went on around him. "You're sure that you want to continue treating him, Eleanor?" My voice had a pleading tone. "I think the kindest thing at this point would be to put him down."

She lit a cigarette, took a deep drag, and glowered at me. "We have to keep trying. He needs more time!" Aside from a few shifts that her friend, Chris Herchmer, had taken to watch O'Brian, Eleanor had not left his side for more than a few moments. Her face was haggard and she had aged years over the past few days. Her shoulders were hunched; her rubber boots dragged with each plodding step she took. I think she knew deep down that she was beaten, but the fiery smouldering in her eyes made me drop the topic of euthanasia.

I continued with supportive care, even though I had long since given up hope. Today, I was questioning if it was humane to continue with further treatment. The only consolation was that O'Brian was suffering in silence. Surely, he couldn't go on much longer.

Eleanor covered him with an old sleeping bag and stripped the wool blanket from her own bed to put on top of it. As I was talking myself into leaving this depressing scene, the rain started. It was just a fine drizzle, but the clouds were hanging low and things promised to get worse rather than better.

"I've got an old tarp that should help keep him dry." Eleanor trudged towards the house. I broke a straw bale and spread it next to O'Brian. Pulling first on his halter, then on his tail, I dragged his lifeless carcass until he was settled on a deep cushion of straw. By the time Eleanor returned with the tarp, I had him propped up on his belly.

"He can't do himself much harm right now. Why don't you go in and go to bed yourself? You need to get some rest."

She fished a cigarette from her pocket and sheltered her head in her jacket against the wind. I could smell the acrid scent of the smoke before I could see it. Eleanor tipped her head back and took a deep drag. "I will...He looks pretty comfortable right at the moment."

I left Eleanor's place that night almost thankful that this ordeal was about to end. O'Brian would surely be dead and gone by morning. I was tired of struggling with him, and I knew that Eleanor was at the end of her rope. By the time I got home, the rain had given way to sleet and the wipers were having trouble keeping up. When I took Lug for a run a half hour later, huge white flakes filled the air and an inch of slush had already accumulated.

I tossed and turned for hours that night. My mind was in constant turmoil, jumping from different things I should have tried with O'Brian to worries about Eleanor's health. I don't know what time I finally drifted off, but I do know that it wasn't long before the telephone woke me again. It was a calving in Lister.

Heavy snow had fallen in the short while I'd been asleep—at least five inches on the street—and the way it was coming down, there'd be twice as much by morning. I kept thinking of O'Brian out there in the snow; surely this would hasten his parting and put an end to Eleanor's struggle.

As far as calvings went, this one was relatively simple and satisfying. The calf had been presented in the breech position with nothing but the tail protruding through the lips of the vulva. Joe Pogany had struggled to straighten it on his own and finally given up. Within a few minutes, I produced the feet that he had been unable to find. Once the legs were straightened, the cow delivered virtually on her own. It was a bonus to watch those first few breaths in the life of a newborn calf and know that I had something to do with making it all possible.

Although I was desperate for more sleep, I found my car taking the long way home. As I drove along the back road towards Canyon, the snow was coming down so heavily that I had a hard time seeing the edge of the road. It was a little after four in the morning when I pulled up in front of Eleanor's gate. Not daring to veer off into the deep bank left by the snowplow, I eased to the edge of the road and pulled on the four-way flashers.

Standing in snow up to my boot tops, I wrestled with the chain on the wooden gate and pried it open enough to squeeze through. I was pleased to see no light in the house, no tracks in the new snow. Eleanor had finally given up the struggle and gone to bed.

I lowered my head and trudged through the drifts, hoping that the battle was over. "Please God, let O'Brian be dead!" I was almost past the house when I shone my flashlight onto the verandah. It didn't register till I had taken a few more steps—the twine was on the door, tying it shut from the outside.

I rushed to untangle the string and push the door open. I could hear cats scatter like a pack of rats at my advance. Taking a deep breath of night air, I stepped inside. There was a stirring of bodies in the room as cats gravitated to the furthest corners; their yellow eyes gleamed back at me from the darkness.

"Eleanor! Eleanor, are you here?"

I shone the light around the room. There was no sign of her. She hadn't been in the house since before the snow had started!

"Damn you, Eleanor! Where the hell are you?"

I rushed out the door, not bothering to tie it shut. Eleanor was out there in the storm. She'd probably had a heart attack or a stroke and been unable to make it back to the house.

I was running by the time I hit the end of the verandah. Somewhere under the snow, my boot landed on a concealed board that was slick from the moisture. My feet flew out from under me and I went sprawling. Soaked to the skin, I picked myself up and kept going. The sleet was still falling in huge wet flakes and water ran down my face as it melted in my hair.

I was in a state of panic when I reached the heap of snow that was obviously O'Brian. There was another mound not ten feet away; I rushed over and plunged my hands through it. I was relieved to find the scattered remains of a bale of hay. My heart thumping, I shone the light around the surrounding area, fully expecting to find Eleanor's body beneath the snow.

Nothing! I began to feel a bit foolish for jumping to conclusions. Maybe Eleanor had gone to stay with Chris. But, I had never known her to spend a night away. No, no way would she leave home at a time like this.

I scraped at the heavy snow in search of the tarp covering O'Brian and was finally able to work an end of the canvas free. I lifted it and the blankets enough to expose O'Brian's body, wanting access to his chest so I could listen to his heart.

There was no movement at all. At first, I was sure he was dead, but no, I could see the vibration of his chest wall. His heart was beating. There it was again. And there, he took a breath. I listened to his heart rate—only twenty-eight beats per minute, but still going and still strong. He just didn't know how to quit!

I grasped the edge of the tarp and gave it a heave, throwing the accumulated snow back as far as possible. When I lifted the blanket and sleeping bag away from his head, I couldn't believe my eyes. Curled up in the crevice between O'Brian's head and legs was Eleanor—fast asleep.

Startled by the flashlight, she looked for all the world like a deer caught in the headlights of an oncoming car. Her eyes filled with terror; she was totally bewildered. She fought to stand, crumpled and fell.

"It's okay, Nell...It's okay! It's Dave! It's Dave!"

I extended my hand to help her up. She sat for a moment trying to orient herself, then clutched O'Brian and pushed herself up.

"I'm sorry to startle you like that, Eleanor, but I was worried sick about you. I had no idea where you were."

She fumbled about in her jacket for her pack of smokes. With still trembling hands, she struck a match to light one.

"Are you all right?" I felt like a fool.

"I'm fine!" Her voice was terse. "I'm just fine."

I went on to examine O'Brian while Eleanor calmed her nerves. His pulse was strong; if anything, I thought he was looking better. O'Brian wasn't going to make this easy.

"I'm sorry that I woke you up so rudely, Eleanor. I had no idea you were in there with him. Did you get any sleep?"

"As a matter of fact, I did." I detected just a trace of a smile. "What do you think of O'Brian?" Straightening her posture, she ran her fingers through her soggy hair. Her jacket was already covered with a garnish of wet snow.

"I don't know what to think of him, Eleanor. He doesn't look any worse. If anything, his eyes are brighter."

"I thought that earlier this evening," she replied, taking a deep drag on her cigarette. We pulled the blankets and tarp over the horse, and I escorted Eleanor to the door of her house. To the best of my knowledge, she spent the rest of the night inside, but God only knows for sure.

I was on my way downstairs the following morning when Doris hollered at me. "Eleanor's on the phone for you!"

"I just thought you'd want to know," she started in a controlled tone, "that O'Brian is up. I went out this morning with a bucket of warm water and a hot bran mash. He took a bit of each." She stopped for a moment and, in my mind's eye, I could see her take a long pull on her cigarette. Her voice became animated. "As soon as I dragged off the tarp and blankets, he stood up. I knew he would. I just knew he would."

O'Brian rallied slowly as his devoted keeper babied him with hot bran mashes and pelleted alfalfa. He never did look like much, but he fit in nicely with the motley collection of critters that Eleanor knew as family.

Jade and Jets

"That damn mare's the only one around here that doesn't earn her keep!" David Rayfield was complaining about the overweight quarter horse that stood in the next box stall munching on a big mouthful of hay.

"You ride her once in a while, don't you?" I asked, as he grabbed her halter.

"Isabel rode her once this spring when we went out for a weekend fishing trip," he growled. "Jade balked, dumped her in the creek, and we came home the same night we left!"

"Is she that flighty or just not good in the mountains?"

"She certainly has a mind of her own." David gave the horse a look of disgust. "It doesn't help that Isabel hardly ever rides her. When she does ride, she lets Jade have her own way all the time."

I carried my bucket and deworming medication from the last stall and stepped inside with her as David snapped the lead shank on the halter and brought her head around to face me. She chewed jealously at the few remaining strands of hay that protruded from her mouth, then swallowed them quickly, as if convinced that we would steal them from her.

Measuring out Jade's medication, I slipped the chain of the twitch over her nose and twisted the handle upward to tighten it. The mare tossed her head in a defiant attempt to shake the twitch loose, snorted, and stared straight ahead, her eyes filled with anticipation.

"She's a big bluffer, really," David said, holding firmly to her halter. "Once she knows who's boss, she's not too hard to work with."

I slipped the transparent plastic tube from the bucket of water and recoiled it in a tight circle. I inserted the tapered end into her left nostril and pushed it smoothly along the floor of her nasal cavity. Jade's eyes focused fully on me, her fear and disgust palpable. I tipped the coil over, rotating the end of the tube upward, and moved it back and forth until she swallowed. Once she had, I puffed air into the tube and advanced it down her esophagus. A gush of gas smelling of fresh-mown hay announced my entry into the stomach. Grabbing the dose syringe, I flushed the worming medication down the tube and followed it with a couple of squirts of water.

"Don't know why we bother with you, Jade!" David rambled on. "You're fatter than a pig and don't do a thing around here to make yourself useful. I should breed you to a grade stallion and get a foal out of you just to make you earn your keep."

The way David was going on about the mare, it was obvious that she had been on his mind for some time. The other seven horses all had a reason for existence—the two yearlings would be sold in a few months, the four Thoroughbred mares were pregnant and would produce next year's foal crop, and the gelding was David's own personal mount, which he rode on a regular basis.

A week later, David showed up at the office at quitting time. For some reason, the afternoon had been relatively slow, and it was a treat to see a flesh and blood customer walk in.

"Just thought I'd stop in and get a couple rolls of that bandage material you use to wrap the mares' tails when you pregnancy test them. That mare of Isabel's has come into heat, and I've decided to breed her to an Appaloosa stud that's just down the road from me. Her freeloader days are over!"

"Whose stallion is it? I wasn't aware that anyone had a stallion in your neck of the woods."

"Joe Strand just bought the horse a couple of weeks ago. He's going to breed his own mares to him, then get him castrated."

"So it's not a registered stallion?"

"Hell no!" David chuckled. "He's six or seven years old and has been running on pasture somewhere out on the prairie until two weeks ago. They used him last year to pasture breed a few mares, and he was supposed to have settled all of them. As long as I get that mare bred, I'll be happy—she's not papered either."

"This sounds like it could be quite a show!"

"If you have nothing better to do, you should come along with me. We may just need you to sew something up before everything's said and done. I'm heading home to get the mare and walk her down right now."

"I wouldn't want to miss this. I'll meet you at your place in fifteen minutes."

I pulled into their driveway to find Isabel holding the mare while David attempted to wrap her long tail. Lug stood on the seat and wagged with excitement. "You forget it, fella, you're just a spectator today."

By the look of the hoof marks in the gravel, they'd been at it for a while and still hadn't finished. "Hold her still, will you, Isabel!" David was not amused when the mare made another circle around the driveway, dragging him behind her. "Damn it, anyway. Why does this stuff keep sliding down to the bottom like a pair of old lady's panty hose?"

I took the bandage material, carefully rewrapped it on the roll, then took one turn around the base of the tail. After applying it, I quickly folded a clump of hair from the base of the bandage back on top and buried it with a subsequent wrap.

"Just keep folding a bit of hair back once in a while; it'll anchor the bandage so it won't slide down. After you do that a couple of times, you should be able to just wrap the bottom part of the tail and not worry about it slipping."

Within a few minutes, Jade's tail was wrapped, and we headed off down the driveway.

"I'll leave this adventure to you guys," Isabel called after us. "I'll have supper ready by the time you get back."

Jade plodded along at David's heels until she realized she was actually leaving home, then whinnied to the mares that raced up and down on the other side of the corral. With legs planted, she turned her head and struggled against David to go back.

"Jade!" He yanked on her lead shank. "I'm not Isabel!"

A few well-placed whacks with the end of the nylon belt convinced Jade she shouldn't protest too much and, with a quick look behind her, she fell in line. We walked the half mile to Joe Strand's place with Jade parading back and forth on the end of the shank, nickering and calling to every horse that we passed along the way.

Joe and his wife, Edna, were waiting at their driveway. As we approached, he spoke to her and she hustled off into the house.

"We're all ready for you! The wife's just getting the ice water ready."

David and I gave one another a questioning look. "Am I missing something?" I whispered.

"I haven't got a clue."

Joe was a short, stocky man in his late fifties. His hair was grey, with the slightest indication that it may have been a dark brown in his earlier years. He had it buzzed close to his head and covered by a New York Yankees' baseball cap pulled down tightly to ears that perched at a forty-five-degree angle to his head. He looked nervous, and he was unsure about how to start with the breeding of his first mare.

"That mare of yours is healthy is she, David?" Joe circled her and eyed her up and down.

"She should be," David scoffed, "other than being too damn fat. This is my vet, Dave Perrin, if you want to ask him."

"No, no, that's fine. She looks good to me. That's a pretty fancy wrap you've got on her tail."

"It'll keep the hair from getting in the stallion's way," David responded.

250

As if on cue, a sudden high-pitched squeal echoed from the barn. Joe glanced hesitantly in that direction, then said, with an obvious lack of enthusiasm, "Well, I guess I better go and see if I can get a halter shank on 'im."

Jade answered with a high-pitched whinny of her own, and there was a new response from within the barn accompanied by the sound of hooves connecting with a wooden wall.

"Settle down, Jets! Settle down!" came Joe's impassioned plea.

"This looks like it could be interesting," I muttered to David, as he gave Jade's halter shank a crank and pulled her around to face us.

The next fifteen minutes were punctuated by squeals and whinnying from both the barn and the yard. Jade circled around and around until the driveway began to look like a plowed field. Mrs. Strand waddled from the house carrying a three-gallon bucket brimming with water and ice cubes. She walked to within ten feet of us, then set it down and shot a concerned look in the direction of the barn.

"This may sound like a stupid question," I asked hesitantly, "but what's the ice water for?"

"Well, to throw on the mare's back after she's been bred." She was obviously surprised by my ignorance. "Joe says it'll make her tuck her back down and keep the stallion's juice from leaking out."

"Oh."

"I don't know where he came up with the fool notion of buying this stallion anyway." She was talking as much to herself as to us. "He went on for weeks about how much money he was going to save in stud fees, but right at the moment those fees would sound pretty cheap!"

An awkward silence followed. I was searching for words to respond to Mrs. Strand when we heard a tremendous commotion. Joe released a tirade of cursing, and there was a sudden flurry of activity at the entrance to the barn.

Jets erupted from the doorway, dragging the almost insignificant Mr. Strand behind him. Once free of the low building, the horse stood up and literally walked on his hind legs across the distance between us. Jets was ready for work, his penis standing erect and perpendicular to his body.

"Get down! Get down, you son of a bitch!" Joe hollered, yanking on the chain lead that was ineffectually fastened to the bottom of the halter.

Jade swung her rear end in Jets's direction. Holding her tail to the side, she squirted small volumes of urine and winked her vulva. Jets squealed and lunged forward, hitting Jade on the side and knocking her down.

"Try and get him under control!" David hollered, as Jade scrambled to her feet, and he struggled to get her away from the still airborne stallion.

For what seemed an age, Joe howled and yanked on the halter shank that kept lifting him from the ground. The horse completely dominated him and threw him about as he pleased. Mrs. Strand danced around, struggling to salvage the precious bucket of ice water but, with every lunge, she spilled more and more onto her own clothing and around the yard.

It took over ten minutes of struggling for Joe to steady the stallion. David had taken Jade down the road out of sight where she pranced and carried on. I grabbed hold of Jets's halter shank and helped anchor him to the ground. Undoing the snap to the lead shank, I slipped the chain portion through the metal eye at the side of the halter and over the horse's nose. Now every time he reared, the chain would carry the full weight of Joe's body on the bridge of his nose.

"We're as ready as we're going to be!" Joe hollered.

As soon as David led Jade near, Jets was airborne once more, carrying Joe along like a fly in the wind. Over the next ten minutes, Jets mounted Jade in every direction but the right one. He knocked her down two more times and had thrown Joe around so mercilessly that the man had all but given up. The only thing in Joe's favour was that Jets himself was wearing down; his nostrils were flared as he fought for air, and sweat poured like water from under his chest. We separated them once again, and I took the mare down the road while David and Joe planned their strategy.

Jade's interest in the event was beginning to fade. She had several bite wounds on the side of her neck and was limping slightly from the last time that Jets had knocked her down. She still occasionally answered his whinny, but acted now as if she would happily walk home.

It was David's hollering that got my attention; they had obviously concocted a plan and were going to have another go at it. I led Jade to the yard once more to find that Jets had been taken behind the barn.

"You hold Jade's head, Dave!" he hollered to me excitedly, "and I'll keep her rear end over and guide the stallion's penis. He's inexperienced and obviously doesn't know where to stick it but, if we can line them up properly, he should be able to breed her."

Jets pranced around the corner of the barn, but this time his front feet were on the ground. Joe was alternately leading him and yanking on the shank to make him conscious of the chain over his nose. The stallion's final approach could almost be described as controlled. He was ten feet away from Jade's rear end when he stood on his hind legs and advanced.

David stood by Jade's hindquarters, his eyes focused on the penis which, this time, was pointing more or less in the right direction. Jets's front feet went over Jade's back, and I thought that this time he had finally figured it out. He thrust once, his penis diverting off the top of Jade's tail. He thrust again, and his penis deviated to the side.

"Get ready with the water, Edna!" Joe bellowed.

With intense concentration, Mrs. Strand held the bucket at waist height; she was focused and ready to throw. Her bucket was now barely half full and her clothes were thoroughly soaked from the spillage. David dove forward in a desperate attempt to grab the stallion's penis and direct it into Jade's vagina. Jets lunged. David let out a holler as the penis made its way up his shirt sleeve; Jets ejaculated into his armpit. As if on command, Mrs. Strand let loose with her water just as David jumped aside. The water cascaded in a perfect arch to come splashing down over his head.

Jets slid off Jade's back and I led her ahead. David stood dripping wet, a look of dejection on his face. Long strands of wet hair dangled forward, exposing the bald forehead that he normally covered carefully with judicial combing. Water dripped off his nose and chin, accumulating in a puddle on the driveway.

We walked in silence on the way home. David didn't speak from the time we left the Strands' driveway until we reached his own, and Jade plodded along behind him without paying the slightest heed to the horses she passed along the way. David trudged to the barn to put Jade in her box stall, and I hopped in my car and drove home.

I dealt with the Rayfields on a regular basis over the ensuing years, and Jade was a permanent fixture during that time. She was just as fat, just as lazy, and just as cantankerous as ever, but not once after that day did I hear David comment on her. He certainly never mentioned wanting a foal out of her again.

The Sample

I hung up the receiver and slouched against the wall. "Looks like lunch is cancelled again today, Doris...unless you're into a quick peanut butter sandwich on stale bread."

"What's up now?" Doris finished wrapping the surgery instruments in the green cotton serge, then tucked and taped the long, pointed flap.

"Sounds like Trixie White's back is acting up again. She bit John when he tried to pick her up, and Emily's fit to be tied."

"Oh that poor dear...first her husband, now the dog. Walter just got out of the hospital again last week, and from what Lois was telling me the other day, he still isn't doing well."

"I know. He's been off work for months now and he looks terrible."

"And of course, there's John...I can't help but think if they'd had more children, life would have been easier. There must be days when that poor girl doesn't know how she can carry on!"

I sorted through the drawer until I came up with Emily White's file, then pulled out Trixie's card. In the last few months, we had dealt with the dog on four occasions. The first two visits had been for back problems, the third had been a broken dewclaw. The final visit, only ten days ago, had been an abscessed anal gland.

Ten minutes later, the door burst open and a tall, gaunt man with a bushy beard strode to the middle of the waiting room. Stopping abruptly, he stood with a blank expression on his face.

255

Clutched tightly to his breast was a sleek-looking miniature dachshund. Her big brown eyes bugged as she surveyed the room. Even from where I was standing, I could see her body vibrating.

"Hello there, John. You've brought Trixie for me to examine, have you?"

I thought I detected a nod of his shaggy head before he followed me to the exam room. I pried Trixie's shaking body from his hands and set her on the table. John stood as rigid as a statue, his hands positioned almost as they had been when carrying the dog, his long, thin, nicotine-stained fingers pointing haphazardly to the ceiling like spindly seedlings growing towards a distant light. On two fingers of his right hand were fresh Band-Aids.

"Have you seen her move her hind legs at all, John?" I watched the poor dog sink to the table without trying to support herself.

John stared straight ahead as if in a trance. He gave no indication that he'd heard my question. I grabbed Trixie's flaccid tail and squeezed it with ever increasing force. Only when the pressure was intense did she attempt to pull away.

Paddling her hind legs in an uncoordinated fashion, she pushed forward and lifted her abdomen from the tabletop, then slowly allowed her legs to slide away until they splayed behind her like a seal. She panicked and her front feet scratched wildly for traction on the stainless steel surface. I lifted her gently to my chest and pulled her against me.

"Easy, Trixie, easy. Settle down now, girl."

Her body was rigid and trembled uncontrollably; her bulging eyes emanated fear and pain. She looked anxiously at John, hoping to be rescued, but he was somewhere else—somewhere in a different time or a different place.

"Doris! Can you give me a hand!"

Doris attempted to get into position to hold Trixie, but John stood his ground in the middle of the action. Reaching from the end of the table, she took the quivering dog from me and spoke reassuringly. "It's okay, Trixie."

Without saying a word, John fished into his pocket, withdrew a pack of cigarettes, and headed outside. Trixie struggled to follow him, but soon gave in to lie quietly in Doris's arms.

"She doesn't look very strong on those hind legs, Dave. Was she this bad last time?"

"Last time she had a lot of pain, but her legs were strong. The X-rays showed several calcified discs, but I couldn't find anything else of significance."

I gently poked over the top of Trixie's spine with a needle. With each prick, the loose skin over her back contracted and wiggled until I reached the end of her ribs. At that point, she yipped and whipped her head around to bite at my hand.

"Watch out!" Doris squawked. The dog's teeth grazed my finger.

"Easy, Trixie, easy girl, I know it hurts. We just have to find out what's wrong with you."

Doris got a better grip on Trixie's head as I continued my examination. There was no doubt that her pain was most intense over the spine at the level of the last rib. Beyond that point, her sensation diminished dramatically. Poking her with the needle further down the spine garnered hardly any response whatsoever.

To test her reflexes, I held the dog and positioned her until the top of her hind legs touched the edge of the table. Her legs hung limply.

"She doesn't feel them, does she?"

"It sure doesn't look like it. A normal dog would have lifted its feet to the table."

I grasped the toes of her right foot and gave them a firm squeeze. The pressure was intense when she finally looked back at me and made a weak effort to withdraw. Pinching the toes on the opposite foot produced similar results.

"I better give Emily a call. This doesn't look good."

She answered the phone on the first ring. "It's Dave, Emily. I've had a good look at Trixie. She's lost a lot of sensation and most of the movement to her hind legs. I need to take some X-rays to confirm my suspicions, but the symptoms suggest a ruptured disc in the middle of her back, about the level of the last rib. I suspect a lot of swelling in the spinal cord itself."

"Oh my, I was afraid things were more serious this time. I've never seen her act like this before. She spent the entire morning huddled under the coffee table...Is there anything we can do for her?"

"I'll get her started on anti-inflammatories right away to try and shrink the swelling, but if you want the best for her, we should get her to the veterinary college at Pullman for surgery. The sooner the pressure over the cord is removed, the more likely she is to regain full function of her hind end."

"Oh, Dave!" Emily sobbed. "There's no way we can consider something like that right now. If Walter weren't off work, we could think about it, but right now it's totally impossible."

"Well, that's what I needed to know. We can treat her medically. It's just that if surgery were an option, we would get best results if it were done soon after the disc prolapse. We'll start her on medication right now and see what happens."

"So you really think surgery could help? Walter has a bad back, and the doctor told him years ago that he may need surgery...He seems to keep managing without it."

"I know from experience how painful disc problems can be, but humans are different from dogs. When we have a bulging disc, it presses on nerves that come off the cord but, in the dog, the pressure is applied on the spinal cord itself. In many cases, unless it's relieved, the loss of function can be permanent."

"Oh my," Emily muttered.

"Trixie can still feel deep pain in her hind legs, so there's a decent chance she'll be able to walk normally and regain control of her bowels. I just want you to realize that her best odds would be with decompression surgery as soon as it could be done."

"So, she could be paralyzed?"

"Yes. It depends to some degree on the damage, and how successful we are at keeping it from getting worse. I'll be able to give you a better idea once I've taken some X-rays."

"You know how much we love that little dog, Dave. I don't know how we'd get along without her. It'd be hard enough for Walter and me if she doesn't make it, but it would be something else for John! He isn't one to show much affection, but he lives for Trixie. He was devastated this morning when she bit him. For his sake, I hope you don't have to keep her there."

"I'm afraid we won't have much choice but to hospitalize her, Emily. We'll need to give her medication by injection and keep her confined so her disc can heal."

"Is John still there?"

"He went outside for a cigarette. I'm assuming he'll be back."

"He'll be back, and he won't be happy about going home without her."

Doris and I had started an intravenous drip and given the first round of injections by the time John returned to the waiting room. His furry face plopped on his left hand, he sat staring vacantly at the Band-Aids on his wounded fingers.

"Trixie has a very serious problem with her back, John. We need to keep her here for treatment or she may never be able to walk again."

He continued to stare grudgingly at his fingers.

"She's in agony, John…you know she wouldn't have bitten you otherwise. Whenever she moves, terrible pains shoot through her back. Sometimes when people are hurting, they strike out at those they love, too. Dogs are no different."

I was hoping for a response—some inkling that my words had been understood. John's face remained expressionless. I studied him for several minutes, certain that wheels were turning somewhere. Surely he would blink, frown, look away, do something. Dealing with him on a daily basis must be difficult—poor Emily. Finally, I shook my head in frustration and returned to Trixie.

The Demerol had done wonders to calm her down. She lay

quietly, her long nose outstretched, her hind legs extended. Her eyes were closed, her breathing more relaxed.

"We'll take those X-rays now, Doris. Just check the developer and make sure the chemicals are up to temperature."

I scooped Trixie from the kennel as gently as possible. Her back was rigid as I moved her; she grunted with each breath. The look in her eyes suggested I had better watch my own fingers.

"Doris, would you grab me a roll of gauze? I don't feel like getting bit right at the moment."

I settled Trixie on the X-ray table, unravelled three feet of gauze, and looped it over her nose. I tied it first on the top of her muzzle, then under her jaw. Finally, I brought it behind her head and tied it again.

"That's a girl, Trixie. We just want to keep you honest."

Centring the beam over her spine at the end of the rib cage, we stretched the dog on her side and exposed the first plate. The shot of her lying on her back was quite another thing. Every time we were ready to shoot, her snakelike body twisted into the shape of a pretzel.

"Now, Doris!" The machine gave a decisive clunk. We had captured Trixie in a moment of immobility.

The X-rays were as good as could be expected without a general anesthetic. The disc space at the end of the thorax was non-existent; a number of other discs were calcified. Trixie was a candidate for similar problems in the years to come. Her X-rays were typical of a very old dog—hardly what one would expect from a four-year-old!

John sat in the waiting room until his parents showed up hours later. When the disheartened family came in to view the films, I tried to sound optimistic. "It's a matter of staying the course and seeing what next week will bring."

Walter stared dejectedly at the view box. His face was ashen; each breath he drew seemed to take a major effort. With his shoulders hunched and his gut hanging sloppily over his belt, just staying erect appeared an onerous task. He gazed sadly at Emily. "I guess we'll just have to wait and see, honey. There isn't much else we can do." Beside him, John stared passively at the view box.

"Well, Dave, we'll leave Trixie in your hands." Emily sighed deeply. "I know you're doing everything you can for her here. We discussed taking her to Pullman; even if we could afford it, we have so much else going on in our lives that there's no way we'd be able to take her."

Walter and Emily ambled through the waiting room with John shuffling reluctantly behind them. The sight of the trio filing through the office became commonplace. They came together at least three times a day during the next week and made special arrangements to visit on Sunday as well. John frequently showed up alone. He would come in and simply sit. He never spoke to other clients, never asked me any questions about Trixie. Numerous times, I invited him to the kennel room to visit his dog, but he didn't accept. Each time, he gazed past me, not willing or not able to acknowledge my presence.

Trixie improved remarkably. For the first two days, her bladder was flaccid and I had to empty it by applying external pressure. As time went on, however, the bladder wall regained its tone and the dog was able to empty it without help. She began to have less and less pain from her back and, by the end of the week, was standing and able to make hesitant but steady steps on her own.

Emily showed up as we were working Trixie's legs in a tub full of warm water. We had been shooting for today for Trixie's discharge, and I wanted to make sure that Emily fully understood everything she would have to do.

"Walking her around like that in our tub should be no problem at all," Emily observed. "She's always liked baths."

"It's very important for her to be confined. If you keep her quiet, she'll have the opportunity to heal properly and this disc won't be a problem in the future."

"Does she have to be in that cage all the time?" Emily looked askance at the three-foot-square steel kennel.

"There's no reason she can't lie quietly on your lap while you're watching television. Just make sure she doesn't jump down or get dropped, or we may be back to where we started."

"And we can keep on feeding her what she normally eats? She gets half a can of Dr. Ballard's twice a day."

"That should be just fine, but I'd like you to add some bran to try and maintain a soft stool. We'll have to watch that she doesn't get constipated for the first little while."

A frown creased Emily's delicate features. "We'll have a hard time reasoning with John that she's to stay confined in that kennel."

"As long as he understands that she shouldn't walk, jump down, or get dropped. You'll be just fine even if John wants to carry her around all day."

"Oh good, I've been worried sick about how to keep those two apart. John's really very gentle with her, and he seems to have forgiven her for biting him."

"Keep your eyes open for anything unusual. Make sure you carry her outside to pee and always have the leash on her. Dogs with spinal cord problems commonly end up with urinary tract infections, so watch how often she pees and check for blood in her urine."

Emily carried Trixie from the office and deposited her in John's lap in the front seat of the car. John sat silently; his hand stroked the dog's head rhythmically. On his face was an expression that could have passed for contentment.

Trixie improved rapidly. By the end of the second week, she was able to stand firmly on her hind legs and coordinate them well enough to walk in a straight line. She showed no evidence of constant discomfort. The Whites were content that, even if she improved no further, she would be able to get around adequately and live a happy life.

A month later, I was on my way up the street for a quick lunch at the Depot Restaurant when I heard Emily's voice ring out. "Dave! Dave, can I talk to you for a second?"

I walked to the corner and waited for her to cross. "Hello, Emily. How are things with Trixie?"

"She's getting steadier on her feet every day, but this morning I noticed this in the bottom of her cage." She rummaged through her purse to produce a plastic bag containing a rag soaked with blood. "That's just a piece of an old sheet that I tore up to put in the bottom of her kennel. I'm afraid she may have something wrong inside. You mentioned that blood in the urine might mean a urinary infection."

"That'd be the most likely explanation." I lifted the cloth to my nose for a quick whiff. "It's not impossible that she could have vomited blood, but this definitely smells like urine."

"Would you like me to have John bring her in again this afternoon? I'm on my break and have to get back to work."

"Would you have time to whip home and get a urine sample? It would really speed things up for us if you could collect some in a shallow pan like a pie plate. Just put it into a clean jar that you sterilize with boiling water. That way, John can bring it in when he comes with Trixie. We'll be able to check it out for signs of infection and get her on antibiotics right away if necessary."

Emily glanced at her watch, then shot a worried look at the store where she worked. "Well, if I rush, I should be able to make it home and get the sample without being late." She tore off down the street and hollered over her shoulder. "I'll call Doris from the store to get an appointment time."

The office was already buzzing when I got back from lunch. My first appointment of the afternoon was a vaccination, and Doris was taking the cat's temperature. A black Lab puffed nervously in the middle of the waiting room; his owner knelt on the floor next to him holding a blood-soaked towel tightly around his foot. Bernie Meekes and Morris Hanson, both local dairymen, stood near the counter chatting patiently with one another as they waited for Doris to return and help them out with the supplies they required.

The Sample

Emily had phoned to say that John would be in with Trixie and the sample. She was concerned at the amount of blood in the urine and was anxious for us to see Trixie as soon as possible. I slipped into my smock and got to work. By the time John arrived, I was still a long way from catching up with the waiting clients.

Thinking that I'd get a jump on treatment, I slipped out between appointments and asked John for the sample so I could spin it in the centrifuge and examine it before checking the dog. He sat stoically, staring straight ahead.

"Excuse me, John!" My voice had enough of an edge that it seemed to penetrate the haze. Mrs. Morris squirmed uncomfortably and shifted her poodle from the seat beside her onto her knee. "Your mother collected a sample for me to examine—a sample of Trixie's urine. Did you bring it?"

His shaggy head rotated slowly from side to side.

"So you forgot to bring the sample?" I struggled to maintain my cool.

This time his head moved up and down. I stomped to the back room and returned with a stainless steel collection bowl. Holding it out in front of John, I waited for him to take it. Mrs. Morris watched our interaction with great interest; she snickered self-consciously as the standoff continued.

"I'd appreciate it if you could collect some pee before we have a look at Trixie. It's important for me to see what's going on in her bladder, and the urine sample will be the best way for me to do that. Do you understand, John?"

He sat for another minute staring at the bowl.

"John!" My face was flushed; my voice betrayed my agitation. The poodle, Pepsi, buried her head in her mistress's bosom. John finally shifted Trixie in his arms to grab the bowl. He headed out the front door, and I ushered Mrs. Morris to the examination room.

By the time I finished trimming Pepsi's nails, John had returned. I rushed to the waiting room to retrieve the sample, concerned that he might spill it on the carpet. I stared in dismay at the bowl in his hand. It was full to the brim with clear, straw-coloured urine. As Trixie shifted her weight, some of the contents tipped into John's lap and onto the bench.

I carried the bowl gingerly to the back and dipped a urine stick into the liquid. Comparing the impregnated tabs with the colour chart on the side of the container, I discovered that everything in the sample was completely within normal range. There wasn't the slightest trace of blood.

My mind was whirling. There was no question that the sample John had brought me was indeed urine, but I was equally sure from both the consistency and the volume that it was not Trixie's.

When I finally plucked the dog from John's lap, he followed me to the exam table. Settling Trixie with her hind legs firmly planted under her, I palpated her abdomen, slipping the contents between my fingers. Her bladder was in fact still full!

"Would you grab me a bowl so we can express a sample, Doris?"

She gave me a strange look. "You mean, she still has some urine in her?"

"Quite a bit, really."

John actually paid attention as I applied pressure to the dog's abdomen. He stared blankly as urine flowed into the container. I glanced at him as I left with the dish full of catsup-coloured fluid to start a sample spinning. Was that a trace of a smile?

Doris followed me into the lab. "How could her urine change so quickly?" I could tell she was genuinely puzzled.

"It didn't! Emily said that the sample she got this morning was almost straight blood, and this one's certainly loaded with it. The other specimen isn't from the same critter."

"What do you mean?"

"Well, there's no way that Trixie could have peed that much this morning to begin with. That bowl was brimming—and look at how much was in her bladder again."

"You don't mean that John...Nooo!"

Microscopic examination revealed that Trixie's urine was loaded with red cells, white cells, and bacteria. I smeared a sample onto a blood agar plate to grow colonies of the bacteria present. The next day, I would replate the culture with antibiotic sensitivity discs to make sure that the medicine I had chosen would kill the organism.

Trixie's recovery was uneventful from that point forward. She was never a hundred percent normal on her hind legs and was prone to urinary infections for the rest of her life. Emily coped with a myriad of family worries and dog problems, but we relieved her of one responsibility. We never asked her to collect another urine sample from Trixie.

Entrapment

"Your vet student is downstairs." Shirley was struggling to keep a straight face. "Says you're expecting her."

I smiled sheepishly. "Pat Clark asked if I'd let his student come in and observe when things are slow at the government office. He thought it would give her experience with something other than regulatory work. Besides, she might be a big help in the off-hours."

Shirley broke into laughter. "She sure might! Have you met her yet?"

"No, she only just started with Pat this week."

"Well, you're in for a treat. They aren't making vets like they used to."

"What's that supposed to mean?"

Shirley trotted off. "Come see for yourself."

Apprehensively, I followed her down the stairs. A very shapely young lady was silhouetted in front of the aquarium. It didn't take long to notice that the Levis she wore were filled out very nicely. Shirley was right; they weren't making vets like they used to.

"Hello," I stammered. "I'm Dave Perrin."

She turned to face me. Her dark blonde shoulder-length hair framed winsome facial features. She regarded me with expressive blue eyes.

"Hi, Dr. Perrin. I'm Marcie Harris." She extended her hand in a firm shake.

"You're going into your final year at the Western College?"

"Yes, doesn't seem possible that this is the last one."

I turned to see Shirley duck around the corner of the surgery. She and Doris were watching the introductions with more interest than I thought necessary.

"I'll be working with Dr. Clark for the entire summer. It doesn't sound like my position will be too onerous. I suspect I'll have quite a bit of free time to see cases with you, if you don't mind my hanging around."

"That sounds fine with me. You can come and go as your job allows…and I can give you a call if we have any interesting cases after hours."

"That's exactly what I was hoping for." Marcie was even more attractive when she smiled. "The more experience I can get this summer, the better. I would have preferred to work in a general practice, but this job with the government pays a lot better. You know what it's like surviving as a student—every nickel counts."

"Boy, do I…hasn't been that long ago for me either." Our eyes met for a brief moment and we both smiled. "Are you finished for the day?"

"Yes. We just got back from inspecting seven imported horses at the American border, and Pat told me to skedaddle."

"I'm going on a horse call if you'd like to tag along."

"Sure. I've got my coveralls in the car."

We left the office a few moments later. As we strolled to my vehicle, I glanced back at the office. Both Doris and Shirley were peering out the surgery window.

"Dave Lougheed is a new client. I met him through the Rayfields, who are good horse clients. They do a lot of riding together, and Rayfield has been bugging Lougheed about tube deworming his horses…Have you had a chance to deworm many critters at college?"

Marcie shook her head. "Only the few that we got to do in medical exercises."

"We'll see how things go. Maybe we can get you doing some before the summer's out."

I wound my way through the orchards of Erickson, past the cemetery, and onto a road that scaled the butt of Goat Mountain. Marcie wasn't saying much, and I found myself searching for small talk and intelligent questions. I found out that she had grown up in B.C. and would love to return. We traversed several sharp switchbacks, climbed a narrow roadway, and turned off onto an even steeper driveway. I parked next to a well-seasoned logging truck.

"Dave's an industrious guy," I commented. "I don't know if he finished high school, but there's not much he won't attempt. He bought that truck and a position to haul logs at the Crestbrook mill ahead of dozens of guys twice his age. He and his wife have built this house from the footings up."

Marcie scanned the nicely finished home and the well-fitted outbuildings and raised her eyebrows in appreciation. A tall, slender man strode briskly towards us from a barn on the brow of the hill. Dressed in a wool Mackinaw and blue jeans, a broad-brimmed brown hat and well-worn boots, he looked every bit the cowboy.

"Brought some help, did you?" The handsome blond gave us a toothy smile as he approached.

"This is Marcie Harris. Marcie...Dave Lougheed." Dave nodded and extended his hand. "Marcie's a student at the vet college...graduates next spring."

"Good for you. Where'd you like to start? We got four horses to worm and then there's Snip, that little filly that I talked to you about. She's been limpin' for better than two weeks now."

"Let's start with the worming. Has the filly been improving, or is the lameness about the same?"

"Hasn't been much change since it happened."

On the way to the barn, I stopped at an upright hydrant and filled my bucket with water. Following Dave, Marcie carried the bottle of dewormer along with the tube, funnel, measuring cup, and an assortment of farrier tools. Four horses stood secured to a hitch rail. Dave untied the lead rope of a heavy-chested quarter horse gelding and led him forward. "Where'd you like to do 'em?"

"Right here's fine; if they act up, just back them into the barn wall." Dave held the horse's head as I applied the chain twitch to his lip and secured it. I passed the handle to Marcie.

"There's a boy, Griz," Dave reassured the horse, while I introduced the tube into his nostril and advanced it down his throat. "Rayfield's been givin' me a hard time about gettin' these guys done...keeps tellin' me I'd save more in hay than it costs me."

He stood by, slowly massaging the gelding's neck as we measured out the dewormer and flushed it down. He had a quiet, confident air about him that rubbed off on his critters. It was evident that his horses were used to doing what they were told. What a joy it was to work with a true horseman.

We treated the other animals one at a time. As he led out an old bay mare, Dave winked at me. "This is my pack horse—can do about anything with old Jem here. Want to let our assistant try?"

I passed the twitch to Marcie, and she stepped forward without hesitation. As if she had performed the procedure a hundred times before, she passed the tube and presented the end for me to flush down the wormer. I looked cheekily at Dave and smiled. This girl knew her stuff.

While working with the other horses, I noticed that the filly's foot was causing discomfort. Her right hind leg was cocked in such a manner as to take the weight off it.

"Can you tell which one she's favouring?" I asked Marcie, as we watched Dave trot towards the house with Snip on his heels. "Give her lots of slack in the lead shank, Dave!"

"It's hard to tell when she's moving."

"Is it front or back?"

"Back."

"Watch her head and her hip...When does her head go up?"

"I think it's going up every time her left hind hits the ground."

"And what about the hip?"

"She drops it every time the foot touches down."

"I agree. Her hip on the right side rises and the head drops whenever she puts weight on her right hind."

Marcie nodded uncertainly.

"That's the horse's way of advancing the sore leg without flexing it so much. She avoids putting as much weight on it that way."

Dave had trotted the filly along the brow of the hill for a third time. "She's real tender over the fetlock...and the tendon at the back seems sore." Puffing for air, he came to a stop in front of us. "I saw her go tearin' across the pasture after Griz; a few minutes later, she came in limpin'. Kinda wondered if it wasn't in the hip to start with, but she's seems sore all over. Kinda hard to tell."

I ran my hand over Snip's leg, feeling for evidence of heat or swelling. The stifle and the hock felt normal to me. As I ran my fingers down the tendon at the back of the hock, however, she lifted her leg and waved it in the air.

"She did the same thing with me...you don't think she's bowed a tendon, do you?" Dave passed the lead shank to Marcie and moved to my shoulder where he could better evaluate what I was doing.

"The foot's warm...I wonder if there's something lower." I lifted her foot and pared away at the horn on the bottom, looking for discoloration that could indicate a stone bruise or puncture.

Dave peered over my shoulder. "See anything?"

"Looks clean as can be."

I applied hoof testers across the back of the heel and squeezed. "She doesn't like that," Dave observed.

Moving the huge plier-like implement to the bottom of the sole, I depressed it once more. The filly reefed her foot free from my grip and flailed it wildly back and forth. Dave grabbed her halter and pulled her up short. "Easy, Snip. Settle down, girl."

"She definitely didn't like that."

"So you think it's in the foot then?" Dave sounded skeptical. "You stick that big pincer on my foot and I'd jump too. Could it be navicular disease? I lost a horse at the coast to navicular."

"You saw how she reacted way up here on the toe…When there's inflammation around the navicular bone, we see pain further towards the heel. Besides, navicular would be far more likely if this were a front foot."

"Where do we go from here?"

"I'd suggest an X-ray of the foot, but we can certainly do a nerve block to rule out problems elsewhere."

"What d'you mean?"

"I can give her a couple of shots that'll numb the nerves in her foot. If she walks sound after that, we know she isn't sore anywhere else."

He contemplated, then smiled at the thought. "Let's try it."

I sent Marcie for fresh water while I returned to the car for my materials. I clipped a ring of hair from around the fetlock joint and had my new assistant do a scrub. As I soaped myself and drew up lidocaine, she doused the lower leg with alcohol. I chose a spot halfway between the fetlock and the top of the hoof and probed deeply with my fingertips.

"Can you feel this tendon?" I waited for Marcie to locate the hard band running up the back of the leg. "Do you remember the name of it?"

"The superficial digital flexor?"

"Right on. If I inject a couple of millilitres of anesthetic in front of it, I should be able to deaden the posterior digital nerve…Lift her other leg for me, Dave."

He hefted Snip's opposite leg, forcing her to bear her entire weight on her sore one. I popped a small-gauge needle in front of the tendon and injected. "Just one second more." She didn't even flinch as I introduced a second needle to freeze the other side.

"Okay, you can put her foot down…We'll let her stand for ten minutes." Dave dropped her foot and the horse shifted her weight from one leg to the other.

My attention strayed to the stack of logs that rested against the corral. "This is a nice load of cedar. You must come across all kinds of great finds when you're making some of your runs."

"Yeah, I do." Dave strolled over and rested his foot on the bottom log. "But wood like this is gettin' hard to find. Got these to split for rails and posts around here, but I'm gonna use a few of 'em makin' my raft for the race."

"What race is that?"

"Haven't you heard of the Yahk raft race? Every year on the last weekend of May they have a race on the Moyie River. I watched it last year—what a riot. My brother and I decided to have a go at it this time. You should think about comin' up with someone to go with. You need a partner—and both guys have to finish."

"Is there much of a prize?"

"Darned if I know, but lots of guys from the bush crews are goin' in it, and I wanna give it a try."

I had been out past Yahk only the week before, and the thought of jumping on a raft and tackling the water when it was raging like that was well down on my list of priorities. "The water's pretty wild right at the moment."

Dave grinned. "That's why they run the race when they do—it's high water."

"Sounds like a logger's delight."

"Not really. Last year there were guys from all over; couple of Yanks from Bonners Ferry won."

I shivered at the thought of that icy water, then turned back to the task at hand. "Let's see how she tracks now." I picked up Snip's foot and applied pressure with the hoof tester once more across her heel.

"That sure made a difference," Dave observed. When I pressed on the toe again, the filly pulled her foot forward and stood firm. "Think she still felt that one."

As Dave again walked her towards the house, I hollered, "Take her out at a trot! Give her lots of free lead once you get started. What do you think, Marcie?"

275

"She may be a bit better. She started jogging a lot quicker this time."

"Is she normal?"

Marcie hesitated as Dave turned the corner by the house and headed back towards us. "She's improved…but I can see her head bob."

"So can I."

Dave stopped in front of us. "What d'you think?"

"Still not normal." I drew up some more lidocaine.

"So what's that mean?"

"It means that it's not navicular and not a bruise over the back of the foot…I think it's improved though. We're on the right track…Let's do another scrub." Once more, Marcie diligently slathered the clipped area with surgical soap.

Dave looked disappointed. "What if she's still limpin' after this?"

"Then we'll try another block higher up to rule out the fetlock."

As he lifted Snip's other leg, I injected local anesthetic in a ring around the front of the foot halfway between the fetlock and the top of the hoof. "You're really goin' for broke this time," Dave grunted. The horse shifted and struggled to get her good leg free. "Okay, let her have it."

We all settled back to watch Snip. She was now bearing weight on both hind legs equally.

"So, how big are these rafts? What are the rules?"

"Far as I know, there aren't many rules, other than you need a life jacket and have to make your raft no more than four feet by eight feet…I think there's something about the length of the paddle, too, but I'll have to check that out."

"Do you haul the logs up to Yahk or make the raft here?"

"We'll be buildin' it here this week. I can give you some cedar if you want to go in it yourself."

I chuckled. "Don't know anyone else crazy enough to want to try it."

Dave's smile spread from ear to ear. "Well, you could always take Marcie here."

Marcie flushed. I could see she didn't like Dave's tone. I knew from experience with the women in my class at the college that you never wanted to goad a female student by telling her what a woman could or could not do. "I don't think she looks very keen on that." My tone was almost hopeful.

"Speak for yourself." Marcie's face was crimson. "If you guys could finish the race, I sure as heck could!"

There was certainly nothing retiring about my perfectly feminine protegé. My face fell as I realized I was getting closer and closer to getting my arse wet.

"Looks like you'll be up here buildin' rafts with us this week." Dave couldn't contain his enjoyment.

"Let's see what's up with Snip." I was intent on changing the direction of this conversation; I couldn't believe the sequence of events. This situation was reminiscent of buying my farm: how did the thing gain so much momentum so quickly? I felt like a passenger on a raging express train, hoping there'd soon be somewhere to bail out.

Dave took off with the filly following easily behind him. She floated along as straight as an arrow. He turned and stopped before us. "That seems to have gotten it. So, it is the foot."

"Sure looks like it…What are the possibilities, Marcie?"

She didn't reply. Her thoughts were focused elsewhere. Man, I bet that river water was cold!

"Looks like time for an X-ray."

"Do you think she broke something?" asked Dave, oblivious to my discomfort.

"That's what we'll have to find out. Even with a bad bruise, I'd have expected her to be improving by now."

While Marcie and I returned to the clinic for the X-ray machine, Dave removed Snip's shoes. We snapped a series of radiographs after packing the underside of her foot with play-dough to remove the shadows around the frog—the soft tissues in the V of a horse's heel.

An hour later, the three of us stood shoulder to shoulder at the view box. Dave's tone was woeful as he peered at the developed film. "Oh man, it's broken all in pieces."

"These are normal." I pointed to a series of lines running to the depth of the third phalanx. "Those are all vascular channels, where blood vessels run through the bone. But this," I said, indicating a small triangular wedge at the front of the bone, "...is a fracture."

"I'll be darned." Dave drew closer to the X-ray and pointed to a lucent line that traversed the bone. "Is this part of it, too?"

"That's another vessel...See how regular it is in comparison?"

"Is she finished as a ridin' horse? My wife'll be some disappointed."

"I don't think so. We can always send these to an equine specialist for an opinion in case I've missed something, but it's my guess that if we get a corrective shoe on her and reduce the movement of the frog, it should heal."

Marcie leaned forward to peer at the still wet radiograph.

"It doesn't seem to be broken into the joint at all, does it?" Her question caught me off guard. My attention had become more focused on her profile than on the lines of the X-ray.

"No...not that I can see." I held up the oblique views for comparison. "She must have just come down wrong on a rock and slabbed that piece off the front."

"Where do we go from here?" Dave asked resolutely.

"Who does your farrier work?"

He smiled. "Do all my own."

"Why am I not surprised? Do you have your own welder?"

"Wouldn't keep my truck on the road without it."

"Well then, I'm sending you home with my textbook on lameness; it's got some good diagrams on how to make up the adaptations. We'll want you to get a shoe all set up as if you were ready to nail it on. Once you have it sprung so that it fits properly, you'll weld a bar across the heel and some quarter clips along the sides. They'll keep the foot from expanding and take some of the pressure off the frog."

"Doesn't sound too difficult."

"I'd keep her in that little corral by herself away from the other horses. The less she moves around on the foot, the quicker it'll heal."

"How long do you think it'll be before we know what'll happen?"

"Three to six months, and you'll have to reset the shoes every month or so."

Dave nodded, then turned to me with a broad grin. "So, what night are you comin' up to build your raft?"

I felt my face flush. I knew my ears would be the colour of ripe watermelon. "What day is the race?"

"Next Saturday."

I glanced at Marcie, wondering what was going through the woman's mind. She smiled and shrugged. "Any night's fine with me."

I checked the appointment book and drew a line through the following Saturday. "Let's make it tomorrow."

No Place for a Woman

All day I'd been dwelling on how I ended up in this spot. I had nothing against a bit of fun, but being spontaneous was certainly not one of my strong points. Normally, it would have taken me weeks to build up to something like entering a raft race. It was only yesterday evening that I got sucked into this. Now I had less than an hour to finish at the clinic, pick up Marcie, and get to Lougheeds' place to build my ark.

The last appointment of the afternoon was Eli, an Airedale puppy owned by Doris's older daughter, Jean, and her husband, Peter. They had driven over from Nelson with their brand-new family addition. The tan, curly-haired baby was a bundle of energy, licking his grandma's hands and chewing on my fingers.

"This is his first checkup," said Jean. "The breeder guarantees that he's healthy and free of deformities. We just want your assurances."

I roughed up the wiry tassels on the top of the pup's head and recoiled as his needle-sharp teeth clamped down on my finger. "Hey, little man, you play pretty rough."

"You don't have to tell me," Peter chuckled, extending arms that were covered with scratches.

Doris held the squirming critter as I checked his temperature and had a look at his recently docked tail. "Sure could have used a couple of stitches," I criticized, noting the scarred stub. I listened

to the sounds of his chest. "Looking good so far," I muttered, as ·
his slender, soft-spoken mistress looked on expectantly.

I palpated his hips and checked his scrotum to make sure both
testicles were down. His ears looked great; his tattoo was legible. I
was set to stamp his forehead with my seal of approval. It was
when I tilted his impish face up to the light to have a closer look
at his eyes that I noticed it—a shining refractory along the margin
of the eyelids.

"Does he ever paw at his eyes?"

"Yeah," answered Peter. "Now that you mention it, he does
quite often. Is there something wrong?"

"I'm afraid so." The pup squirmed in Doris's grip as I rotated
his lid and peered closer. A row of extra hairs was poking straight
towards the surface of the cornea. "It's a condition called distichi-
asis—a fancy name for a second set of lashes."

"Oh, my." Jean looked first to her mother, then to her husband.
"Is that serious?"

"I've seen many dogs that have a hair or two rubbing that
never bother. These are complete sets; I'd almost bet they'll be
trouble."

"Oh, Mom, what should we do?" Jean was near tears. Doris
shrugged and looked at me questioningly.

"It's a heritable condition that the breeder should guarantee
against. There's no question you can demand your money back—
or another puppy."

I already knew what Jean was going to say before she opened
her mouth. "Oh, Peter, we can't take him back!"

"What would you suggest?" Peter asked matter-of-factly.

"I guess you have to decide if you want *a* puppy or *this* puppy.
If you want *a* puppy, then you should go to the breeder and get
your money back—Eli could end up being a lot of hassle and
expense. I can get Doris to type up a letter for you to take to them.
If you want *this* puppy, then we'll have to manage him."

"Manage him?"

"Some dogs don't have as much trouble with this condition as others. You'll have to watch carefully for signs of irritation and erosion of the surface of the eye. An ulcer could affect his sight and lead to permanent injury. If the lashes bother constantly, then it may be best to remove them surgically."

Jean regarded Peter for a moment, then resolutely affirmed, "He's not going back."

"You should see if the breeder is prepared to help you out in some way. They may want him seen by their own veterinarian. We'll write you a letter."

I scratched out a sample for Doris to type, then ran upstairs to change and grab a bite to eat. I poured out a bowl of granola before realizing there were only a few drops of milk left in the carton. I had put a considerable dent in my simple fare by the time Doris showed up.

"Does that look okay?" she asked, handing me a neatly typed document.

I read over the letter, then quickly scrawled my name. It was amazing what a year of practice had done to my signature.

"Don't know why I brought it up here," Doris huffed. "I can scratch a line as well as you."

"I know you can. I saw the one you put on that spay certificate for Mrs. Greer the other day."

She flushed and changed the subject. "Where are you off to in such a rush? Have you got something planned with Marcie?"

I looked at Doris. Did I detect just a hint of jealousy? "We're going up to Dave Lougheed's tonight to check out his shoeing job and to build a raft for the Yahk race."

She looked surprised. "Is that why you have Saturday scratched off?"

I nodded. Gagging down the remainder of the dry grain, I felt the lump pass the length of my esophagus. I quickly filled a glass with water and swallowed a few gulps.

"Barb and I will have to come out to Yahk and watch you,"

Doris said, heading for the door. "She's my adventuresome daughter. She's been talking about going in that race for years."

The Lougheed brothers were already busy by the time we got there. "I've got the logs bucked up for you. We selected 'em all about the right size," Dave said, looking up from nailing a cross-tie for his own raft. "Just use my saw and knock off all the knots…Square the sides a bit, and the four logs you have there will make it the perfect width."

Within a half-hour, we had flattened the logs and slid them into place for assembly. I had fashioned the notches for the front cross-tie, and the chain saw was screaming as I prepared the one at the back. Marcie set the two-by-six in place and pounded in the nails. She had no problem hitting them square on the head.

A green Ford pickup pulled into the yard. I shut down the saw and looked up from my task. A tall, husky man disembarked. Adjusting a broad-brimmed cowboy hat, he strolled casually towards the construction site. "Just about have 'em done, eh?" He stroked the bushy red beard that adorned his face.

"Yeah," replied Dave. "Ron and I are done…Dave and Marcie there are getting close."

"George, have you met Dave? He's the new vet in town." We shook hands.

My partner finished pounding the last spikes into the two-by-six. "This is Marcie."

George gave her a broad smile. "Glad to meet ya."

"So are you finished your raft yet?" Dave asked George.

"Moberg and I finished it on Sunday. Looks pretty darn good—we'll make good time with it. So, who's your partner in the race, Doc?"

"Marcie," I replied.

George gaped at me in total disbelief. "Are you serious? That's no place for a woman."

Marcie flushed, then picked up the other two-by-six and began pounding spikes. I couldn't help but notice that she swung the hammer more vigorously as George continued with his advice.

"Seriously, Doc, it's for guys." George lowered his voice. "Got nothin' against women. They have their place…but it sure as hell ain't on a raft in the middle of a river."

Marcie was sullen and said little as we watched Dave sculpt the front of our raft. I was waiting for her to give George a broadside about his thoughts on women, but she seemed determined to handle him with actions rather than words.

The day before the race, I had run completely out of clean jeans. Laundry day could be delayed no longer. I was picking up the last of the dirty clothes that were strewn around the apartment.

"You have company downstairs." Doris was puffing.

"Who is it? I thought we were done for the day."

"He says he's an old roommate of yours from college."

"Cory?"

"Yes, that's right."

I thumped down the stairs two at a time with Lug following close behind. I hadn't seen Cory since he and I and two other classmates had borrowed some money and splurged on a trip to Barbados right after we graduated.

"Well, hello there, stranger!" I grasped his hand in a firm shake. "What are you doing in this neck of the woods? I thought you were somewhere in the States."

Cory produced one of his winning smiles. "I'm finished down there. If you can believe it, I'm one of the new equine residents at Saskatoon. I don't start for a couple of weeks, so I thought I'd come out here to look you up."

"Great! Glad you did." Cory was a farm boy from southern Saskatchewan; he loved the prairie. His going back to Saskatoon didn't surprise me but, in the four years we had spent studying together, I didn't peg him for a horse buff. "Damn, if I'd known you were coming, I'd have had an excuse to stay out of the raft race."

"Raft race? What's that about?"

"Did you come in from Cranbrook?"

"Yeah, through there and a place called Yahk."

"You remember the river along the road?" He nodded vaguely. "Well, we're going to be floating on a raft from Yahk to the American border."

"Why don't you sign Cory up, too?" suggested Doris. "That would be a real B.C. experience."

"Cory, have you met my assistant?"

"Yes, Doris introduced herself earlier."

"How could we sign Cory up? He can't go by himself."

"I told you Barb was dying to go. I talked to her last night, and she was green with envy that Marcie was entering. Barb's always been a bit of a tomboy. She'd love to be one of the first women in that race. I can fix it up with her if you like."

Within the hour, Cory and I were on our way to see Dave Lougheed. One more raft was in the making.

The Yahk Raft Race

To say that the crew was apprehensive would be an understatement. Marcie stared soberly at the road ahead. In the back seat of my Volkswagen, Cory and Barb were subdued and had yet to speak after the initial introductions. I was beginning to wonder about Doris's assertion that her daughter was looking forward to the raft race. Right now, I was certain that each of us was wondering the same thing: How in the world did I end up in this situation?

I slowed the car as I started up the incline towards Kitchener. Approaching the village, the Goat River made a lazy curve. Littered with uprooted trees, it was running brown with silt. All eyes focused on the raging torrent. No one spoke. I looked in the rear-view mirror at Cory and gave him an encouraging smile. He slowly shook his head as he viewed the carnage below.

I held up the twenty-sixer that I had stashed under the seat. The half-and-half mixture of dark rum and Coke suddenly looked like the main component of our first-aid kit. "We're gonna be needing this before the afternoon's out."

Cory held up its mate. "We may need it before much longer."

Out of the corner of my eye, I saw a dark green Ford pickup. It rapidly overtook us and swished past. I turned my head in time to catch sight of a red beard and broad-brimmed cowboy hat. George Huscroft was boogying right along, his raft tied across the truck box. His wife, Linda, gave us a hearty wave. George

appeared determined to cross the finish line first, one way or another. He hung his arm out the window in an easy salute as the truck disappeared in the distance.

The Yahk junction held new significance today. As we approached it, we got our first sighting of the Moyie River. "Well guys, there she is. If we make it this far, we'll know that our rafts will float."

I pulled over to the shoulder and we all stared in awe at the challenge before us. An uprooted cottonwood floated by. "Lougheed says this is the highest the river's been in years."

Cory clutched his bottle of rum and Coke as if it had suddenly taken on new meaning. He had just finished taping a section of plastic rope to each of our two bottles. There was no way that we'd be parting with them voluntarily.

Barb looked nervous. "You guys know I can't swim?"

We didn't take our eyes off the raging river. "We'll make darn good and sure your life jacket's tight," Cory declared enthusiastically.

Barb glared at him, then returned her focus to the water that licked at the foundation of the bridge. "How did I let Mother talk me into this?"

Another pickup loaded with its unwieldy cargo whipped past us. "There's one from Idaho." Its structure was different from any raft I'd seen so far. Smaller logs to the side were positioned like outriggers to offset two huge logs in the centre. "Man, they've gone to a lot of trouble."

"I'll be happy if ours stays afloat," muttered Barb.

We all broke into laughter and I pulled back onto the highway. That water sure looked foreboding.

Yahk was bustling with activity. The one day of the year when the Yahk Motel got to light up its No Vacancy sign had arrived. The parking lots in front of the Grouse Mountain and Yahk General Stores were plugged with vehicles. Cars were already parked on both sides of the road between the two bridges. I hadn't seen so many people materialize here since I'd repaired the pony's leg in the rocky field on the other side of the river. An involuntary shiver ran up my spine at the memory.

I crossed the bridges and followed the flow of traffic to a pasture a few hundred yards up the highway. A wisp of a grey-haired man dressed in denim and a floppy-brimmed cowboy hat directed vehicles through the gate in the barbed-wire fence. I stopped and waited as a Dodge truck with massive off-road tires lumbered through the ditch and onto the highway. Music blared as it passed. We looked up into a cab that was stuffed with teenagers.

"I get the feeling there's a different crowd out here." How well I recognized the tone in Cory's voice; after spending four years together, I knew when he was having second thoughts.

In the pasture I pulled to a stop, about where Dave Lougheed had told us to meet him. Cars were jammed in solid; people were coming and going between and around them. Everywhere I looked, men were busily building their rafts. Chain saws roared; the smell of blue smoke permeated the air.

"Over there." Marcie pointed towards the end of a narrow alley between cars, where Dave's heavily laden Ford pickup was parked. Next to him, on the other side of an old apple tree, was George. I pulled ahead of them and parked the vehicle out of harm's way.

" 'Bout time you guys showed up." George tipped back a bottle containing a Coke-coloured liquid and took several healthy glugs. "You'd better get started takin' in some antifreeze or ya won't last long out there."

Dave and his brother were sprawled on the ground under the pickup untying the ropes that secured the three rafts. "You better hurry up and register to get your numbers. Ron and I are close to the front—number 5. George was already way back when he signed up. Head over to the river 'n' you'll see the booth. Joe Gagne will take your money 'n' sign you up."

Cory and I headed off across the field in search of the registration table. Marcie and Barb loitered uncomfortably next to the car, taking in the commotion around them. Although neither would have admitted it, I'm sure they were thinking this venture was looking more and more like a guy thing.

The closer to the river we got, the more intense was the activity. It appeared that half of the rafts had been constructed right there on the spot from whatever materials the participants had dragged along. A few looked as if they would be lucky to have a couple of logs nailed together by start time.

"Look at that one." A brand-new white Ford three-quarter-ton with dual wheels backed in front of us. On board was a vessel that made our raft look like a toy. Constructed of four huge pine logs, the thing must have weighed a ton. "They'll need a crane for that one. Look at the oar locks and those fancy padded seats."

"These guys plan on being comfortable," Cory muttered as the truck jockeyed for position at the unloading site. "What's with the chrome railings?"

Rafts were stacked everywhere next to a fifty-foot section of beach. Four or five were leaning against the huge cottonwoods that lined the bank of the river. "How in the world do they ever launch them all?" I asked Cory. "It doesn't look like there's room for more than a few at a time." His face mirrored his discomfort. I had a feeling that our prairie dog was longing for the open plains.

A crowd of contestants was hanging around the sign-up table. I recognized Wayne Keirn's booming voice above the din. "You just wait Paladichuk! Me and Adams got your number! We'll whip ya again this year."

"In your dreams you will, Keirn!" responded Frank Paladichuk, the local building inspector. "You know that the only reason you beat me last year is I lost my paddle."

"Lost your paddle...Hell man, you threw it at me!" Wayne burst into laughter and gave the burly, dark-haired man a playful shove. The logger and the building inspector had obviously crossed oars in the past.

Wayne turned to leave. "Whoa, Frank, look at this; we got a

giant in the race! With long arms like Dr. Dave's against us, you'll have to do a little work for a change."

Frank picked up his receipt from the sign-up table and backed off with a broad smile. "You wait and see who'll have to work, Keirn. You're dead meat!"

Wayne passionately grabbed my arm. "You watch this guy, Dave. He doesn't take well to bein' passed. Last year he threw everything he had on board at us. Damn near split my head open with a full beer—even tried to whack me with his paddle." Frank ignored him.

I paid the twenty-dollar entry fee. Our raft was number 21; Cory and Barb's was 22.

By the time two o'clock rolled around, more than thirty rafts were piled along the narrow stretch of beach that gave access to the swirling river. Marcie and I stood side by side as the first four rafts were dragged into place. Contestants nervously made last-minute adjustments and took final drags on the bottles that gave them courage. I glanced at my partner; she was sure putting on a brave front.

"Dave and Cory, we need a hand." Lougheed had backed the truck as near as the crowd allowed. With the help of bystanders, we carried his raft and set it behind the first one in line. We dumped our own rafts in a heap.

The man with the fancy white truck was ready to unload, too. A dozen guys grabbed either side of the gargantuan barge and staggered ahead to drop it on the ground. "Boy, that's heavy," said one of the men in front of me. "Must be made of wet logs."

Paul McCartney strode from the front line. Whipping out his tape, he quickly measured the craft. "You can't take that in…It's too big!"

"What difference does it make?" The owner, a slender, fair-haired fellow, was ready for an argument.

Paul pulled off his baseball cap, ran his fingers through his red hair, and jutted out his jaw. "I'm a race official…Says right in the rules that the raft can be no bigger than four-by-eight. Yours is better 'n seven-by-twelve—either cut it off or haul it away. I'll let you go on the width, but you gotta cut it to length."

Paul flitted from raft to raft, checking them for size. Nattering non-stop, the man followed in his wake. I chuckled when he eventually gave up and headed back to his truck to consult with his partner.

"On your mark!" The voice over the megaphone startled me. Although I knew it was inevitable that we would reach this point, it was still too soon. "Get set!" The crowd around me surged forward. "Launch!"

The navigators of the first four rafts struggled to get them out into the current free of the rocky shore. The two further upstream shot forward as their crews perched at the front and pushed mightily with their oars. One crashed into the front of the lead raft before it could launch, and a spirited exchange of profanity ensued. The crowd roared as a contestant on the first raft swung his paddle at the interlopers and was yanked overboard. Onlookers pushed the raft off with its lone occupant; I watched in fascination as the bobbing crewman struggled against the current to get back on board.

"One minute!" Four more rafts were moved into position. Dave and Ron stood on the front of number 5 and jammed their paddles in downstream to hold their position against the current.

"Ya better make good time, Lougheed! We'll pass ya by the second bridge." George took another swig of his rum and Coke. He gave me an elbow in the ribs as we watched the next wave of competitors push off. "Yahoo!" he hollered. "Look at that!" He jumped up and down with excitement as the raft next to the Lougheeds split in two only feet from shore. The collection of fence posts that had been tacked together disintegrated, and a pair of teenage boys clung helplessly to the logs that remained. The crowd hooted unapologetically as the debris was swept from sight and the next rafts were dragged forward.

293

A chain saw fired up behind us. The illegal twelve-foot barge was being pruned. Pieces of chrome lay on the ground beside it; the chairs had been thrown into the back of the truck. Another corporate venture was in the process of downsizing.

George clapped me on the back and started in with his familiar refrain. "Ya got a lot of guts goin' in this thing with a woman, Perrin." His cheeks were flushed. He stumbled and grabbed my arm for support as we stepped back to get out of the way of incoming rafts.

"You better slow down on that antifreeze, George, or you'll be lucky to even get out there."

He grinned. "We'll see who'll get out there. This is no place for a woman. Ya better get a few shots of booze into 'er or you'll be lucky to drag 'er off shore."

George and his partner, John Moberg, got off to an impressive start. Paddling like mad, they put at least seventy feet between them and the closest competitor in their heat.

Bodies materialized out of nowhere to help move our raft into position. Marcie shuffled forward to the front of the platform. I passed her the bottle, and she took a healthy swig. I chugged a couple of mouthfuls myself and closed my eyes as it burned its way down.

"Jam your paddle into the rocks as I move us out!" I hollered over the roar of the water and the hooting of the crowd. Pushing the raft as far into the current as I dared, I stood on shore, clinging to my paddle and the rear cross-tie. Marcie's eyes were the size of hubcaps as she struggled to dig her paddle into the rocky bottom and hold the raft straight.

Cory and Barb were right next to us. I knew they were wishing they were part of the audience. Out of the corner of my eye, I noted that the now semi-legal vessel from the white truck was fourth in our heat.

"Launch!"

The order caught me off guard. Both members of the third team pushed off, determined to get the advantage. I could see they were already in the current; they were going to be ahead of us. I heaved. The front end of our raft dunked under the water, and Marcie's legs disappeared beneath a wave. We were hung up on a huge boulder somewhere under the middle log.

Cory and Barb's launch began smoothly, but they crashed into our bow just as I struggled to lift us free. Our raft took off. Barb screeched in horror as theirs spun fully around and headed sideways into the current. The crowd howled with pleasure when she grabbed Cory's arm and held on for dear life.

I dove forward as our raft twisted into the current. The boulders under my feet gave way and I sprawled into the icy water. I gasped when the cold engulfed me, struggled to my feet, and made a desperate lunge. My hand caught on a cross-member, and I dragged my torso onto the raft. Ten feet from the start line, and I was already wet from top to bottom.

The crowd was heckling with delight—probably at our expense. I knelt on the logs at the back and struggled to straighten our craft as we drifted sideways. Cory was about fifty feet ahead of us; the third raft was well ahead of them. I turned in search of the fourth raft in time to see the crew abandon ship. Constructed of those green pine logs, their barge had sunk on the spot.

"Look out!" I yelled. Marcie ducked as we skimmed the shore under branches from a partially submerged hawthorn clump that scraped down the side of our raft. "Let's get further out into the stream!" I paddled madly to force the unresponsive craft away from shore.

"We have to at least make it past the bridge!" Marcie pointed at the yellow metal structure that offered the first chance for spectators to view the progress of the race. The rails were jammed with people shouting encouragement. The entire understructure was cluttered with children who had climbed out on the girders for a better view of the action.

I shifted my legs, trying to find a comfortable position. From this point on, the only possibility of warmth would come from the bottle at my side. My toes squished inside wet sneakers; my sopping clothing clung to my skin. We were well in the middle of the river by the time we reached the bridge. As we passed under, I glimpsed Doris, camera in hand. She was hanging over the rail waving wildly and cheering us on.

The river curved gently to the right and ran full length through the village. We paddled less than a stone's throw from back yards choked with onlookers. At the edge of town, we passed under the rickety old bridge that I had recently crossed to visit a sick cow on the Cotton property. The wiry man who owned the ranch hung over the rail with dozens of neighbourhood children. He waved cheerfully and hollered, "Good luck, Doc!"

I raised my paddle in a salute. "Thanks, Tom. We're going to need it!"

At this point, the river ran straight and free of obstacles. Allowing the current to have its way with our raft, we raced along at a good clip. To the left was a wooded ridge covered with fir and larch; to the right were open meadows and occasionally a house or outbuilding. Every once in a while, we caught a glimpse of the highway and patches of onlookers.

Two rafts were still in sight ahead of us. One belonged to Barb and Cory; every now and then, they would wave. The last thing on my mind was overtaking anyone—survival was the order of the day. As the river flowed faster, however, we navigated into the middle and gained on them. Now side by side, we hollered back and forth. Marcie and I even paddled a bit to pull ahead. We crossed under the highway bridge into a long, open stretch and zipped past the Mohawk service station. "This is the spot we stopped earlier!" I shouted above the roar of the river. "We must be a third of the way."

I passed Marcie the bottle of hooch. She took a long draught and handed it back. Rum had never tasted this good before. The

Moyie picked up speed and rushed into a rambling curve. Huge rocks and clumps of trees suddenly materialized in the middle of the river.

"It's dividing!" I cried. "Which way should we go?...Hard to the right!" My shoulders ached as I dug my paddle deep into the water to try and pull us clear of the island. The nose of our raft rammed hard against a clump of alder. We spun completely around, narrowly missing rocks that would certainly have swamped us. Marcie looked horrified. I grabbed onto a cross-tie and held on. We surged through the rapids—now backwards, now sideways—totally at the whim of the raging water.

The current slowed by the time the branches of river rejoined. Cory and Barb were twenty feet to our right; the lead raft had navigated left and was almost out of sight ahead of us. Our raft straightened itself. I glanced at Marcie, smiled meekly, and passed her the bottle. It almost looked as if we were under control by the time we reached a stretch of the river that parallelled the highway. There was Doris with her camera, waving for all she was worth.

I observed Marcie as she paddled. She actually seemed to be enjoying this. For the most part, she was still dry. If it hadn't been for that initial dousing I gave her during the launch, she could have come through the race unscathed. As for me, I was uncomfortably cold and trying to convince myself that I still had feeling in my toes.

The pace picked up again as the river was pinched between a pair of rocky ridges. "Look at that!" I pointed to the narrow stretch ahead. The guy on the raft ahead of us suddenly stood up, then disappeared from sight. I craned my neck and stood to better see what was going on. The raft in front of us was now empty, the crew nowhere to be seen.

"Cory! Barb!" I waved my paddle to get their attention.

"Marcie! Look out...Go right! Go right!" I pointed excitedly at the obstacle in front of us—a fir tree that had fallen into the stream. Visible several feet above the surface of the water near the bank, it was totally submerged towards the middle. Given our present course, there was no way to avoid it. Hugging the bank was our only hope—maybe we could lie down and squeak under it. I strained on my paddle, trying to navigate our unresponsive craft.

Cory and Barb were struggling to get far enough out to avoid the end of the tree. But Marcie and I had done too little, too late. There would be only inches to spare when our raft reached the tree. "Jump, Marcie!" I stood on the cross-tie near the back of the raft, balancing with my paddle. If I leaped over at just the right moment, maybe I could stay aboard.

Barb screeched. I turned in time to see the front of their raft ride up on the snag. In a flash, the torrent buried the back end, and the nose reared up. Our hapless comrades disappeared in a swirl of white froth.

Marcie slipped over the side into the river. Seconds later, the front of our raft passed under the snag. One corner caught a branch that dangled in the water. I jumped. The raft spun and I was launched into the air moments before my belly flop. When I broke to the surface, I was fighting for breath in the frigid water, but still clinging to my paddle. I scanned the river for the others. Twenty feet away, Marcie was fighting to reach the bank. Cory floated along in the middle and there, thank God, was Barb struggling towards the other shore.

Bobbing like a cork in the current, I spotted our raft, only to lose it again in the swells. I was heading for shore when I spied Barb and Cory's raft not far ahead. I swam for it, threw my paddle on board, and dragged myself after it. Gasping for breath, I knelt on the uneven surface and hollered at my companions. Cory began to swim toward me. I could see, with a sense of satisfaction, that Barb had already made shore. Marcie saw me and stopped swimming. "Pick me up, Dave!" she yelled. I was impressed. Why wouldn't she just head for solid ground?

I was extending my paddle to Cory when the front of the raft struck a massive cottonwood snag and spun erratically. I was almost thrown back in the drink. I rolled over, grasping for anything to keep me on board. I was looking straight up into the overhanging branches of the snag. There, clinging like a pair of monkeys to the upper limbs, were the former occupants of the third raft in our heat. They were stranded high and dry in the middle of the river.

Cory struggled desperately against the current to get closer to me. I lay on my belly and extended my paddle as far as I could reach. After a half-dozen attempts, he was able to grab hold; I dragged him on board like a half-dead flounder.

"Did you lose your bottle?" he gasped. I nodded sadly.

With a spurt of adrenaline, I crossed to the other side of the river. The flow had abated; for as far as I could see, there was nothing but smooth sailing. By the time we hauled Marcie on board, her lips were blue. She gave me a weak smile as I grabbed her hand and helped her up. She huddled in a heap at the front of the raft, her teeth chattering uncontrollably. I was about to ask her if she wanted to quit, when she pointed to a piece of flat wood floating near us. "Grab that!" she cried. "I need something to paddle with."

The last we saw of Barb, she had been heading through the underbrush. I could just picture Doris standing next to her car ready to snap our pictures. What was she going to think when paddles and an empty raft floated past? She would freak when we came by without her daughter.

Rounding the corner towards the road, we picked up speed again. Jagged rocks lined both sides of the river. A chill ran up my spine as I recognized the landmarks. "Paddle hard! We have to be on the inside." This was Keeney's Hole—the hairpin turn everyone had been warning us about. Here the water rushed toward the outside of the curve, where a tremendous collection of logs had been heaped by the force of the current. According to Dave, this spot was notorious for ending the hopes of many contestants in past events. Cars were parked everywhere on the side of the road; people were whooping and waving. This was action central.

Marcie stroked with her driftwood, while I strained with my paddle. We looked longingly towards the inside of the corner where alders poked through the surface of calmer water, but the force of the current seemed impossible to resist. My hands were already blistering and my back ached. "Oh crap!" Cory cursed. "We haven't got a hope."

Working in the fastest water we had encountered since the start of the race, we positioned ourselves in the middle of the torrent. We rounded the corner sideways, paddling frenetically to keep from being forced into the concretion of logs. I could feel the current dragging us closer and closer to the far edge as we followed the curve. We skimmed the jam only a few feet from protruding snags. Almost past the worst of the danger, we spotted George clinging to the branches of an enormous fir tree. I swung my paddle jauntily and splashed him.

"Whooeee! George, is this the finish line?"

"Damn it, Dave! I'm drownin'!" he blurted.

The look on his face said it all. He was exhausted. As he clung to the branch over his head, his legs and torso were being whipped under the jam by the force of the water. It was obvious that even holding on was taking its toll. I watched him in anguish as we swept past and around the corner.

Here the water slowed considerably and widened enough to reduce the force of the current. "Let's beach it!" We maneuvered as close to the edge of the river as possible, jumped into the water, and struggled to drag the raft to shore. My legs were like rubber and I stumbled on the rocky bottom. I couldn't feel my feet.

I left Cory and Marcie with the raft. As good as it felt to have ground beneath me, I found walking almost impossible. I thrashed along the shore like a drunk, slipping often and falling full length into the water. I made my way along the shore as far as I could, then headed across country. The terrain would have made the going rough at the best of times. Alders, willows, and thorn bushes grew in profusion, creating an absolute jungle. I was hanging up everywhere, falling repeatedly. I had to find George!

Closer to the river, the entire shore was a bog. Wading through waist-deep water, I stumbled onto the jam and lurched from log to log, hoping he was still there. I could see the orange of his life jacket bobbing at the edge of the huge snag at the front of the heap. At least three and a half feet at the butt, the log was fifty or sixty feet long. Stout branches jutted out randomly over the upper half.

I carefully picked my way along the trunk. It was slippery in places; I would have been leery of my footing even under normal conditions. Advancing with baby steps, I was almost to him. As I planted my foot, a piece of loose bark let go; my leg went flying out from under me and half my body dipped again into the water. I grabbed frantically for the branches and pulled myself back up.

I was directly above George but he didn't realize it. His eyes were closed, both hands tightly gripped around a branch that protruded above his head. He looked for all the world as if he no longer cared whether he lived or died. His lips were blue, his flesh so grey that his fiery red beard appeared artificial by contrast.

I braced myself and grabbed his life preserver. His eyes opened when I unhooked it from a snag behind him and started to reef him up. He looked at me in a daze. "I can't move my legs, Doc...so damn cold." He thrashed wildly as I began to make headway against the current. "Don't let go, Dave...Don't let go!" He grabbed a branch further up on the tree and I pulled again.

By the time I had hoisted him to the top of the log, we were both done in. People who had been observing from the road arrived to help carry him. "I thought I was gonna drown, Doc," he mumbled. "Don't know how much longer I coulda held on."

We were almost at the highway when Barb and Doris pushed through the crowd. "Are you all right?" Doris asked.

"Yeah, everyone's still in one piece."

"Are you guys quitting?" Doris looked disappointed.

"I think we still have a raft and a paddle," I replied, eyeing the river pensively. "At least, I hope Cory and Marcie still have them."

"Then you *are* going to finish?"

"If I have anything to say about it…It's only a few miles more."

Still wearing her life jacket, Barb looked at her mother, then back at the river. "Get going," Doris ordered. "They told me you and Marcie were the first women who ever entered. How can you quit now?"

Climbing onto that raft again was one of the most difficult things I had done in ages, but we had come this far and we were going to finish. Soaked and miserable, the four of us crowded on board and floated downstream. Our weight was substantial: the raft was partially submerged.

I rested my hand on Marcie's arm. She was shivering. "How are you faring?" I asked. She merely smiled and nodded an acknowledgement. She had hardly said a word since we were thrown into the drink. I decided that she wasn't exactly moody, but I would certainly classify her as the strong, silent type.

Cory had recovered a paddle from debris below the log jam; he and Marcie stroked half-heartedly at the front. Barb sat shivering in the middle of the raft. I slipped into the water and hung on the back, kicking as much as I could with legs that were numb and feeling strangely detached from my body.

On a fast-flowing straight stretch, we had easy going and zipped rapidly along. About a mile downstream, the terrain levelled and we drifted calmly through a quiet stretch of water. "Look!" Marcie hollered. "Is that ours?" There in a back eddy floated a raft that was still in one piece. When we got closer, I pushed off and swam to it.

"It's not the one we built, but it'll get us to the finish line!" With renewed enthusiasm, I maneuvered it close enough to the other raft for Marcie to jump on. I ripped a board from the side to use as a paddle and we were away. The final fifteen minutes flew by. I was surprised to round a bend and find spectators frantically waving us to the right side of the river. We had made it to the finish line at the American border.

Paddling hard, we struggled towards shore. Hundreds of people were lined up ten deep along the bank. "Grab the lines!" a man hollered. He threw out a half-inch plastic cord. My fingers were reluctant to close, but I caught it and held on. Two more ropes landed on the deck, and Marcie scrambled to snatch one.

Clinging to them tenaciously, we gravitated towards the shore and the men who struggled along the rocky beach to drag us in. Two fellows wearing hip waders jumped into the water and captured our raft. Marcie and I straightened our rigid bodies and tripped onto the boulder-strewn beach.

We turned to see Cory and Barb come shooting down the river. They were further from shore; one line after the other was thrown and missed. A shout of delight went up when Cory finally grasped one and was ripped into the drink. The raft flew past with Barb still on board, grabbing desperately for ropes that landed well beyond her reach.

Everyone watched spellbound as two men stumbled along the bank, playing Cory like a sturgeon in the raging water. The crowd hooted when Barb finally gripped a rope and splashed into the Moyie within American territory. We lost sight of her as she and her rescuers disappeared around the bend.

Marcie and I tackled the fifty-foot embankment that led towards the cheering crowd. My legs refused to cooperate. Helping hands appeared everywhere as we struggled with the rope up the well-worn trail.

We had climbed several feet when Marcie's legs gave way; she came barrelling in my direction. I caught her in my arms and we sprawled in a heap. I hugged her and raised her arm in victory. The crowd roared. We hesitantly picked ourselves up and made it to the top.

Another cheer went up when a man in the uniform of a U.S. Customs officer escorted Barb back to Canadian territory.

We had survived the gruelling race, finishing in just under two hours. Although we were well behind the winning time of a hundred and five minutes, we were proud of our accomplishment. The first two women to enter the race had both finished in style.

We were picking our way through the crowd when a hand clapped me on the back. "Sure glad ya came along when ya did this afternoon." Tipping back his cowboy hat, the irascible redhead extended an offering of rum and Coke. "Not sure how much longer I coulda held on," he slurred.

"Thanks, George." I gladly accepted the drink.

"Ya know, Doc, that partner of yours did pretty good out there today...Maybe ya should keep her around."

I looked in Marcie's direction. She and Barb were standing arm in arm as Doris snapped their picture. Marcie was laughing out loud at something Barb was saying. I smiled. "You know, George, you might just be right."

About the Author

Born in the *Silver City*—Trail, British Columbia—Dave Perrin was raised in Casino, a small community nestled in the hills. He attended school in Trail and moved on to Selkirk College, the University of British Columbia, and the Western College of Veterinary Medicine at Saskatoon, Saskatchewan.

Photo by Geri Buchanan

He graduated in 1973 and practised in the Creston Valley until 1998. After a year in Hawaii, where he began writing his first book, *Don't Turn Your Back in the Barn,* he returned to the family home. He lives on a small farm in Lister with his wife, four children, and an assortment of animal friends.

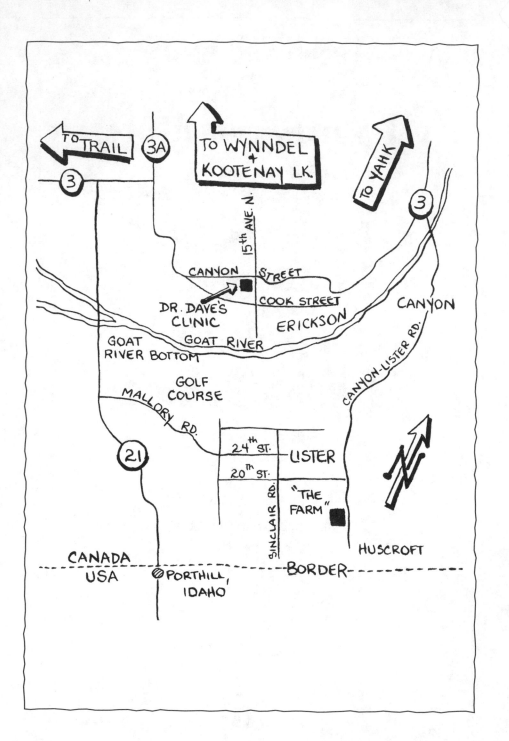